# PMP® Exam

## Practice Test and Study Guide

SEVENTH EDITION

**J. LeRoy Ward, PMP®**

ESI International • Arlington, Virginia

Published by

**ESI International**
901 North Glebe Road, Suite 200
Arlington, Virginia  22203

First Edition 1997
Second Edition 1998
Third Edition February 2001
Fourth Edition October 2001
Fifth Edition July 2003
Sixth Edition June 2005
Seventh Edition June 2006
Printed in the United States of America

ISBN 978-1-890367-44-2

# CONTENTS

# PREFACE

ESI International has been helping people prepare for the project management professional (PMP®) certification exam since early 1991. During the last 14 years, it has become quite clear that most prospective exam takers (myself included when I studied for the exam in the summer of 1990) ask two questions when they decide to earn PMP® certification: "What topics are covered on the exam?" and "What are the questions like?" Not surprisingly, some of the most sought-after study aids are practice tests, which are helpful in two ways: first, taking practice tests increases your knowledge of the kinds of questions, phrases, terminology, and sentence construction that you will encounter on the "real" exam; and second, taking practice tests provides an opportunity for highly concentrated study by exposing you to a breadth of project management content generally not found in a single reference source.

We initiated the development of this specialty publication with only one simple goal in mind: to help you study for, and pass, the PMP® certification exam. Because the Project Management Institute (PMI®) does not sell "past" exams to prospective certification candidates for study purposes, the best anyone can do is to develop practice test questions that are as representative of the real questions as possible. And that is exactly what we have done.

ESI has an enviable cadre of instructors and consultants who not only know project management but also have taken the exam themselves and regularly teach others how to prepare for it. We decided to draw on this group of respected, knowledgeable professionals to help develop this publication. Additionally, many of our clients regularly report their exam-taking experiences, so we can update the questions in this publication in both form and substance.

The result of our collective effort is the *PMP® Exam: Practice Test and Study Guide*. This seventh edition—like the preceding six—contains study hints, a list of exam topics, and 40 multiple-choice questions for each of the nine knowledge areas presented in *A Guide to the Project Management Body of Knowledge Third Edition*, better known as the *PMBOK® Guide*, as well as 40 questions in the area of Professional and Social Responsibility, for a grand total of 400.

---

"PMI" is a service and trademark of the Project Management Institute, Inc., which is registered in the United States and other nations. "PMBOK" is a trademark of the Project Management Institute, Inc., which is registered in the United States and other nations. "PMP" is a certification mark of the Project Management Institute, Inc., which is registered in the United States and other nations.

And as in previous editions, this edition includes a plainly written rationale for each correct answer, along with a supporting reference list. Our reference list alone took many weeks to compile. If you had nothing but the list of exam topics and the references, you would be well on your way to passing the exam.

You will find a reference to one or more of the five process groups—Initiating, Planning, Executing, Monitoring and Controlling, or Closing—and the Professional and Social Responsibility domain at the end of each rationale. Those references are important because they give you an understanding of the types of exam questions that fall within each of these six major project management performance domains.

This seventh edition includes many scenario-based questions, which comprise approximately 50 percent of the questions found on the PMP® exam. It omits many of the purely definitional questions; PMI® has gradually eliminated these types of questions from the exam.

We have included questions specifically related to the *PMBOK® Guide*'s nine knowledge areas and the various inputs, tools and techniques, and outputs described in the processes and subprocesses of those areas. Additionally, we have reduced the length of many of our questions, especially in the Professional and Social Responsibility section, to more accurately represent the real exam. Finally, in response to a number of requests we have included a completely original, 200-question practice test; none of these questions are found in the other sections of this book.

We have retained the helpful Study Matrix in this edition as well. The matrix is included as an appendix. The matrix, which is based on PMI®'s *Role Delineation Study,* will help you use the 200-question exam to its full advantage. The matrix provides a way for you to assess your strengths and weaknesses in each performance domain and to identify areas that require further study.

A special note to those who speak English as a second language (ESL): Our experience in teaching project management programs around the world has shown that most of our ESL clients understand English well enough to pass the PMP® exam *as long as they know the content.* Nevertheless, in an effort to avoid adding to your frustration before taking the exam, we have painstakingly reviewed each question and answer in the practice test to ensure that we did not use words, terms, or phrases that could be confusing to those who are not fluent in English.

Although the language issue may concern you, and rightfully so, the only difference between you and those who speak English as their first language is the amount of time it takes to complete the exam. I know of only one person who did not have enough time, and that individual was able to complete all but two questions. We would suggest, therefore, that if you can grasp the content expressed in this publication, a few colloquialisms or ambiguous terms on the real exam will not ultimately determine whether you pass or fail: Your subject matter knowledge will do that!

Earning the PMP® certification is a prestigious accomplishment. But studying for it need not be difficult if you use the tools available. You may want to include our companion piece, *PMP® Challenge!,* in your study plan if you have not already done so. In an easy flash-card format, it too provides many opportunities to become thoroughly familiar and comfortable with the project management body of knowledge. We would also like to recommend our CD audio set entitled "The Portable PMP® Prep: Conversations on Passing the PMP® Exam" if you are fluent in American English.

Good luck on the exam!

# ABOUT THE AUTHOR

**J. LeRoy Ward,** a project management professional with 29 years of experience in project management, is Executive Vice President of ESI International. He is responsible for all ESI corporate client engagements worldwide, including training in instructor relations and international partnerships. A PMP® since 1990, Mr. Ward developed ESI's popular *PMP® Exam Preparation* course and has taught it, and other courses, to people from more than 50 countries. He is the author of several books and articles on project management and is a frequent speaker at conferences around the world. He holds B.S. and M.S. degrees from Southern Connecticut State University and an M.S.T.M. degree, with distinction, in computer systems management from The American University.

# About ESI

**ESI International,** an IIR company, is a training and consulting firm founded as Educational Services Institute in 1981.  For the past 24 years, our professionals have helped other professionals acquire knowledge and competencies in project management, business analysis, and contract management.

Our one-of-a-kind curriculum has become the world's premier professional development program in project management.  More than 750,000 professionals from 100 countries have benefited from ESI's professional development programs.  Our Project Management Professional Development program, which leads to a Master's Certificate in Project Management from The George Washington University, comprises seven core courses and dozens of electives.   We have presented our programs to many of the world's largest corporations in the telecommunications, software development, lumber and paper products, oil exploration and refining, insurance, financial services, computer manufacturing, and banking industries.  In 2004, we presented more than 4,500 courses to more than 18,000 attendees on six continents.

ESI also develops and teaches sessions specially requested by clients.  Some sessions replicate our public courses; others are customized—in content, emphasis, or duration—to the client's specific needs.

In addition to training, ESI International also provides online appraisal instruments in project management, business analysis, and contract management, and online practice tests for the PMP® and CAPM™ credentials.

**Call toll free at 1 (888) ESI-8884 for a course catalog, or visit our Web site at http://www.esi-intl.com for more information.**

"CAPM" is a trademark of the Project Management Institute, Inc.

# CONTRIBUTING AUTHOR

**Dr. Ginger Levin,** a consultant and educator, has more than 30 years' experience in project management. From 1970 to 1984, she held several U.S. government positions, managing a variety of information systems and transportation projects. Since 1984, she has been active in project management and organizational development, consulting for both government and the private sector. In 1996, for example, she prepared courseware for the Project Management Institute in the nine project management knowledge areas described in the *PMBOK® Guide*. She is an Adjunct Professor and the Program Specialist in Project Management for the University of Wisconsin—Platteville, and the author or coauthor of several books and numerous papers in project management. Dr. Levin holds a D.P.A. and an M.S.A. from The George Washington University and a B.B.A. from Wake Forest University.

# ACKNOWLEDGMENTS

I am always amazed at the number of people it takes to get a publication out the door, and I would be remiss in not acknowledging the dedicated efforts of my colleagues who helped prepare what I consider to be a most important publication for PMP® exam takers.

My special thanks to **Rosalie Lacorazza,** editor, for her skillful and highly professional effort under an extraordinarily tight time frame, as well as for managing the entire project, **Nicole Peters** for assisting in the document update, and **Barbara Raab** for her cover design. Special thanks is extended to **Joe Czarnecki**, who manages all of ESI's product development projects.

I also would like to thank my friends and colleagues, who, through the years, have participated in this publication. They include **Rick Bilbro, Paul Chaney, Mike Farr, Leonard Krapcha, Bill Pursch, Ben Sellers, Ron Whitehead, Chester Zhivanos, Dixie Richards, Anne Feldman, Mary Saxton, Jeanne Trapani, Kim Briggs, Ron Guappone, Rodney Henderson, Trinh Le,** and **Carl Pritchard.** Their contributions to the various editions of this publication were critical to the success of this current edition, and I once again thank them for their help and encouragement.

Finally, I would like to thank **Ginger Levin,** who has been the lead contributing author for the past several editions of this manuscript, as well as a participant in earlier editions. Ginger has been a friend and colleague of mine for more than 10 years. She is a prolific writer, presenter, and thinker in the field of project management and has contributed mightily to the success of our PMP® preparation programs at ESI. I am truly indebted to her.

# INTRODUCTION

The PMP® exam contains 200 questions, of which 25 questions will not be included in the pass/fail determination. These "pretest" items, as PMI® calls them, will be randomly placed throughout the exam to gather statistical information on their performance to determine their use for future exams. Accordingly, to pass the PMP® exam, candidates must answer a minimum of 106 of the 175 scored questions, or roughly 61 percent.[1] Of the 175 scored questions, 20 questions (11.6%) relate to initiating, 40 questions (22.7%) relate to planning, 48 questions (27.5%) relate to executing, 37 questions (21%) relate to monitoring and controlling, 15 questions (8.6%) relate to closing, and 15 questions (8.6%) relate to professional and social responsibility. We have followed a similar distribution in our practice test so that it is representative of the PMP® exam.[2]

To use the study guide effectively, work on one section at a time. It does not matter which you choose first. Start by reading the study hints. They provide useful background on the content of the PMP® exam and identify the emphasis placed on various topics. Familiarize yourself with the major topics listed. Then answer the 40 practice questions, recording your answers on the sheet provided. Finally, compare your answers with those in the answer key. The rationales provided should clarify any misconceptions you may have had, and the process group designations will give you an understanding of the types of questions you might see on the exam that relate to those process groups. For further study and clarification, you may want to consult the bibliographic reference.

After you have finished answering the questions that follow each section, it is time to take the completely rewritten and original, 200-question practice test. Note your answers on the sheet provided, compare your answers to the answer key, and use the Study Matrix in the Appendix to determine what areas you need to study further.

---

[1] Remember, the 106 questions you need to get correct must be from the 175 scored questions. Simply getting 106 questions correct does not mean a passing grade if one or more of these come from the 25 "pretest" questions. Our suggestion, therefore, is to try to get at least 131 correct when you take the exam. When taking the 200-question exam in this book, we suggest you try to get 160 correct.

[2] The distribution has been applied to all 200 questions in our practice test in this Guide.

To make the most of this book, use it regularly. Take and retake the practice test. Photocopy the answer sheet in order to have a clean one each time you retake the test. Convene a study group to compare your answers with those of your colleagues. This method of study is a powerful one. You will learn more from your colleagues than you ever thought possible! Make sure you have a solid understanding of the exam topics that are provided in each section. Consult our extensive bibliography, or other sources you have found useful, for further independent study. And, most important, create a study plan and stick to it. Your chances of success are raised dramatically when you dedicate yourself to your goal.

# ACRONYMS

| | |
|---|---|
| AC | actual cost |
| AD | activity duration |
| ADM | arrow diagramming method |
| BAC | budget at completion |
| CEO | chief executive officer |
| CPI | cost performance index |
| CPM | critical path method |
| CV | cost variance |
| EAC | estimate at completion |
| EMV | expected monetary value |
| ERP | enterprise resource planning |
| ETC | estimate to complete |
| EV | earned value |
| EVM | earned value management |
| GERT | graphical evaluation and review technique |
| IFB | invitation for bid |
| ISO | International Organization for Standardization |
| JIT | just-in-time |
| LCC | life-cycle cost |
| MBO | management by objectives |
| MRP | material requirements planning |
| OBS | organizational breakdown structure |
| PDM | precedence diagramming method |
| PERT | program evaluation and review technique |
| *PMBOK® Guide* | *A Guide to the Project Management Body of Knowledge* |
| PMI® | Project Management Institute |
| PMIS | project management information system |
| PMO | program management office |
| PMP® | project management professional |
| PRC | project review committee |
| PV | planned value |
| RFP | request for proposal |
| ROI | return on investment |

| | |
|---|---|
| SD | standard deviation |
| SPC | statistical process control |
| SPI | schedule performance index |
| SV | schedule variance |
| SWOT | strengths-weaknesses-opportunities-threats |
| TCPI | to complete performance index |
| VAC | variance at completion |
| WBS | work breakdown structure |

# PROJECT INTEGRATION MANAGEMENT

## Study Hints

The Project Integration Management questions on the PMP® certification exam address critical project management functions that ensure coordination of the various elements of the project.  As the *PMBOK® Guide* explains, the processes in integration management are *primarily* integrative.  Project Integration Management involves making trade-offs among competing objectives to meet or exceed stakeholder needs and expectations and addresses project initiation with the development of a project charter and a preliminary project scope statement, project plan development, project plan execution, monitoring and controlling the project work, integrated change control, and closing the project.  These seven processes not only interact with one another but also interact with processes in the other eight knowledge areas.  It is important to note PMI®'s view that integration occurs in other areas as well.  For example, project scope and product scope need to be integrated, project work needs to be integrated with other ongoing work of the organization, and deliverables from various technical specialties need integration.

The Project Integration Management questions are relatively straightforward.  Most people find them to be fairly easy.  But because they cover so much material, including all five of the process groups, you do need to study them carefully to become familiar with PMI®'s terminology and perspectives.  *PMBOK® Guide* Figure 4-1 provides an overview of the structure of Project Integration Management.  Know this chart thoroughly.

Following is a list of the major Project Integration Management topics.  Use it to help focus your study efforts on the areas most likely to appear on the exam.

# Major Topics

*Project, program, and portfolio definitions*

*Project management definition*

*Project life cycle*

*Project management office*

*Project process groups*

- Initiating
- Planning
- Executing
- Monitoring and Controlling
- Closing

*Develop project charter*

*Enterprise environmental factors*

*Organizational process assets*

*Develop preliminary project scope statement*

*Develop project management plan*

*Project management methodology*

*Stakeholders*

*Project management information system (PMIS)*

*Earned value technique*

*Expert judgment*

*Project management plan*

*Direct and manage project execution*

*Corrective and preventive action*

*Deliverables*

*Work performance information*

# Major Topics (continued)

*Interpersonal skills*

- Leadership
- Communicating
- Negotiating and conflict management
- Problem solving
- Influencing the organization
- Motivation

*Standards and regulations*

*Management by objectives*

- Three-step process

*Project environment*

- Culture and social environment
- International and political environment
- Physical environment

*Monitor and control project work*

*Forecasts*

*Integrated change control*

*Change requests*

*Change control system*

- Change control board

*Configuration management system*

- Purpose
- Basic steps in configuration management

*Close project*

*Administrative closure procedure*

*Contract closure procedure*

*Lessons learned*

# Practice Questions

INSTRUCTIONS: Note the most suitable answer for each multiple-choice question in the appropriate space on the answer sheet.

1. Your company's project review committee (PRC) asked you to present your project's objectives, requirements, and deliverables at its next meeting. You need to prepare which one of the following documents?

   a. Project charter
   b. Product description
   c. Preliminary project scope statement
   d. WBS

2. You are managing a large project with 20 key internal stakeholders, 8 contractors, and 6 team leaders. You must devote attention to effective integrated change control. This means you are concerned primarily with—

   a. Reviewing, approving, and controlling changes
   b. Maintaining baseline integrity, integrating product and project scope, and coordinating change across knowledge areas
   c. Integrating deliverables from different functional specialties on the project
   d. Establishing a change control board that oversees the overall project changes

3. Management wants your project to yield high-value results at a low cost. Your internal client wants all the features identified regardless of the cost. When working with stakeholders, you should—

   a. Group stakeholders into categories for easy identification
   b. Proactively curtail stakeholder activities that might affect the project adversely
   c. Be sensitive to the fact that stakeholders often have very different objectives and that this makes stakeholder management difficult
   d. Recognize that roles and responsibilities may overlap

4. Your project has a budget of $1.5 million for the first year, $3 million for the second year, $2.2 million for the third year, and $800,000 for the fourth year. Most of the project budget will be spent during—

   a. Develop project plan
   b. Direct and manage project execution
   c. Integrated change control
   d. Project initiation

5. You are leading a team to establish a project selection and prioritization method. The team is considering many different management concerns, including financial return, market share, and public perception. The most important criteria for building a project selection model is—

   a. Capability
   b. Realism
   c. Ease of use
   d. Cost

6. When you established the change control board for your avionics project, you established specific procedures to govern its operation. The procedures require all approved changes to be reflected in the—

   a. Performance measurement baseline
   b. Change management plan
   c. Quality assurance plan
   d. Project management plan

7. You are beginning a new project staffed with a virtual team that is located in five countries. To help avoid conflict in work priorities among your team and the functional managers, you ask the project sponsor to prepare a—

   a. Memo to team members informing them that they work for you now
   b. Project charter
   c. Memo to the functional managers informing them that you have authority to direct their employees
   d. Human resource management plan

8. In which of the following processes will you use such project performance information as actual costs and deliverables completed?

   a. Direct and manage project execution
   b. Integrated change control
   c. Performance reporting
   d. Scope verification

9. Your company is embarking on a project to completely eliminate defects in its products. You are the project manager for this project, and you have just finished the concept phase. The deliverable for this phase is the—

   a. Project plan
   b. Statement of work
   c. Project charter
   d. Resource spreadsheet

10. Your project management office implemented a project management methodology that emphasizes the importance of integrated change control. It states that change requests can occur in all the following forms *except—*

    a. Indirect
    b. Legally mandated
    c. Informal
    d. Internally initiated

11. You are a team member on a project whose project manager believes that people are motivated only by money and need to be supervised closely, otherwise they will not do as directed. This project manager's approach is characterized by which one of the following theories?

    a. Ouchi's Theory of Inconsequential Behavior
    b. McGregor's Theory X
    c. Maslow's Theory of Micromanagement
    d. Vroom's Expectancy Theory

12. All the following are examples of mathematical models *except—*

    a. Integer programming
    b. Dynamic programming
    c. Economic model
    d. Multiobjective programming

13. You have been assigned to manage a large enterprise resource planning (ERP) project in your organization. You realize that detailed planning, execution, and closing processes are prerequisites for success. To support the project from initiation through closing you should use—

    a. A make-or-buy analysis
    b. Lessons learned and other historical information from previous projects
    c. Benefit-cost analysis
    d. The project management information system

14. You are implementing a project management methodology for your company that requires you to establish a change control board. Which one of the following statements *best* describes a change control board?

    a. Recommended for use on all (large and small) projects
    b. Used to review, evaluate, approve, delay, or reject changes to the project
    c. Managed by the project manager, who also serves as its secretary
    d. Composed of key project team members

15. You prepared a project management plan and a project schedule. Key stakeholders accepted the plan. It is time to distribute it. Both the project management plan and schedule should be distributed to—

    a. All stakeholders in the performing organization
    b. All project stakeholders
    c. Project team members and the project sponsor
    d. People identified in the communications management plan

16. You realize that leadership without management or management without leadership probably will produce poor project results. Which one of the following key responsibilities *best* represents project leadership?

    a. Developing a vision and strategy, and motivating people to achieve them
    b. Getting things done through other people
    c. Using charismatic power to motivate others even if they don't like the work
    d. Using all types of power, as appropriate, as motivational tools

17. You have been directed to establish a change control system for your company, but must convince your colleagues to use it. To be effective, the change control system must include—

    a. Procedures that define how project documents may be changed
    b. Specific change requests expected on the project and plans to respond to each one
    c. Performance reports that forecast project changes
    d. A description of the functional and physical characteristics of an item or system

18. According to Herzberg's Motivator-Hygiene Theory, when achievement, recognition, responsibility, and advancement or promotion are *not* present, employees will—

    a. Become alienated with the organization and leave
    b. Lack motivation but will not be dissatisfied with their work
    c. Lack motivation and become dissatisfied with their work
    d. Become dissatisfied only if they do not receive salary increases

19. You are a member of a project selection committee using the discounted cash-flow approach. Using this approach, the project is acceptable if the—

    a. Sum of the net present value of all estimated cash flow during the life of the project equals the profit
    b. Net present value of the inflow is greater than the net present value of the outflow by a specified amount or percentage
    c. Gross present value of all future expected cash flow divided by the initial cash investment is greater than one
    d. Payback period occurs by the second year of the project

20. You are project manager for a systems integration effort and need to procure the hardware components from external sources. Your subcontracts administrator has told you to prepare a product description, which is also called a—

    a. Statement of work
    b. Contract scope statement
    c. Request for proposal
    d. Contract

21. Because your project is slated to last five years, you believe rolling wave planning is appropriate. It provides information about the work to be done—

    a. Throughout all project phases
    b. For successful completion of the current project phase
    c. For successful completion of the current and subsequent project phases
    d. In the next project phase

22. Configuration management describes procedures for applying technical and administrative direction and surveillance. Which one of the following tasks is *not* performed in configuration management?

    a. Identifying functional and physical characteristics of an item or system
    b. Controlling changes to characteristics
    c. Performing an audit to verify conformance to requirements
    d. Allowing automatic approval of changes

23. You are managing a project to introduce a new product to the marketplace that is expected to have a very long life. In this situation, the concept of being *temporary,* which is part of the definition of a project—

    a. Does not apply because the project will have a lasting result
    b. Does not apply to the product to be created
    c. Recognizes that the project team will outlive the actual project
    d. Does not apply because the project will not be short in duration

24. Although your company's project life cycle does not mandate when a project review should be conducted, you believe it is important to review performance at the conclusion of each phase. The objective of such a review is to—

    a. Determine how many resources are required to complete the project according to the project baseline
    b. Adjust the schedule and cost baselines based on past performance
    c. Obtain customer acceptance of project deliverables
    d. Determine whether the project should continue to the next phase

25. You are part of a team that is preparing a project plan for your company's new wireless VCR product line. Which one of the following is an example of a constraint that you should consider?

    a. Records of past performance
    b. Financial reports from similar projects
    c. Predefined budget
    d. Lessons learned from previous projects

26. A number of tools and techniques are helpful in integrated change control. If you want to implement an integrated change control process, you should use—

    a. Configuration management software
    b. A project management information system
    c. Project status review meetings
    d. Project management methodology

27. You have just conducted a project kickoff meeting with your team members and other stakeholders. One of the stakeholders asked a question about project failure. You responded by saying—

    a. The risk of failing to achieve the objectives is greatest at the start of the project
    b. The probability of failure increases throughout the life cycle as more team members work on the project
    c. The number of scope changes will increase project risk
    d. The risk of project failure can be mitigated by using matrix management

28. Ideally, a project manager should be selected and assigned at which point in the project life cycle?

    a. During the initiating processes
    b. During the project planning process
    c. At the end of the concept phase of the project life cycle
    d. Prior to the beginning of the development phase of the project life cycle

29. Implemented change requests are an output from—

    a. Develop project management plan
    b. Direct and manage project execution
    c. Integrated change control
    d. Monitor and control project work

30. You want to minimize the impact of changes on your project, yet you want to ensure that change is managed when and if it occurs. This can be done through each of the following ways *except*—

    a. Rejecting requested changes when appropriate
    b. Approving changes and incorporating them into a revised baseline
    c. Documenting the complete impact of requested changes
    d. Ensuring that project scope changes are reflected in changes to product scope

31. According to the expectancy theory of motivation—

    a. Poor performance is the natural outcome of poor training
    b. Managers should not expect too much of workers
    c. Motivation to act is linked to an outcome that is expected to have value
    d. Managers should expect that employees who are paid more will work harder

32. You are responsible for a project management training curriculum that is offered throughout the organization. In this situation, your intangible deliverables are—

    a. Employees who can apply the training effectively
    b. Training materials for each course
    c. Certificates of completion for everyone who completes the program
    d. The training curriculum as advertised in your catalog

33. You are a personnel management specialist recently assigned to a project team working on a team-based reward and recognition system. The other team members also work in the human resources department. The project charter should be issued by—

    a. The project manager
    b. The client
    c. A sponsor external to the project
    d. A member of the program management office (PMO) who has jurisdiction over human resources

34. Administrative closure should not be delayed until project completion because—

    a. Useful information may be lost
    b. The project manager may be reassigned
    c. Project team members may be reassigned by that time
    d. Sellers are anxious for payments

35. The most appropriate management style to use to encourage your staff to pool its knowledge about project issues to make the best decisions possible is—

    a. Laissez-faire
    b. Democratic
    c. Autocratic
    d. Directive

36. Project management processes describe project work, while product-oriented management processes specify the project's product. Therefore, a project management process and a product-oriented management process—

    a. Overlap and interact throughout the project
    b. Are defined by the project life cycle
    c. Are concerned with describing and organizing project work
    d. Are similar for each application area

37. The administrative closure procedure addresses actions and activities concerning all of the following *except*—

    a. Completion or exit criteria for the project
    b. Stakeholder approval requirements for changes and deliverables
    c. Verification that the deliverables have been provided and accepted
    d. Documentation that completed deliverables have been accepted

38. Your project is proceeding according to schedule. You have just learned that a new regulatory requirement will cause a change in one of the project's performance specifications. To ensure that this change is incorporated into the project plan, you should—

    a. Call a meeting of the change control board
    b. Change the WBS, project schedule, and project plan to reflect the new requirement
    c. Prepare a change request
    d. Immediately inform all affected stakeholders of the new approach to take on the project

39. The highest level of Maslow's theory of motivation characterized by responsibility, a sense of accomplishment, and a sense of competence is called—

    a. Self-actualization
    b. Social
    c. Esteem
    d. Physiological

40. You are the new head of the project management office. There have been many arguments among project managers regarding the detail to be included in any WBS. You prepare a guideline that states that the WBS—

    a. Should be three levels to avoid confusing the client
    b. Should be included as part of the scope management plan regardless of its detail
    c. Should be developed, but only to the second level for small projects
    d. Should be developed to the level at which control will be exercised

## Answer Sheet

1. a b c d     21. a b c d
2. a b c d     22. a b c d
3. a b c d     23. a b c d
4. a b c d     24. a b c d
5. a b c d     25. a b c d
6. a b c d     26. a b c d
7. a b c d     27. a b c d
8. a b c d     28. a b c d
9. a b c d     29. a b c d
10. a b c d     30. a b c d
11. a b c d     31. a b c d
12. a b c d     32. a b c d
13. a b c d     33. a b c d
14. a b c d     34. a b c d
15. a b c d     35. a b c d
16. a b c d     36. a b c d
17. a b c d     37. a b c d
18. a b c d     38. a b c d
19. a b c d     39. a b c d
20. a b c d     40. a b c d

# Answer Key

### 1. c. Preliminary project scope statement

The preliminary project scope statement provides stakeholders with a common understanding of the scope of the project and is a source of reference for making future project decisions. [Initiating]

PMI®, *PMBOK® Guide*, 2004, 86

### 2. a. Reviewing, approving, and controlling changes

Integrated change control consists of coordinating and managing changes across the project. Activities that occur within the context of integrated change control include scope control, scope verification, schedule control, cost control, quality control, risk monitoring and control, and contract administration. [Monitoring and Controlling]

PMI®, *PMBOK® Guide*, 2004, 363

### 3. c. Be sensitive to the fact that stakeholders often have very different objectives and that this makes stakeholder management difficult

A project stakeholder is an individual or organization who is actively involved in the project or whose interests may be affected, either positively or negatively, as a result of project execution or successful project completion. Stakeholders also may exert influence on the project and its results. Managing stakeholder expectations is difficult because stakeholders often have different, conflicting objectives. [Monitoring and Controlling]

PMI®, *PMBOK® Guide*, 2004, 26

### 4. b. Direct and manage project execution

It is during this phase that all the interfaces affecting the project must be coordinated and that the product or service of the project is created. [Executing]

PMI®, *PMBOK® Guide*, 2004, 91

### 5. b.  Realism

The model should reflect the objectives of the company and its managers; consider the realities of the organization's limitations on facilities, capital, and personnel; and include factors for risk—the technical risks of performance, cost, and time and the market risk of customer rejection. [Initiating]

Meredith and Mantel 2006, 43

### 6. d.  Project management plan

The project management plan must be updated continually to reflect project modifications, and those changes must be communicated to appropriate stakeholders in a timely manner.  [Monitoring and Controlling]

PMI®, *PMBOK® Guide*, 2004, 96

### 7. b.  Project charter

Although the project charter cannot stop conflicts from arising, it can provide a framework to help resolve them because it describes the project manager's authority to apply organizational resources to project activities. [Initiating]

Meredith and Mantel 2006, 239

### 8. c.  Performance reporting

Work performance information is the outcome of activities performed to accomplish the project.  Work performance information is collected as part of the direct and manage project execution process, and should be used in the performance reporting process to meet performance objectives defined in the project management plan and project scope statement, and to provide stakeholders with information about how resources are being used to achieve project objectives.  [Executing and Monitoring and Controlling]

PMI®, *PMBOK® Guide*, 2004, 91

### 9. c.  Project charter

This document signifies official sanction by top management and starts the planning, or development, phase.  The project charter formally recognizes the existence of the project and provides the project manager with the authority to apply organizational resources to project activities.  [Initiating]

PMI®, *PMBOK® Guide*, 2004, 81–82

**10. c.  Informal**

Requested changes are an input to integrated change control.  Although occurring in many forms, they must be formal requests developed within the context of a change control system consisting of documented procedures.  [Monitoring and Controlling]

PMI®, *PMBOK® Guide*, 2004, 93

**11. b.  McGregor's Theory X**

McGregor observed two types of managers and classified them by their perceptions of workers.  Theory X managers thought that workers were lazy, needed to be watched and supervised closely, and were irresponsible.  Theory Y managers thought that, given the correct conditions, workers could be trusted to seek responsibility and work hard at their jobs.  [Executing]

McGregor 1960, 33–35; Verma 1996, 68–69

**12. c.  Economic model**

Economic models include benefit measurement methods, comparative approaches, scoring models, and benefit contribution.  [Initiating]

PMI®, *PMBOK® Guide*, 2004, 85

**13. d.  The project management information system**

This system supports the project from the initiating through the closing phases, and generally consists of a standard set of automated tools available within the organization and integrated into a system.  [Planning]

PMI®, *PMBOK® Guide*, 2004, 86

**14. b.  Used to review, evaluate, approve, delay, or reject changes to the project**

The change control board's powers and responsibilities should be well defined and agreed upon by key stakeholders.  On some projects, multiple change control boards may exist with different areas of responsibility.  [Monitoring and Controlling]

PMI®, *PMBOK® Guide*, 2004, 98 and 353

**15. d. People identified in the communications management plan**

The communications management plan defines who receives what kinds of information and the level of detail to be provided to each person. For example, managers in the performing organization may require only the more general information from the project management plan, whereas sellers may need the more detailed portions of the plan that pertain to their operations. [Planning]

PMI®, *PMBOK® Guide*, 2004, 227

**16. a. Developing a vision and strategy and motivating people to achieve them**

Leadership involves developing a vision of the future and strategies to achieve that vision, positioning people to carry out the vision, and helping people energize themselves to overcome any barriers to change. [Executing]

PMI®, *PMBOK® Guide*, 2004, 15

**17. a. Procedures that define how project documents may be changed**

A change control system is a collection of formal, documented procedures that define the process used to control change and approve project documents. It includes the paperwork, tracking systems, and approval levels necessary to authorize changes. It also provides guidance on when changes can be approved without formal review. [Planning and Monitoring and Controlling]

PMI®, *PMBOK® Guide*, 2004, 90 and 96

**18. c. Lack motivation and become dissatisfied with their work**

Herzberg advanced the theory that hygiene factors, such as the poor attitude of a supervisor, lead to dissatisfaction but not usually to decreased motivation. When motivators, such as responsibility and recognition, are lacking, they lead to job dissatisfaction, but when such motivators are present, they tend to motivate a person in the performance of his or her work. [Executing]

ESI October 2004, 6-12; Verma 1996, 64–65

**19. b. Net present value of the inflow is greater than the net present value of the outflow by a specified amount or percentage**

The discounted cash-flow approach—or the present value method—determines the net present value of all cash flow by discounting it by the required rate of return. The impact of inflation can be considered. Early in the life of a project, net cash flow is likely to be negative because the major outflow is the initial investment in the project. If the project is successful, cash flow will become positive. [Initiating]

Meredith and Mantel 2006, 50–51

**20. a. Statement of work**

Many projects involve one organization (the seller) doing work under contract to another (the buyer). In such circumstances, the buyer provides the initial product scope description, which is also called a statement of work. [Initiating]

PMI®, *PMBOK® Guide*, 2004, 82 and 280

**21. c. For successful completion of the current and subsequent project phases**

Rolling wave planning provides progressive detailing of the work to be accomplished throughout the life of the project. [Planning]

PMI®, *PMBOK® Guide*, 2004, 128 and 374

**22. d. Allowing automatic approval of changes**

Allowing for automatic approval of defined changes is a function of the change control system, not configuration management. Configuration management ensures that the description of the project product is correct and complete. [Monitoring and Controlling]

PMI®, *PMBOK® Guide*, 2004, 90

**23. b. Does not apply to the product to be created**

A project is completed when its objectives have been achieved or when they are recognized as being unachievable and the project is terminated. In this case, the end will occur when the product is finished. Thus, the concept of *temporary* applies to the project life cycle—not the product life cycle. [Planning]

PMI®, *PMBOK® Guide*, 2004, 5

### 24. d. Determine whether the project should continue to the next phase

The review at the end of a project phase is called a phase exit, stage gate, or kill point. The purpose of this review is to determine whether the project should continue to the next phase, to detect and correct errors while they are still manageable, and to ensure that the project remains focused on the business need it was undertaken to address. [Initiating]

PMI®, *PMBOK® Guide*, 2004, 23, 43–44

### 25. c. Predefined budget

Constraints are factors that limit the project management team's options. A predefined budget will likely limit the team's options with regard to scope, staffing, and schedule. [Planning]

PMI®, *PMBOK® Guide*, 2004, 355

### 26. d. Project management methodology

The project management methodology is a key tool and technique for integrated change control to aid the team in implementing this process for the project. [Monitoring and Controlling]

PMI®, *PMBOK® Guide*, 2004, 85

### 27. a. The risk of failing to achieve the objectives is greatest at the start of the project

Because the level of uncertainty is highest at the beginning of a project, the probability of failure is equally as high. As the project progresses, uncertainty and the chance of failure diminish.

PMI®, *PMBOK® Guide*, 2004, 20

### 28. a. During the initiating processes

If the project manager is selected and assigned to the project during initiation, several of the usual start-up tasks of the project are simplified. In addition, becoming involved with project activities from the beginning helps the project manager understand where the project fits within the organization in terms of its priority relative to other projects and the ongoing work of the organization. [Initiating]

Meredith and Mantel 2006, 117; PMI®, *PMBOK® Guide*, 2004, 43

### 29. b.  Direct and manage project execution

These are the approved change requests that have been implemented by the project team during project execution.  [Executing]

PMI®, *PMBOK® Guide*, 2004, 93

### 30. d.  Ensuring that project scope changes are reflected in changes to product scope

Integrated change control requires maintaining the integrity of baselines by releasing only approved changes into project products or services.  It also ensures that changes to product scope are reflected in the project scope definition.  This is done by coordinating changes across the entire project.  [Monitoring and Controlling]

PMI®, *PMBOK® Guide*, 2004, 96–97

### 31. c.  Motivation to act is linked to an outcome that is expected to have value

The strength of a tendency to act in a certain way depends on both the strength of an expectation that this act will be followed by a given outcome and the value of that outcome.  [Executing]

Vroom 1995, 20; Verma 1996, 73

### 32. a.  Employees who can apply the training effectively

Most deliverables are tangible, such as buildings or roads; but intangible deliverables also can be provided.  Information on work performance is collected during project execution and becomes an input to the performance reporting process for the project.  [Executing]

PMI®, *PMBOK® Guide*, 2004, 91

### 33. c.  A sponsor external to the project

The project charter should be issued by a project initiator or sponsor outside the project but at a level appropriate to the project's needs.  Because it provides the project manager with the authority to apply organizational resources to project activities, the project charter should not be issued by the project manager.  Functional managers should have approval authority.  [Initiating]

PMI®, *PMBOK® Guide*, 2004, 81

### 34. a. Useful information may be lost

Closure includes collecting project records, ensuring that the records accurately reflect final specifications, analyzing project or phase success and effectiveness, and archiving such information for future use. Each phase of the project should be properly closed while important project information is still available. [Closing]

PMI®, *PMBOK® Guide*, 2004, 66 and 100

### 35. b. Democratic

A democratic management style provides maximum participation for the development of creative solutions in the group. Watch out, however, for the "tyranny of the majority," where voting can drown a creative voice. This style would not be effective in an emergency situation where fast action is required. [Executing]

Frame 1995, 78–79

### 36. a. Overlap and interact throughout the project

Project management processes and product-oriented management processes must be integrated throughout the project's life cycle, given their close relationship. In some cases, it's difficult to distinguish between the two. For example, knowing how the project will be created aids in determining the project's scope. [Executing]

PMI®, *PMBOK® Guide*, 2004, 38

### 37. d. Documentation that completed deliverables have been accepted

Such documentation is prepared as an output from scope verification. The administrative closure procedure provides a step-by-step methodology that addresses stakeholder approval requirements for changes and all levels of deliverables; confirmation that the project has met sponsor, customer, and other stakeholder requirements; verification that the deliverables have been provided and accepted; and satisfaction and validation that completion and exit criteria have been met. [Closing]

PMI®, *PMBOK® Guide*, 2004, 101–102

**38. c. Prepare a change request**

The change request should detail the nature of the change and its effect on the project. Documentation is critical to provide a record of the change and who approved it, in case differences of opinion arise later. A requested change is an output from the direct and manage project execution process and an input to integrated change control. [Monitoring and Controlling]

PMI®, *PMBOK® Guide*, 2004, 93 and 98

**39. c. Esteem**

Other examples of esteem needs include self-respect, recognition, and a sense of equity. [Executing]

Maslow 1954, 80–92; Verma 1996, 60–63

**40. d. Should be developed to the level at which control will be exercised**

The WBS is a baseline scope document. As such, it should be included in the project management plan at the level at which control will be exercised. [Planning]

PMI®, *PMBOK® Guide*, 2004, 88

# PROJECT SCOPE MANAGEMENT

## Study Hints

The Project Scope Management questions on the PMP® certification exam cover a diverse, yet fundamental, set of project management topics. Project planning, work breakdown structures, project life cycle, scope statement, scope verification, scope management plan, and scope changes are among the topics covered.

PMI® views Project Scope Management as a five-step process that consists of scope planning, scope definition, creation of the WBS, scope verification, and scope control. *PMBOK® Guide* Figure 5-1 provides an overview of this structure. Know this chart thoroughly.

The Project Scope Management questions on the exam are straightforward. Historically, most people have found them to be relatively easy; however, do not be lulled into a false sense of security by past results. These questions cover a wide breadth of material, and you must be familiar with the terminology and perspectives adopted by PMI®.

Following is a list of the major Project Scope Management topics. Use it to help focus your study efforts on the areas most likely to appear on the exam.

## Major Topics

*Scope planning*

*Project scope management plan*

*Scope definition*

*Product analysis*

*Alternatives analysis*

*Stakeholder analysis*

*Project scope statement*

*Work breakdown structure*

- Benefits
- Uses
- Development
- Other structures

*WBS dictionary*

*Scope baseline*

*Scope verification*

*Inspection*

*Accepted deliverables*

*Scope control*

*Scope change control system*

*Variance analysis*

*Cost of capital*

## Practice Questions

INSTRUCTIONS:  Note the most suitable answer for each multiple-choice question in the appropriate space on the answer sheet.

1. Progressive elaboration of product characteristics on your project must be coordinated carefully with the—

   a. Proper project scope definition
   b. Project stakeholders
   c. Scope change control system
   d. Customer's strategic plan

2. You are examining multiple scope change requests on a project you were asked to take over because the previous project manager decided to resign.  To assess the degree to which the project scope will change, you need to compare the requests to which project document?

   a. Preliminary scope statement
   b. WBS
   c. Project plan
   d. Scope management plan

3. A critical project may require formal, thorough, and time-intensive scoping activities, while a routine project involves less documentation and scrutiny.  This statement shows that—

   a. Effort expended on scoping activities should be commensurate with the project's size, complexity, and importance
   b. The project management methodology is a key tool and technique used in the scope planning process
   c. Expert judgment is required as an input to scope definition but is required only for complex projects
   d. A change request should be prepared to enable the routine project to use less documentation and have less scrutiny

4. An example of an organizational process asset that could affect how project scope is managed is—

   a. Personnel policies
   b. Marketplace conditions
   c. Historical information on previous projects
   d. Organizational culture

5. The components of the project scope management plan include all the following processes *except*—

   a. How formal verification and acceptance of deliverables will be obtained
   b. How change requests to the scope management plan will be processed
   c. How to prepare a detailed project scope statement
   d. How to create the WBS

6. A key tool and technique used in scope definition is—

   a. Templates, forms, and standards
   b. Decomposition
   c. Stakeholder analysis
   d. Project management methodology

7. Alternatives identification often is useful in project planning. An example of a technique that can be used is—

   a. Sensitivity analysis
   b. Decision trees
   c. Mathematical model
   d. Lateral thinking

8. Product analysis techniques include all the following *except*—

   a. Value engineering
   b. Value analysis
   c. Functional analysis
   d. Bill of materials

9. The baseline for evaluating whether requests for changes or additional work are contained within or outside the project's boundaries is provided by the—

   a. Project management plan
   b. Project scope statement
   c. Project scope management plan
   d. WBS dictionary

10. Rather than use a WBS, your team developed a bill of materials to define the project's work components. A customer review of this document uncovered that a scope change was needed, and a change request was subsequently written. This is an example of a change request that was the result of—

    a. An external event
    b. An error or omission in defining the scope of the product
    c. A value-adding change
    d. An error or omission in defining the scope of the project

11. Your management has stated that your project is not to exceed $500,000 and ideally should cost less than $450,000. These are examples of—

    a. Project objectives
    b. Project assumptions
    c. Project requirements
    d. Funding limitations

12. Your project is now under way, and you recognize that, given the nature of project work, scope change is inevitable. You meet with your team and decide to establish a project scope change control system, which is—

    a. A collection of formal, documented procedures to define the steps by which official project documents may be changed
    b. A documented process used to apply technical and administrative direction and surveillance to identify and document functional and physical characteristics of items, record and report change, control change, and audit the items and system to verify conformance to requirements
    c. A set of procedures by which project scope and product scope may be changed
    d. Mandatory for use on projects so that the scope management plan cannot be changed without prior review and sign-off

13. The level of configuration management and change control to be implemented on the project should be—

    a. Part of the scope change control system
    b. Stated in the project scope statement
    c. Determined based on the initial requests for changes
    d. Part of the project management information system

14. You want to structure your project so that each project team member has a discrete work package to perform. The work package is a—

    a. Deliverable at the lowest level of the WBS
    b. Task with a unique identifier
    c. Required level of reporting
    d. Task that can be assigned to more than one organizational unit

15. Approved change requests may result in the need to—

    a. Update the organizational breakdown structure
    b. Update the scope management plan
    c. Define corrective action as part of scope control
    d. Define preventive action as part of scope control

16. The first level of decomposition of the WBS may be displayed by using all but which one of the following?

    a. Phases of the project life cycle
    b. Subprojects
    c. Major deliverables
    d. Project organizational units

17. Your customer signed off on the requirements definition document and scope statement of your video game project last month. Today she stated she would like to make it an interactive game that can be played on a television and on a computer. This represents a requested scope change that, at a minimum—

    a. Should be reviewed according to the integrated change control process
    b. Results in a change to all project baselines
    c. Requires adjustments to cost, time, quality, and other objectives
    d. Results in a lesson learned

18. Each WBS component should be assigned a unique identifier from a code of accounts in order to—

    a. Link the WBS to the bill of materials
    b. Enable the WBS to follow a similar numbering system to that of the organization's units as part of the organizational breakdown structure
    c. Sum costs, schedule, and resource information
    d. Link the WBS to the project management plan

19. A key input to the scope verification process is the—

    a. WBS
    b. WBS dictionary
    c. Accepted deliverables
    d. Approved change requests

20. An example of an enterprise environmental factor used as an input to scope planning is—

    a. An organization's culture
    b. Historical information on previous projects
    c. Organizational policies
    d. Organizational procedures

21. You have been appointed project manager for a new project in your organization and must prepare a project plan. You decide to prepare a WBS to show the magnitude and complexity of the work involved. No WBS templates are available to help you. To prepare the WBS, your first step should be to—

    a. Determine the cost and duration estimates for each project deliverable
    b. Identify the deliverables and related work
    c. Identify the components of each project deliverable
    d. Determine the key tasks to be performed

22. Other terms used for inspections include all the following *except*—

    a. Walkthroughs
    b. Audits
    c. Performance reports
    d. Product reviews

23. You are leading a project team to identify potential new products for your organization. One idea was rejected by management because it would not fit with the organization's core competencies. You need to recommend other products using management's guideline as—

    a. An assumption
    b. A risk
    c. A specification
    d. A technical requirement

24. Change is inevitable on projects. Uncontrolled changes are often referred to as—

    a. Rework
    b. Scope creep
    c. Configuration items
    d. Emergency changes

25. In scope control it is important to determine the cause of any unacceptable variance relative to the scope baseline. This can be done through—

    a. Root cause analysis
    b. Control charts
    c. Inspections
    d. Project performance measurements

26. Which one of the following projects has the most attractive BCR (benefit cost ratio)?

    | Project | Benefits | Costs |
    | --- | --- | --- |
    | A | 100 | 50 |
    | B | 1,000 | 500 |
    | C | 10,000 | 5,000 |

    a. Project A
    b. Project B
    c. Project C
    d. None, the BCR for each is the same

27. Modifications may be needed to the WBS and WBS dictionary because of approved change requests. This shows that—

    a. Replanning is an output from scope control
    b. Scope creep is common on projects
    c. Rebaselining subsequently will be necessary
    d. Replanning is a tool and technique for scope control

28. Which of the following ensures that requested changes to both product scope and project scope are thoroughly considered before they are processed through the integrated change control process?

    a. Scope change control system
    b. Configuration management system
    c. Change control board
    d. Configuration status audits

29. Scope verification—

    a. Improves cost and schedule accuracy, particularly on projects using innovative techniques or technology
    b. Is the last activity performed on a project before handoff to the customer
    c. Documents the characteristics of the product or service that the project was undertaken to create
    d. Differs from quality control in that scope verification is concerned with the acceptance—not the correctness—of the work results

30. Specifying the project's technical requirements is an important step because such requirements—

    a. Describe the characteristics of the deliverable in ordinary language
    b. Are used by the project staff to target efforts
    c. Are useful to both the project staff and the customers
    d. Are designed to ensure that customers know what they are getting from a project

31. Any step recommended to bring expected future performance in line with the project management plan is called—

    a. Performance evaluation
    b. Corrective action
    c. Preventive action
    d. Defect repair

32. Written change orders should be required on—

    a. All projects, large and small
    b. Only large projects
    c. Projects with a formal configuration management system in place
    d. Projects for which the cost of a change control system can be justified

33. Your team has been working on a contract for three years. Yesterday you were informed that your client depleted its resources and will terminate the contract for convenience. Your first action is to—

    a. Submit the work products to date to your client's representative
    b. Document lessons learned
    c. Establish and document the level and extent of completion
    d. Shut down the project office and reassign all personnel

34. Of the following, which one is *not* an input to scope change control?

    a. WBS
    b. Performance reports
    c. Deliverables
    d. Project scope management plan

35. The project scope statement is important in scope control because it—

    a. Provides the scope baseline
    b. Provides information on project performance
    c. Alerts the project team to issues that may cause problems in the future
    d. Is expected to change throughout the project

36. You are the project manager for a subcontractor on a major contract. The prime contractor has asked that you manage your work in a detailed manner. Your first step is to—

    a. Follow the WBS that the prime contractor developed for the project and use the work packages you identified during the proposal
    b. Develop a subproject WBS for the work package that is your company's responsibility
    c. Establish a similar coding structure to the prime's to facilitate use of a common project management information system
    d. Develop a WBS dictionary to show specific staff assignments

37. Your project selection team is using payback period as a method to determine which projects to undertake. You disagree with this approach citing that the major shortcoming of using payback period is—

    a. It is often difficult to identify all costs incurred on a project
    b. Project cost estimates are overly optimistic, thus skewing the analysis
    c. It does not take into account cash flows after the payback period and it is not a measure of profitability
    d. It relies too heavily on economic value added approaches to determine net present value

38. Your project has been defined as clinical trials for a new drug that improves memory. As the project proceeds, the product is described more explicitly as four Phase I trials, five Phase II trials, and six Phase III trials. This situation provides an example of—

    a. Quality function deployment
    b. Close alignment of project activities with the WBS
    c. Value analysis
    d. Progressive elaboration of the product description

39. Work performance information includes all the following *except*—

    a. Personnel training results
    b. Costs authorized and incurred
    c. Resource utilization data
    d. Completed deliverables

40. Your project is estimated to have overall profitability of 15% based on direct and indirect costs of $1.5 million. Your company's chief financial officer argues that the same $1.5 million invested in an alternative project would yield a rate of return equal to 20%, which is also called the—

    a. Cost of capital
    b. Net present value
    c. Payback period
    d. Economic value added

# Answer Sheet

| | | | | | | | | | | |
|---|---|---|---|---|---|---|---|---|---|---|
| 1. | a | b | c | d | | 21. | a | b | c | d |
| 2. | a | b | c | d | | 22. | a | b | c | d |
| 3. | a | b | c | d | | 23. | a | b | c | d |
| 4. | a | b | c | d | | 24. | a | b | c | d |
| 5. | a | b | c | d | | 25. | a | b | c | d |
| 6. | a | b | c | d | | 26. | a | b | c | d |
| 7. | a | b | c | d | | 27. | a | b | c | d |
| 8. | a | b | c | d | | 28. | a | b | c | d |
| 9. | a | b | c | d | | 29. | a | b | c | d |
| 10. | a | b | c | d | | 30. | a | b | c | d |
| 11. | a | b | c | d | | 31. | a | b | c | d |
| 12. | a | b | c | d | | 32. | a | b | c | d |
| 13. | a | b | c | d | | 33. | a | b | c | d |
| 14. | a | b | c | d | | 34. | a | b | c | d |
| 15. | a | b | c | d | | 35. | a | b | c | d |
| 16. | a | b | c | d | | 36. | a | b | c | d |
| 17. | a | b | c | d | | 37. | a | b | c | d |
| 18. | a | b | c | d | | 38. | a | b | c | d |
| 19. | a | b | c | d | | 39. | a | b | c | d |
| 20. | a | b | c | d | | 40. | a | b | c | d |

# Answer Key

### 1. a.  Proper project scope definition

Progressive elaboration of product characteristics must be coordinated carefully with proper scope definition, particularly when the project is performed under contract.  When properly defined, the project scope—the work to be done—should remain constant even when the product characteristics are elaborated progressively.  [Planning]

PMI®, *PMBOK*® *Guide*, 2004, 6

### 2. b.  WBS

The WBS, along with the detailed scope statement and the WBS dictionary, defines the project's scope baseline, which provides the basis for any changes that may occur on the project.  [Planning]

PMI®, *PMBOK*® *Guide*, 2004, 117

### 3. a.  Effort expended on scoping activities should be commensurate with the project's size, complexity, and importance

Defining and managing project scope influences the project's overall success.  Each project requires a careful balance of tools, data sources, methodologies, processes and procedures, and other factors.  It is important to ensure that the effort required for scope planning is appropriate for the specific project.  [Planning]

PMI®, *PMBOK*® *Guide*, 2004, 107

### 4. c.  Historical information on previous projects

Organizational process assets include formal and informal policies, procedures, and guidelines impacting project scope management. Historical information about previous projects is one example and may be located in the lessons learned knowledge base.  [Planning]

PMI®, *PMBOK*® *Guide*, 2004, 107–108

### 5. b.  How change requests to the scope management plan will be processed

The scope management plan provides the project team with guidance on how to define, document, verify, manage, and control project scope.  In addition to the other three processes above, it describes how requests for changes to the detailed project scope statement will be processed.  [Planning]

PMI®, *PMBOK® Guide*, 2004, 108

### 6. c.  Stakeholder analysis

During scope definition, stakeholder needs, wants, and expectations are analyzed and reduced to requirements.  Stakeholder analysis identifies the influence and interests of the stakeholders and provides this documentation.  [Planning]

PMI®, *PMBOK® Guide*, 2004, 109–110

### 7. d.  Lateral thinking

Lateral thinking and brainstorming are examples of general management techniques that can be used to generate different approaches to execute and perform the project's work.  [Planning]

PMI®, *PMBOK® Guide*, 2004, 110

### 8. d.  Bill of materials

Product analysis techniques vary by application area, and each application area generally has accepted methods to translate project objectives into tangible deliverables and requirements.  Other product analysis techniques include product breakdown, systems analysis, and systems engineering.  [Planning]

PMI®, *PMBOK® Guide*, 2004, 110

### 9. b.  Project scope statement

Project boundaries identify generally what is included within the project, and state explicitly what is excluded from the project, if a stakeholder might assume that a particular product, service, or result could be a project component.  Project boundaries are described as part of the detailed project scope statement.  [Planning]

PMI®, *PMBOK® Guide*, 2004, 110–111

**10. d.  An error or omission in defining the scope of the project**

The bill of materials provides a hierarchical view of the physical assemblies, subassemblies, and components needed to build a manufactured product, whereas the WBS is a deliverable-oriented grouping of project components used to define the total scope of the project.  Using a bill of materials where a WBS would be more appropriate may result in an ill-defined scope and subsequent change requests.  [Monitoring and Controlling]

PMI®, *PMBOK® Guide*, 2004, 117

**11. a.  Project objectives**

Project objectives include the measurable success criteria of the project.  They may have a variety of business, cost, schedule, technical, and quality objectives and can include cost, schedule, and quality targets.  [Planning]

PMI®, *PMBOK® Guide*, 2004, 111

**12. c.  A set of procedures by which project scope and product scope may be changed**

In addition to complying with any relevant contractual provisions, scope change control must be integrated with the project's overall change control system and with any systems in place to control project and product scope.  [Monitoring and Controlling]

PMI®, *PMBOK® Guide*, 2004, 121

**13. b.  Stated in the project scope statement**

Project configuration management requirements are stated or referenced as part of the detailed project scope statement.  The degree and level of detail to which the scope statement defines the work to be performed and what is excluded can assist the team in scope control.  [Planning]

PMI®, *PMBOK® Guide*, 2004, 112

**14. a.  Deliverable at the lowest level of the WBS**

A work package is the lowest or smallest unit of work division in a project or WBS.  Typically, a work package contains about 80 hours of work.  [Planning]

PMI®, *PMBOK® Guide*, 2004, 114

**15. b.  Update the scope management plan**

Approved change requests are an input to the scope definition process resulting in an update to the project scope management plan.  [Planning]

PMI®, *PMBOK® Guide*, 2004, 112

**16. d.  Project organizational units**

The WBS includes all the work that needs to be done to complete the project.  The organizational breakdown structure (OBS) includes the organizational units responsible for completing the work.  [Planning]

PMI®, *PMBOK® Guide*, 2004, 115

**17. a.  Should be reviewed according to the integrated change control process**

A requested change is an output from scope control.  Such a change should be handled according to the integrated change control process and may result in an update to the scope baseline.  [Monitoring and Controlling]

PMI®, *PMBOK® Guide*, 2004, 122

**18. c.  Sum costs, schedule, and resource information**

The key document generated from the create WBS process is the actual WBS.  Each WBS component is assigned a unique identifier in order to provide a structure for hierarchical summation of costs, schedule, and resource information.  [Planning]

PMI®, *PMBOK® Guide*, 2004, 117

**19. b.  WBS dictionary**

The WBS dictionary is a collection of work package descriptions that includes, among other things, planning information such as schedule dates, cost budgets, and staff assignments.  [Planning and Monitoring and Controlling]

PMI®, *PMBOK® Guide*, 2004, 118

**20. a.  An organization's culture**

Other enterprise environmental factors that are inputs to scope planning are the organization's infrastructure, tools, human resources, personnel policies, and marketplace conditions that could affect how project scope is managed.  [Planning]

PMI®, *PMBOK® Guide*, 2004, 107

**21. b.  Identify the deliverables and related work**

This is the first step in the decomposition of a project.  The deliverables should be defined in terms of how the project will be organized.  For example, the major project deliverables may be used as the first level with the phases of the project repeated at the second level.  [Planning]

PMI®, *PMBOK® Guide*, 2004, 115

**22. c.  Performance reports**

Inspection includes a variety of activities aimed at ensuring that the deliverables meet requirements and product acceptance criteria.  They may be called reviews, product reviews, audits, and walkthroughs.  [Monitoring and  Controlling]

PMI®, *PMBOK® Guide*, 2004, 119

**23. a.  An assumption**

Assumptions are factors that, for planning purposes, are considered to be true, real, or certain.  They are listed in the project scope statement.  [Planning]

PMI®, *PMBOK® Guide*, 2004, 111 and 352

**24. b.  Scope creep**

Project scope creep is typically the result of uncontrolled changes.  Scope control works to control the impact of any project scope changes.  [Monitoring and Controlling]

PMI®, *PMBOK® Guide*, 2004, 119

**25. d. Project performance measurements**

Variance analysis is a tool and technique for scope control. Project performance measurements are used to assess the magnitude of variance, to determine the cause of the variance, and to decide whether corrective action is required. [Monitoring and Controlling]

PMI®, *PMBOK® Guide*, 2004, 121

**26. d. None, the BCR for each is the same**

BCR is calculated as $\dfrac{\text{Benefits}}{\text{Cost}}$. In each project the BCR = 2, which means that for each dollar of costs we are receiving two dollars of benefits.

Ward 2000, 18

**27. d. Replanning is a tool and technique for scope control**

Approved changes will most likely impact, and cause updates to, the WBS, WBS dictionary, project scope statement, and project scope management plan. Such updates are the result of replanning, which is a tool and technique for scope control. [Monitoring and Controlling]

PMI®, *PMBOK® Guide*, 2004, 121

**28. b. Configuration management system**

The formal configuration management system is an important tool and technique for scope control and is part of the project management information system for the project. [Monitoring and Controlling]

PMI®, *PMBOK® Guide*, 2004, 121

**29. d. Differs from quality control in that scope verification is concerned with the acceptance—not the correctness—of the work results**

An output from scope verification is documentation that the customer has accepted completed deliverables. [Monitoring and Controlling]

PMI®, *PMBOK® Guide*, 2004, 119

### 30. b. Are used by the project staff to target efforts

To develop the project plan, needs are formulated as functional requirements. Technical requirements emerge from the functional requirements because the latter generally do not offer enough precise guidance to the project staff. [Planning]

Frame 1995, 116–117

### 31. b. Corrective action

Recommended corrective action is an output from scope control. In addition to bringing expected future performance in line with the project management plan, it also serves to bring expected future performance in line with the project scope statement. [Monitoring and Controlling]

PMI®, *PMBOK® Guide*, 2004, 122

### 32. a. All projects, large and small

A system is needed for careful monitoring of changes made to the requirements. Use of written change orders encourages the individuals asking for changes to take responsibility for their requests and reduces frivolous requests that may adversely affect the project. [Monitoring and Controlling]

Frame 1995, 153

### 33. c. Establish and document the level and extent of completion

Stakeholders' official acceptance of project scope is part of the scope verification process. If a project is terminated before it is complete, the degree to which the project has been completed should be established and documented. [Monitoring and Controlling]

PMI®, *PMBOK® Guide*, 2004, 118

### 34. c. Deliverables

Deliverables that have been fully or partially completed are an input to scope verification. [Monitoring and Controlling]

PMI®, *PMBOK® Guide*, 2004, 118

### 35. a. Provides the scope baseline

The project scope statement, along with the WBS and WBS dictionary, is a key input to scope control. [Monitoring and Controlling]

PMI®, *PMBOK® Guide*, 2004, 120

**36. b. Develop a subproject WBS for the work package that is your company's responsibility**

Work packages are items at the lowest level of the WBS. A subproject WBS breaks down work packages into greater detail. A subproject WBS generally is used if the project manager assigns a scope of work to another organization, and the project manager at that organization must plan and manage the scope of work in greater detail. [Planning]

PMI®, *PMBOK® Guide*, 2004, 115

**37. c. It does not take into account cash flows after the payback period and it is not a measure of profitability**

Because payback period is not a measure of profitability, analysts prefer the discounted cash flow methods of capital budgeting.

Friedman 1994, 441

**38. d. Progressive elaboration of the product description**

The product description delineates the product or service characteristics that the project was undertaken to create. This description will generally have less detail in early phases and more detail in later ones. By the time execution begins, this description must be finalized. [Planning]

PMI®, *PMBOK® Guide*, 2004, 111

**39. a. Personnel training results**

Work performance information is any data or information describing work accomplishment, including cost, quality, and schedule performance. Personnel training schedule is an administrative matter not directly related to work accomplishment. [Monitoring and Controlling]

PMI®, *PMBOK® Guide*, 2004, 94

**40. a. Cost of capital**

Cost of capital is the rate of return a business could earn if it invested in another project of equivalent risk.

Friedman 1994, 132

# PROJECT TIME MANAGEMENT

## Study Hints

The Project Time Management questions on the PMP® certification exam focus heavily on the program evaluation and review technique (PERT), the critical path method (CPM), and the precedence diagramming method (PDM); the differences between these three techniques; and the appropriate circumstances for their use. The exam tests your knowledge of how PERT/CPM networks are constructed, how schedules are computed, what the critical path is, and how networks are used to analyze and solve project scheduling, and resource allocation and leveling issues. There is a good chance that you will be presented with a network diagram that will be the subject of five or more questions. Therefore, detailed knowledge of network scheduling is critical. There also seems to be a focus on fast-tracking as a method to accelerate the project schedule. You must know the advantages offered by networks over bar charts and network diagrams, and understand the two ways in which networks can be represented (activity-on-arrow and activity-on-node). You also should understand the concept of float (or slack) and how it presents challenges and opportunities to project schedulers.

Because a thorough understanding of networks and scheduling is required to successfully answer questions on Project Time Management, you should take a course relating to that topic, preferably the ESI *Scheduling and Cost Control* course. If you cannot take a course, you may want to consult the user's manual for one of the more popular desktop software project management packages. Typically, you will find plenty of illustrations and short, easy-to-understand scheduling exercises at the level of detail required to correctly answer the exam questions.

The *PMBOK® Guide* separates the function of Project Time Management into six processes: activity definition, activity sequencing, activity resource estimating, activity duration estimating, schedule development, and schedule control. Review *PMBOK® Guide* Figure 6-1 before taking the ESI practice test. Know this chart thoroughly.

Following is a list of the major Project Time Management topics. Use it to help focus your study efforts on the areas most likely to appear on the exam.

# Major Topics

*Activity definition*

*Activity resource estimating*

- Resource requirements
- Resource breakdown structure
- Resource calendars

*Activity duration estimating*

- Expert judgment
- Analogous estimating
- Parametric estimates
- Three-point estimates
- Reserve analysis

*Network systems*

- PERT
- CPM
- PDM
- GERT

*Ways to represent networks*

- Activity sequencing
- Milestone events
- Critical path
- Project duration
- Activity-on-arrow networks
  - Dummy activities
- Activity-on-node networks
  - Lag and lead
  - Slack or float
  - Activity relationships
- Dependency determination

*Schedule development*

- Crashing and fast-tracking
- Resource leveling
- Monte Carlo analysis
- Critical chain method
- Schedule baseline
- Advantages of scheduling tools
- Schedule management plan

# Major Topics (continued)

***Schedule control***

- Schedule change control system
- Variance analysis
- Performance measurements
- Schedule updates

## Practice Questions

INSTRUCTIONS:  Note the most suitable answer for each multiple-choice question in the appropriate space on the answer sheet.

Use the network diagram below to answer questions 1 through 4.  Activity names and duration are provided.

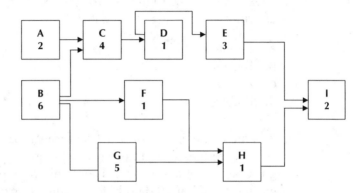

1. What is the duration of the critical path in this network?

    a.   10
    b.   12
    c.   14
    d.   15

2. What is the float for Activity G?

    a.   −2
    b.   0
    c.   1
    d.   4

3. If a project planner imposes a finish time of 14 on the project with no change in the start date or activity durations, what is the total float of Activity E?

    a.   −1
    b.   0
    c.   2
    d.   Cannot be determined

4. If the imposed finish time in question 3 above is removed and reset to 16 and the duration of Activity H is changed to 3, what is the late finish for Activity G?

   a.  −11
   b.  11
   c.  −13
   d.  13

5. Given the change to the network based on question 4 above, what activities are on the critical path?

   a.  B-F-H-I
   b.  B-C-E-I
   c.  A-C-D-I
   d.  B-G-H-I

6. You are managing a construction project for a new city water system. The contract requires you to use special titanium piping equipment that is guaranteed not to corrode. The titanium pipe must be resting in the ground a total of 10 days before connectors can be installed. In this example, the 10-day period is defined as—

   a.  Lag
   b.  Lead
   c.  Float
   d.  Slack

7. Of the following, which one is not a tool or technique used for schedule control?

   a.  Variance analysis
   b.  Project management software
   c.  What-if scenario analysis
   d.  Schedule change control system

8. Schedule control is one important way of avoiding delays. To plan and execute schedule recovery, corrective action frequently requires—

   a.  Making unpopular decisions
   b.  Immediately rebaselining
   c.  Root-cause analysis
   d.  Resource leveling

9. Project schedule development is an iterative process. If the start and finish dates are not realistic, the project probably will not finish as planned. You are working with your team to define how to manage schedule changes. You documented your decisions in which one of the following?

   a. Schedule change control procedures
   b. Schedule management plan
   c. Schedule risk plan
   d. Service-level agreement

10. If a project is to employ two people each for 40 hours at a labor rate of $30 per hour with overhead included, and a third person for 30 hours during the same period but at a loaded labor rate of $50 per hour, the PV for the week is—

    a. $2,400
    b. $3,600
    c. $3,660
    d. $3,900

11. Your lead engineer estimates that a work package will most likely require 50 weeks to complete. It could be completed in 40 weeks if all goes well, but it could take 180 weeks in the worst case. What is the PERT estimate for the expected duration of the work package?

    a. 45 weeks
    b. 70 weeks
    c. 90 weeks
    d. 140 weeks

12. Your customer wants the project to be completed six months earlier than planned. You believe you can meet this target by overlapping project activities. The approach you plan to use is known as—

    a. Concurrent engineering
    b. Fast-tracking
    c. Leveling
    d. Crashing

13. Activity A has a duration of three days and begins on the morning of Monday the 4th. The successor activity, B, has a finish-to-start relationship with A. The finish-to-start relationship has three days of lag, and activity B has a duration of four days. Sunday is a nonworkday. What can be determined from these data?

    a. The total duration of both activities is 8 days.
    b. Calendar time between the start of A to the finish of B is 11 days.
    c. The finish date of B is Wednesday the 13th.
    d. Calendar time between the start of A to the finish of B is 14 days.

14. One way to shorten your project schedule is to assign five people to each activity in the project design phase instead of two. Although you are considering this approach, your design phase project team would double in size as a result. This approach tends to—

    a. Reduce productivity
    b. Increase productivity
    c. Reduce the need for senior-level staff members, thereby reducing overall resource costs
    d. Improve production proportionately more than the increase in resources

15. "I cannot test the software until I code the software." This expression describes which of the following dependencies?

    a. Discretionary
    b. Rational
    c. Preferential
    d. Mandatory or hard

16. It is important to update the schedule baseline carefully because—

    a. Revisions require management approval
    b. Historical data will be lost for the project schedule
    c. Root-cause analysis must be performed
    d. Schedule recovery cannot be planned for activities delineated later in the schedule

17. Your approved project schedule was based on resource leveling due to a scarcity of resources. Management has now mandated that the project be completed as soon as possible. Which of the following methods will you use to recalculate the schedule?

    a. Resource manipulation
    b. Reverse resource allocation
    c. Critical chain scheduling
    d. Resource reallocation

18. Based on an approved change, the customer increased the project scope by 65%. This increased your cost estimate fivefold. Now you must change the scheduled start and finish dates in your approved project schedule. Your first step should be to—

    a. Rebaseline the schedule
    b. Modify the contract
    c. Update the schedule baseline
    d. Add resources

19. You are remodeling your kitchen and decide to prepare a network diagram for this project. Your appliances must be purchased and available for installation by the time the cabinets are completed. In this example, these relationships are—

    a. Start-to-finish
    b. Finish-to-start
    c. Start-to-start
    d. Finish-to-finish

20. Decomposition is a technique used for both WBS development and activity definition. Which statement best describes the role decomposition plays in activity definition as compared to creating the WBS?

    a. Final output is described in terms of work packages in the WBS.
    b. Final output is described as deliverables or tangible items.
    c. Final output is described as schedule activities.
    d. Decomposition is used the same way in scope definition and activity definition.

21. Which of the following formulas provides the most accurate result for computing activity duration (AD)?

    a. $AD = \dfrac{\text{Work quantity}}{\text{Production rate}}$

    b. $AD = \dfrac{\text{Work quantity}}{\text{Number of resources}}$

    c. $AD = \dfrac{\text{Production rate}}{\text{Work quantity}}$

    d. $AD = \dfrac{(\text{Production rate})\,(\text{Work quantity})}{\text{Number of resources}}$

22. To practice effective schedule control, your project team must be alert to any issues that may cause problems in the future. To best accomplish this, the team should—

    a. Review performance reports
    b. Allow no changes to the schedule
    c. Update the schedule management plan on a continuous basis
    d. Hold status reviews

23. Several tools and techniques are available for activity sequencing. The tool or technique selected can be determined by several factors. If the project manager decides to include *subnetworks* or a *fragment network* as part of his or her scheduling technique, what would that decision say about the project?

    a. The work is unique requiring special network diagrams at various stages.
    b. Software that manages resources is available over an existing electronic network.
    c. Several identical or nearly identical series of activities are repeated throughout the project.
    d. Multiple critical paths exist in the project.

24. In order to meet regulatory requirements, you need to crash your project schedule. Your first step is to compute—

    a. The cost and time slope for each critical activity that can be expedited
    b. The cost of additional resources to be added to the project's critical path
    c. The time that will be saved in the overall schedule when tasks are expedited on the critical path
    d. Three probabilistic time estimates of PERT for each critical path activity

25. Working with your team to provide the basis for measuring and reporting schedule progress, you agree to use the—

    a. Schedule management plan
    b. Network diagram
    c. Project schedule
    d. Technical baseline

26. Unlike bar charts, milestone charts show—

    a. Scheduled start or completion of major deliverables and key external interfaces
    b. Activity start and end dates of critical tasks
    c. Expected durations of the critical path
    d. Dependencies between complementary projects

27. A benefit of using a schedule change control system is that it includes the—

    a. Requirements for reporting schedule performance
    b. Requirements for measuring schedule performance
    c. Methods for assessing the magnitude of schedule variations
    d. Approval levels necessary for authorizing schedule changes

28. An activity has an early start date of the 10th and a late start date of the 19th. The activity has a duration of four days. There are no nonworkdays. From the information given, what can be concluded about the activity?

    a. Total float for the activity is nine days.
    b. The early finish date of the activity is the end of the day on the 14$^{th}$.
    c. The late finish date is the 25$^{th}$.
    d. The activity can be completed in two days if the resources devoted to it are doubled.

29. In project development, schedule information such as who will perform the work, where the work will be performed, activity type, and WBS classification are examples of—

    a. Activity attributes
    b. Constraints
    c. Data in the WBS repository
    d. Refinements

30. Which of the following is a primary input to schedule activity definition?

    a. Project management plan
    b. Project scope statement
    c. WBS
    d. Project management information system

31. A schedule performance index of less than 1.0 indicates that the—

    a. Project is running behind the monetary value of the work it planned to accomplish
    b. Earned value physically accomplished thus far is 100%
    c. Project has experienced a permanent loss of time
    d. Project may not be on schedule, but the project manager need not be concerned

32. Several types of float are found in project networks. Float that is used by a particular activity and does not affect the float in later activities is called—

    a. Extra float
    b. Free float
    c. Total float
    d. Expected float

33. All the following statements regarding critical chain analysis are true *except—*

    a. Deterministic and probabilistic approaches are combined
    b. The first step is to use conservative estimates for activity durations
    c. Duration buffers are added on the critical path
    d. It focuses on managing buffer activity durations

34. The risk register is an input to which of the following processes?

    a. Activity duration estimating
    b. Activity resource estimating
    c. Activity sequencing
    d. Activity definition

35. The primary difference between the precedence diagramming method (PDM) and the arrow diagramming method (ADM) is that ADM—

    a. Uses four types of dependencies
    b. Uses only finish-to-start dependencies
    c. Uses nodes to represent activities
    d. Uses only start-to-finish dependencies

36. You are planning to conduct the team-building portion of your new project management training curriculum outdoors. You are limited to scheduling the course at certain times of the year, and the best time for the course to begin is mid-July. One of the more common date constraints to use as you develop your project schedule is—

    a. Start no earlier than
    b. Finish no later than
    c. Fixed late start
    d. Fixed early finish

37. Activity A has a pessimistic *(P)* estimate of 36 days, a most likely *(ML)* estimate of 21 days, and an optimistic *(O)* estimate of 6 days. What is the probability that activity A will be completed in 16 to 26 days?

    a. 55.70%
    b. 68.26%
    c. 95.46%
    d. 99.73%

38. You are managing a project to redesign a retail store layout to improve customer throughput and efficiency. Much of the project work must be done on site and will require the active participation of store employees who are lifelong members of a powerful union that has a reputation for labor unrest. One important component of your schedule must be—

    a. A resource capabilities matrix
    b. Buffers and reserves
    c. A resource calendar
    d. A resource histogram

39. If, when developing a project schedule, you want to define a distribution of probable results for each schedule activity and use it to calculate a distribution of probable results for the total project, the most common technique to use is—

    a. PERT
    b. Monte Carlo analysis
    c. Linear programming
    d. Concurrent engineering

40. Project managers should pay attention to critical and subcritical activities when evaluating project time performance. One way to do this is to analyze 10 subcritical paths in order of ascending float. This approach is part of—

    a. Variance analysis
    b. Simulation
    c. Earned value management
    d. Trend analysis

## Answer Sheet

1.  a  b  c  d
2.  a  b  c  d
3.  a  b  c  d
4.  a  b  c  d
5.  a  b  c  d
6.  a  b  c  d
7.  a  b  c  d
8.  a  b  c  d
9.  a  b  c  d
10. a  b  c  d
11. a  b  c  d
12. a  b  c  d
13. a  b  c  d
14. a  b  c  d
15. a  b  c  d
16. a  b  c  d
17. a  b  c  d
18. a  b  c  d
19. a  b  c  d
20. a  b  c  d

21. a  b  c  d
22. a  b  c  d
23. a  b  c  d
24. a  b  c  d
25. a  b  c  d
26. a  b  c  d
27. a  b  c  d
28. a  b  c  d
29. a  b  c  d
30. a  b  c  d
31. a  b  c  d
32. a  b  c  d
33. a  b  c  d
34. a  b  c  d
35. a  b  c  d
36. a  b  c  d
37. a  b  c  d
38. a  b  c  d
39. a  b  c  d
40. a  b  c  d

# Answer Key

### 1. d.  15

The total duration for the path B-C-D-E-I is 15.  The duration of any of the other paths in the network is less than 15.  [Planning]

Meredith and Mantel 2006, Chapter 8

### 2. c.  1

Float = (late finish – early finish) or

(late start – early start)

Activity G      LF = 12    (12 – 11) = (1)

                 EF = 11

                 LS = 7     (7 – 6) = (1)

                 ES = 6

Legend

| ES | EF |
|----|----|
| LS | LF |

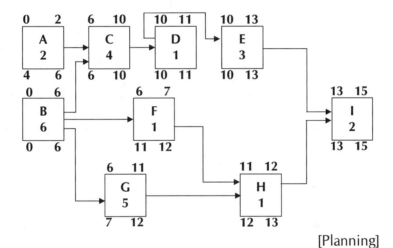

[Planning]

Meredith and Mantel 2006, Chapter 8

### 3. a. −1

The imposed finish date becomes the late finish for Activity I. The late dates for each activity need to be recalculated. The dates for Activity E become—

ES = 10
EF = 13
LS = 9
LF = 12

Total float = LS − ES or 9 − 10 = (−1) or
LF − EF or 12 − 13 = (−1)

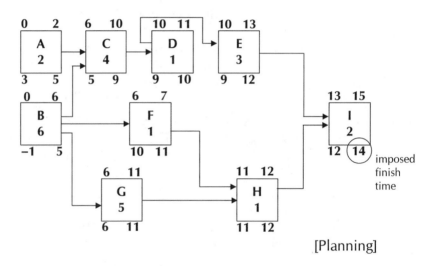

[Planning]

Meredith and Mantel 2006, Chapter 8

## 4. b. 11

The late dates for all activities need to be recalculated given the changed duration. Activity G's revised late dates are—

LF = 11
LS = 6

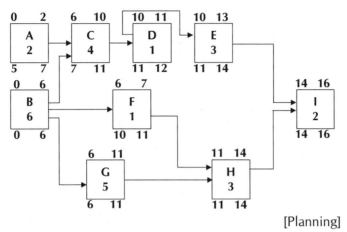

[Planning]

Meredith and Mantel 2006, Chapter 8

## 5. d. B-G-H-I

The activities B-G-H-I have a total duration of 16. Any other path in the network has a duration less than 16.

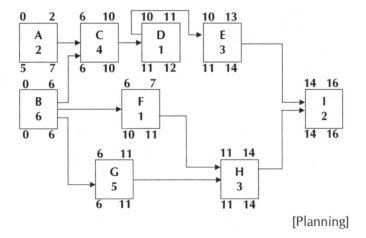

[Planning]

Meredith and Mantel 2006, Chapter 8

### 6. a. Lag

For example, in a finish-to-start dependency with a 20-day lag, the successor activity cannot start until 20 days after the predecessor has finished.  [Planning]

PMI®, *PMBOK® Guide*, 2004, 134

### 7. c. What-if scenario analysis

What-if scenario analysis is a tool used in schedule development. [Planning]

PMI®, *PMBOK® Guide*, 2004, 125

### 8. c. Root-cause analysis

Corrective action is anything that brings expected future schedule performance in line with the project plan.  Root-cause analysis is one of many tools available to identify the cause of variation.  [Monitoring and Controlling]

PMI®, *PMBOK® Guide*, 2004, 155

### 9. b. Schedule management plan

The schedule management plan is part of the overall project plan and defines how schedule changes will be managed.  Whether it's formal or informal, highly detailed or broadly framed, it is generally based on specific project needs.  [Planning]

PMI®, *PMBOK® Guide*, 2004, 124

### 10. d. $3,900

40 hours $\times$ $30 per hour $\times$ 2 = $2,400

30 hours $\times$ $50 per hour $\times$ 1 = $1,500

PV = $2,400 + $1,500 = $3,900

[Monitoring and Controlling]

Lewis 1991, 171–172

**11. b. 70 weeks**

$$E(t) = \frac{\text{Optimistic} + (4 \times \text{Most likely}) + \text{Pessimistic}}{6}$$

$$= \frac{40 + 200 + 180}{6} = \frac{420}{6} = 70 \text{ weeks}$$

[Planning]

PMI®, *PMBOK® Guide*, 2004, 142

**12. b. Fast-tracking**

Fast-tracking is a way to accelerate the project schedule. [Planning]

PMI®, *PMBOK® Guide*, 2004, 146 and 360

**13. b. Calendar time between the start of A to the finish of B is 11 days.**

The duration of A, which is three, is added to the duration of B, which is four, for a total of seven. The three days between the activities is lag and not duration. The lag is a constraint and must be taken into account as part of the network calculations, but it does not consume resources. The total time by the calendar is 11 days as counted from the morning of Monday the 4th. The lag occurs over Thursday, Friday, and Saturday. Sunday is a nonworkday, so activity B does not start until Monday the 11th. Therefore, the calendar time is 11 days, and activity B ends on Thursday the 14th. [Planning]

Dreger 1992, 49

**14. a. Reduce productivity**

Projects can experience communication overload as additional resources are added. A communication overload reduces productivity and causes production to improve proportionately less than the increase in resources. [Planning]

PMI®, *PMBOK® Guide*, 2004, 224

**15. d. Mandatory or hard**

Mandatory dependencies describe a relationship in which the successor activity cannot be started because of physical constraints until the predecessor activity has been finished. For example, software cannot be tested until it has been developed (or coded). [Planning]

PMI®, *PMBOK® Guide*, 2004, 133

### 16. b.   Historical data will be lost for the project schedule

Some schedule delays are so severe that an update to the schedule baseline is needed to provide realistic data in which to measure performance.  The initial schedule baseline is saved before creating the new schedule baseline to prevent loss of historical data against which to determine variances.  [Monitoring and Controlling]

PMI®, *PMBOK® Guide*, 2004, 155

### 17. d.   Resource reallocation

While resource leveling will often result in a project duration that is longer than the preliminary schedule, it can also be used to get a schedule back on track by reassigning activities from noncritical to critical path activities. [Planning]

PMI®, *PMBOK® Guide*, 2004, 147

### 18. c.   Update the schedule baseline

Schedule revisions result in changes to the project's scheduled start or finish dates.  Only changes that are the result of approved changes are incorporated into the project's baseline.  [Monitoring and Controlling]

PMI®, *PMBOK® Guide*, 2004, 155

### 19. d.   Finish-to-finish

The completion of the work of the successor activity depends upon the completion of the work of the predecessor activity.  [Planning]

PMI®, *PMBOK® Guide*, 2004, 132

### 20. c.   Final output is described as schedule activities.

In the create WBS process, final output is described as deliverables or tangible items.  [Planning]

PMI®, *PMBOK® Guide*, 2004, 128

**21. a.** $AD = \dfrac{\text{Work quantity}}{\text{Production rate}}$

First, the volume or quantity of work to be completed must be measured. In other words, the scope of the activity must be defined. Next, the productivity rate as it relates to the work quantity must be determined. Dividing the work quantity by the production rate yields an estimate of the activity duration. [Planning]

AGCA 1994, 30

**22. a. Review performance reports**

Performance reports provide information on schedule performance, such as which planned dates have been met and which have been missed, thereby alerting the team to problems that may arise in the future. [Monitoring and Controlling]

PMI®, *PMBOK® Guide*, 2004, 153

**23. c. Several identical or nearly identical series of activities are repeated throughout the project.**

When identical network descriptions are repeated throughout a project, templates of those activities can be developed. If those series of tasks are repeated several times, the template can be updated several times. Software can be used with the templates to facilitate documenting and adapting them for future use. [Planning]

PMI®, *PMBOK® Guide*, 2004, 133

**24. a. The cost and time slope for each critical activity that can be expedited**

Slope = (Crash cost – Normal cost)/(Crash time – Normal time). This calculation shows the cost per day of crashing the project. The slope is negative to indicate that as the time required for a project or task decreases, the cost increases. If the costs and times are the same regardless of whether they are crashed or normal, the activity cannot be expedited. [Planning]

Meredith and Mantel 2003, 447

### 25. c. Project schedule

The approved project schedule is a key input to schedule control. It is the schedule baseline, and it provides the basis for measuring and reporting schedule performance. [Monitoring and Controlling]

PMI®, *PMBOK® Guide*, 2004, 153

### 26. a. Scheduled start or completion of major deliverables and key external interfaces

Milestones are singular points in time, such as the start or completion of a significant activity or group of activities. [Planning]

PMI®, *PMBOK® Guide*, 2004, 149

### 27. d. Approval levels necessary for authorizing schedule changes

The schedule change control system defines procedures for changing the project schedule and includes the documentation, tracking systems, and approval levels required for authorizing schedule changes. [Monitoring and Controlling]

PMI®, *PMBOK® Guide*, 2004, 153

### 28. a. Total float for the activity is 9 days.

Total float is computed by subtracting the early start date from the late start date, or $19-10=9$. To compute the early finish date given a duration of 4, we would start counting the activity on the morning of the 10th; therefore, the activity would be completed at the end of day 13, not 14 (10, 11, 12, 13). If we started the activity on its late start date on the morning of the 19th, we would finish at the end of day 22, not 25. Insufficient information is provided to determine whether this activity can be completed in 2 days if the resources are doubled. [Planning]

Dreger 1992, 45–51

### 29. a. Activity attributes

Identifying activity attributes is helpful for further selection and sorting of planned activities. They are used for schedule development and for report formatting purposes. [Planning]

PMI®, *PMBOK® Guide*, 2004, 130

**30. c. WBS**

The WBS and WBS dictionary are the primary inputs to schedule activity definition and are used to develop the activity list. [Planning]

PMI®, *PMBOK® Guide*, 2004, 128

**31. a. Project is running behind the monetary value of the work it planned to accomplish**

The SPI represents how much of the originally scheduled work has been accomplished at a given period in time, thus providing the project team with insight as to whether the project is on schedule. [Monitoring and Controlling]

Fleming and Koppelman 2000, 113–115

**32. b. Free float**

Free float is defined as the amount of time an activity can be delayed without delaying the early start of any immediately succeeding activities. [Planning]

PMI®, *PMBOK® Guide*, 2004, 362

**33. b. The first step is to use conservative estimates for activity durations**

When using critical chain techniques, the initial project schedule is developed and calculated using nonconservative estimates with required dependencies and defined constraints as inputs. [Planning]

PMI®, *PMBOK® Guide*, 2004, 147

**34. a. Activity duration estimating**

The risk register is an input to activity duration estimating as part of the project management plan and is used to directly support the schedule development process. [Planning]

PMI®, *PMBOK® Guide*, 2004, 144

**35. b. Uses only finish-to-start dependencies**

Unlike PDM, which uses four types of dependencies, ADM uses only one form, finish-to-start. As such, dummy activities are often used to show dependencies between activities not on the same physical path. [Planning]

PMI®, *PMBOK® Guide*, 2004, 132–133

### 36. a.  Start no earlier than

Imposed dates on schedule activity starts or finishes can be used to restrict the start or finish to occur either no earlier than a specified date or no later than a specified date.  Although all four date constraints typically are available in project management software, *start no earlier than* and *finish no later than* constraints are used most commonly.  [Planning]

PMI®, *PMBOK® Guide*, 2004, 362

### 37. b.  68.26%

First, compute the standard deviation:

$$\sigma = \frac{P-O}{6} \text{ or } \frac{36-6}{6} = 5 \text{ days}$$

Next, compute PERT expected time:

$$\frac{P+4(ML)+O}{6} \text{ or } \frac{36+4(21)+6}{6} = 21 \text{ days}$$

Finally, determine range of outcomes using 1σ:

$$21-5 = 16 \text{ days, and } 21+5 = 26 \text{ days}$$

Simply defined, 1σ is the amount on either side of the mean of a normal distribution that will contain approximately 68.26% of the population. [Planning]

ESI October 2004, 3-3 and 3-11

### 38. c.  A resource calendar

Project and resource calendars identify periods when work is allowed.  Project calendars affect all resources.  Resource calendars affect a specific resource or a resource category, such as a labor contract that requires certain workers to work on certain days of the week.  [Planning]

PMI®, *PMBOK® Guide*, 2004, 138 and 141

### 39. b.  Monte Carlo analysis

Simulation is a tool and a technique for schedule development by which multiple project durations with different sets of activity assumptions are calculated.  Monte Carlo analysis is the most commonly used simulation technique.  [Planning]

PMI®, *PMBOK® Guide*, 2004, 146

**40. a. Variance analysis**

Performance of variance analysis during the schedule monitoring process is a key element of time control. Float variance is an essential planning component for evaluating project time performance. [Monitoring and Controlling]

PMI®, *PMBOK® Guide*, 2004, 154

# PROJECT COST MANAGEMENT

## Study Hints

You do not have to be a certified public accountant to successfully answer the Project Cost Management questions on the PMP® certification exam. PMI® addresses cost management from a project manager's perspective, which is much more general than that of an accountant. However, these questions are not easy. Far from it! Exam takers find the Project Cost Management questions more difficult than most of the others because they address such a broad range of cost issues (for example, basic and capital budgeting, cost estimating, earned value, and creating and interpreting S-curves) and require a significant amount of study time. You should become familiar with introductory finance and accounting concepts, such as those presented in basic project management texts or primers published in both of those areas.

You may find questions relating to contract cost management. Because cost considerations are heavily affected by contract type and Project Procurement Management is one of the nine *PMBOK® Guide* areas on which you will be tested, time spent studying that area will help prepare you for the cost questions on the exam and vice versa. In addition, the *PMBOK® Guide* discusses performance reporting, which also is applicable to cost control.

The exam may include several questions that require you to know and solve specific, albeit simple, formulas. You *must* have a thorough knowledge of earned value—what it is and how it is computed; you also should be knowledgeable about variance analysis.

PMI® views Project Cost Management as a three-step process comprising cost estimating, cost budgeting, and cost control. See *PMBOK® Guide* Figure 7-1 for an overview of this structure. Know this chart thoroughly.

***Important:*** PMI® allows the use of standard six-function (+, −, ×, ÷, √, %) business calculators. These calculators must be silent and have a self-contained power source. They are *not* to include a printing mechanism or a full alphabetic character set. Programmable calculators, which are instruments that can store mathematical formulas, are prohibited. Bring your own calculator—even if the testing center has calculators available for your use or if a calculator feature is included in the testing software. Also ensure that your calculator has new batteries before you take the test.

Following is a list of the major Project Cost Management topics. Use it to help focus your study efforts on the areas most likely to appear on the exam.

# Major Topics

*Project cost management*

*Life-cycle cost (LCC)*

*Cost estimating*

- WBS
- WBS dictionary
- Cost estimating methods
  - ☐ Analogous estimating
  - ☐ Parametric modeling
  - ☐ Bottom-up estimating
  - ☐ Vendor bid analysis
  - ☐ Reserve analysis
- Accuracy of estimates
  - ☐ Order of magnitude
  - ☐ Budget
  - ☐ Definitive

*Other basics of cost management terminology*

- Law of diminishing returns
- Variable versus fixed costs
- Direct versus indirect costs
- Contingency/management reserve
- Working capital

*Depreciation of capital*

- Straight line
- Accelerated

*Value analysis*

*Cost risk and contract type*

*Cost management plan*

*Cost budgeting*

*Cost baseline*

*Cost control*

- Cost change control system
- Performance reviews
- Variance management

## Major Topics (continued)

---

***Earned value management (EVM)***

- Five valuable numbers
- The most rudimentary building blocks
- Cost variance (CV)
- Schedule variance (SV)
- Cost performance index (CPI)
- Schedule performance index (SPI)
- Budget at completion (BAC)
- Estimate to complete (ETC)
- Estimate at completion (EAC)
- Variance at completion (VAC)
- 50–50 rule of progress reporting

---

# Practice Questions

INSTRUCTIONS: Note the most suitable answer for each multiple-choice question in the appropriate space on the answer sheet.

You are using earned value progress reporting for your current project in an effort to teach your software developers the benefits of earned value. You plan to display project results on the cafeteria bulletin board so that the team knows how the project is progressing. Use the current status, listed below, to answer questions 1 through 4:

PV  =  $2,200
EV  =  $2,000
AC  =  $2,500
BAC  =  $10,000

1. According to earned value analysis, the SV and status of the project described above is—

    a.  −$300; the project is ahead of schedule
    b.  +$8,000; the project is on schedule
    c.  +$200; the project is ahead of schedule
    d.  −$200; the project is behind schedule

2. What is the CPI for this project, and what does it tell us about cost performance thus far?

    a.  0.20; actual costs are exactly as planned
    b.  0.80; actual costs have exceeded planned costs
    c.  0.80; actual costs are less than planned costs
    d.  1.25; actual costs have exceeded planned costs

3. The CV is—

    a.  +$300
    b.  −$300
    c.  +$500
    d.  −$500

4. What is the EAC for this project, and what does it represent?

    a.  $12,500; the revised estimate for total project cost (based on performance thus far)
    b.  $10,000; the revised estimate for total project cost (based on performance thus far)
    c.  $12,500; the original project budget
    d.  $10,000; the original project budget

91

5. Your first task on your project is to prepare a cost estimate. You decided to use analogous estimating. Which of the following is *not* characteristic of analogous estimating?

   a. Supports top-down estimating
   b. Is a form of expert judgment
   c. Has an accuracy rate of $\pm 10\%$ of actual costs
   d. Involves using the cost of a previous, similar project as the basis for estimating current project cost

6. You are managing a three-year project with a $3 million budget. If project requirements change, you expect additional funds to become available toward the end of each fiscal year. You may use these funds for your project. You decide to establish a cost change control system to—

   a. Define when to add contingency funds to the project
   b. Define the procedures by which the cost baseline may be changed
   c. Determine why a cost variance has occurred
   d. Determine whether a budget update is required

7. You must consider direct costs, indirect costs, overhead costs, and general and administrative costs during cost estimating. Which of the following is *not* an example of a direct cost?

   a. Salary of the project manager
   b. Subcontractor expenses
   c. Materials used by the project
   d. Electricity

8. If the cost variance is the same as the schedule variance and both numbers are greater than zero, then—

   a. The cost variance is due to the schedule variance
   b. The variance is favorable to the project
   c. The schedule variance can be easily corrected
   d. Labor rates have escalated since the project began

9. You are responsible for preparing a cost estimate for a large World Bank project. You decide to prepare a bottom-up estimate because your estimate needs to be as accurate as possible. Your first step is to—

   a. Locate a computerized tool to assist in the process
   b. Use the cost estimate from a previous project to help you prepare this estimate
   c. Identify and estimate the cost for each individual work item
   d. Consult with subject matter experts and use their suggestions as the basis for your estimate

10. Consider the following—

| Phase | Estimate |
|---|---|
| Concept | $15,000 |
| Initiation | $10,000 |
| Design | $10,000 |
| Development | $30,000 |
| Finish | $ 8,000 |
| Operations and Maintenance | $40,000 |
| Disposition | $12,000 |

What are the total project life-cycle costs?

a. $58,000
b. $73,000
c. $98,000
d. $125,000

11. Management has grown weary of the many surprises, mostly negative, that occur on your projects. In an effort to provide stakeholders with an effective performance metric, you will use the "to complete performance index (TCPI)." Its purpose is to—

a. Determine the schedule and cost performance needed to complete the remaining work within management's financial goal for the project
b. Determine the cost performance needed to complete the remaining work within management's financial goal for the project
c. Predict final project costs
d. Predict final project schedule and costs

12. When you review cost performance data on your project, different responses will be required depending on the degree of variance from the baseline. For example, a variance of 10% might not require immediate action, whereas a variance of 100% will require investigation. A description of how you plan to manage cost variances should be included in the—

a. Cost management plan
b. Change management plan
c. Performance measurement plan
d. Variance management plan

13. If operations on a work package were estimated to cost $1,500 and finish today but, instead, have cost $1,350 and are only two-thirds complete, the cost variance is—

   a.  +$150
   b.  −$150
   c.  −$350
   d.  −$500

14. On your project, you need to assign costs to the time period in which they are incurred. To do this, you should—

   a.  Identify the project components so that costs can be allocated
   b.  Use the project schedule as an input to cost budgeting
   c.  Prepare a detailed and accurate cost estimate
   d.  Prepare a cost performance plan

15. As of the fourth month on the Acme project, cumulative planned expenditures were $100,000. Actual expenditures totaled $120,000. How is the Acme project doing?

   a.  It is ahead of schedule.
   b.  It is in trouble because of a cost overrun.
   c.  It will finish within the original budget.
   d.  The information is insufficient to make an assessment.

16. Each time you meet with your project sponsor, she emphasizes the need for cost control. To address her concerns, you should provide—

   a.  Performance measurements
   b.  Cost baseline updates
   c.  Resource productivity analyses
   d.  Trend analysis statistics

17. You receive a frantic phone call from your vice president who says she is going to meet with a prospective client in 15 minutes to discuss a large and complex project. She asks you how much the project will cost. You quickly think of some similar past projects, factor in a few unknowns, and give her a number. What type of estimate did you just provide?

   a.  Definitive
   b.  Budget
   c.  Order-of-magnitude
   d.  Detailed

18. You have a number of costs to track and manage because your project is technically very complex. They include direct costs and indirect (overhead) costs. You have found that managing overhead costs is particularly difficult because they—

    a. Are handled on a project-by-project basis
    b. Represent only direct labor costs
    c. Represent only equipment and materials needed for the project
    d. Are usually beyond the project manager's control

19. If you want to calculate the ETC based on your expectations that similar variances to those noted to date will not occur, you should use which of the following formulas?

    a. $ETC = BAC - EV^c$
    b. $ETC = (BAC - EV^c)/CPI^c$
    c. $ETC = AC^c + EAC$
    d. $ETC = AC^c + BAC - EV$

20. Your approved cost baseline has changed because of a major scope change on your project. Your next step should be to—

    a. Estimate the magnitude of the scope change
    b. Issue a budget update
    c. Document lessons learned
    d. Execute the approved scope change

21. Which of the following is a tool for analyzing a design, determining its functions, and assessing how to provide those functions cost effectively?

    a. Pareto diagram
    b. Value analysis
    c. Configuration management
    d. Value engineering

22. It is expensive to lease office space in cities around the world. Office space can cost approximately USD $80 per square foot in Tampa, Florida. And it can cost approximately ¥50,000 per square meter in Tokyo. These "averages" can help a person determine how much it will cost to lease office space in these cities based on the amount of space leased. These estimates are examples of—

    a. Variance analysis
    b. Parametric estimating
    c. Bottom-up estimating
    d. Reserve analysis

23. The cumulative CPI has been shown to be relatively stable after what percentage of project completion?

    a. 5% to 10%
    b. 15% to 20%
    c. 25% to 35%
    d. 50% to 75%

24. There are a number of different earned value rules that can be established as part of the cost management plan. Which one of the following is *not* an example of such a rule?

    a. Code of accounts allocation provision
    b. Formulas to determine the ETC
    c. Earned value credit criteria
    d. Definition of the WBS level

25. The undistributed budget is part of the—

    a. Management reserve
    b. Performance measurement baseline
    c. Level-of-effort cost accounts
    d. General and administrative accounts

26. Overall cost estimates must be allocated to individual activities or work packages to establish the project cost baseline. In an ideal situation, a project manager would prefer to prepare estimates—

    a. Before the budget request
    b. After the budget is approved
    c. Using a parametric model
    d. Using a bottom-up estimating method

27. Your project manager has requested that you provide him with a forecast of project costs for the next 12 months. He needs this information to determine if the budget should be increased or decreased on this major construction project. In addition to the usual information sources, which of the following should you also consider?

    a. Cost estimates from similar projects
    b. WBS
    c. Project schedule
    d. Approved change requests

28. Control accounts—

    a. Are charge accounts for personnel time management
    b. Summarize project costs at level 2 of the WBS
    c. Identify and track management reserves
    d. Represent the basic level at which project performance is measured and reported

29. Which of the following calculations *cannot* be used to determine EAC?

    a. EV to date plus the remaining project budget
    b. AC to date plus a new estimate for all remaining work
    c. AC to date plus the remaining budget
    d. AC to date plus the remaining budget modified by a performance factor

30. By reviewing cumulative cost curves, the project manager can monitor—

    a. EV
    b. PV
    c. CVs
    d. CPI

31. According to learning curve theory, when many items are produced repetitively—

    a. Unit costs decrease geometrically as production rates increase linearly
    b. Unit costs decrease as production rates increase
    c. Unit costs decrease in a regular pattern as more units are produced
    d. Costs of training increase as the level of automation increases

32. Performance review meetings are held to assess schedule activity and work package or control account status and progress. Typically, they are used in conjunction with all but which of the following performance reporting techniques?

    a. Variance analysis
    b. Trend analysis
    c. Time reporting systems
    d. Earned value analysis

33. Increased attention to return on investment (ROI) now requires you to complete a financial analysis of the payback period on your project. Such an analysis identifies the—

    a. Ratio of discounted revenues over discounted costs
    b. Future value of money invested today
    c. Amount of time before net cash flow becomes positive
    d. Point in time where costs exceed profit

34. The method of calculating the EAC by adding the remaining project budget (modified by a performance factor) to the actuals to date is used most often when the—

    a. Current variances are viewed as atypical ones
    b. Original estimating assumptions are no longer reliable because conditions have changed
    c. Current variances are viewed as typical of future variances
    d. Original estimating assumptions are considered to be fundamentally flawed

35. Recently you were named the project control officer responsible for regularly measuring project performance. You recommended using earned value management to estimate final project costs to the project manager because it—

    a. Tests the "official" position of the project manager against a statistically forecasted range of final possibilities based on actual project performance
    b. Provides management with the final BAC, PV, and EV
    c. Shows specific tasks in which cost overruns are expected to occur and, thus, focuses the project manager's attention on critical tasks
    d. Ensures that management reserve or contingency will not be needed

36. You have been asked to prepare two cost estimates—one for the project life-cycle costs and one for the total life-cycle costs. Which estimate will be higher?

    a. Project life-cycle costs
    b. Total life-cycle costs
    c. They are the same
    d. The answer depends on the type of project being performed

37. A revised cost baseline may be required in cost control when—

    a. CVs are severe, and a realistic measure of performance is needed
    b. Updated cost estimates are prepared and distributed to stakeholders
    c. Corrective action must be taken to bring expected future performance in line with the project plan
    d. EAC shows that additional funds are needed to complete the project even if a scope change is not needed

38. As project manager, you identified a number of acceptable tolerances as part of your earned value management system. During execution, some "unacceptable" variances occurred. After each "unacceptable" variance occurred, you did which one of the following first?

    a. Updated the budget
    b. Prepared a revised cost estimate
    c. Adjusted the project plan
    d. Documented lessons learned

39. All the following are outputs from the cost estimating process *except*—

    a. Activity cost estimates
    b. Requested changes
    c. Cost management plan updates
    d. Cost baseline

40. The cumulative cost curve for planned and actual expenditures—

    a. Helps monitor project performance at a glance
    b. Is used for calculating the CPI
    c. Is also known as a histogram
    d. Forecasts total project expenditures

## Answer Sheet

1. a b c d
2. a b c d
3. a b c d
4. a b c d
5. a b c d
6. a b c d
7. a b c d
8. a b c d
9. a b c d
10. a b c d
11. a b c d
12. a b c d
13. a b c d
14. a b c d
15. a b c d
16. a b c d
17. a b c d
18. a b c d
19. a b c d
20. a b c d

21. a b c d
22. a b c d
23. a b c d
24. a b c d
25. a b c d
26. a b c d
27. a b c d
28. a b c d
29. a b c d
30. a b c d
31. a b c d
32. a b c d
33. a b c d
34. a b c d
35. a b c d
36. a b c d
37. a b c d
38. a b c d
39. a b c d
40. a b c d

# Answer Key

### 1. d.  −$200; the project is behind schedule

SV is calculated as EV − PV (in this case, $2,000 − $2,200).  A negative variance means that the work completed is less than what was planned for at that point in the project.  [Monitoring and Controlling]

Dreger 1992, 282

### 2. b.  0.80; actual costs have exceeded planned costs

CPI is calculated as EV/AC (in this case, $2,000/$2,500).  EV measures the budgeted dollar value of the work that has actually been accomplished, whereas AC measures the actual cost of getting that work done.  If the two numbers are the same, work on the project is being accomplished for exactly the budgeted amount of money (and the ratio will be equal to 1.0).  If actual costs exceed budgeted costs (as in this example), AC will be larger than EV and the ratio will be less than 1.0.  CPI is also an index of efficiency.  In this example, an index of 0.80 (or 80 percent) means that for every dollar spent on the project only 80 cents worth of work is actually accomplished.  [Monitoring and Controlling]

Frame 1994, 253

### 3. d.  −$500

CV is calculated as EV − AC (in this case, $2,000 − $2,500).  A negative CV means that accomplishing work on the project is costing more than was budgeted.  [Monitoring and Controlling]

Fleming 1988, 258

### 4. a.  $12,500; the revised estimate for total project cost (based on performance thus far)

EAC is calculated as BAC/CPI (in this case, $10,000/0.80).  It is now known that the project will cost more than the original estimate of $10,000.  The project has been getting only 80 cents worth of work done for every dollar spent (CPI), and this information has been used to forecast total project costs.  This approach assumes that performance for the remainder of the project will also be based on a CPI of 0.80.  [Monitoring and Controlling]

Frame 1994, 253

**5. c.  Has an accuracy rate of $\pm 10\%$ of actual costs**

A frequently used method of cost estimating, the analogous technique relies on experience and knowledge gained to predict future events.  This technique provides planners with some idea of the magnitude of project costs but generally not within $\pm 10\%$.  [Planning]

PMI®, *PMBOK® Guide*, 2004, 164

**6. b.  Define the procedures by which the cost baseline may be changed**

The cost change control system includes the documentation, tracking systems, and approval levels needed to authorize a change.  [Monitoring and Controlling]

PMI®, *PMBOK® Guide*, 2004, 172

**7. d.  Electricity**

Direct costs are incurred for the exclusive benefit of a project (for example, salary of the project manager, materials used by the project, and subcontractor expenses).  Indirect costs, also called overhead costs, are allocated to a project by its performing organization as a cost of doing business (for example, security guards, fringe benefits, and electricity).  [Planning]

PMI®, *PMBOK® Guide*, 2004, 278

**8. b.  The variance is favorable to the project**

A positive schedule variance indicates that the project is ahead of schedule.  A positive cost variance indicates that the project has incurred less cost than estimated for the work accomplished; therefore, the project is under budget.  [Monitoring and Controlling]

Lewis 1991, 173

**9. c.  Identify and estimate the cost for each individual work item**

Bottom-up estimating is derived by first estimating the cost of the project's elemental tasks at the lower levels of the WBS and then aggregating those estimates at successively higher levels of the WBS.  The project manager typically includes indirect costs, general and administrative expenses, profit, and any reserves when calculating the total project cost estimate. [Planning]

PMI®, *PMBOK® Guide*, 2004, 165

**10. b. $73,000**

Total project life-cycle costs include all costs associated with project completion. Operations and maintenance and disposition costs are not part of the project life cycle but are considered a part of total life-cycle cost.

Ward 2000, 167

**11. b. Determine the cost performance needed to complete the remaining work within management's financial goal for the project**

The TCPI takes the value of work remaining and divides it by the value of funds remaining to obtain the cost performance factor needed to complete all remaining work according to a financial goal set by management. [Monitoring and Controlling]

Fleming and Koppelman 2000, 137–138

**12. a. Cost management plan**

The management and control of costs focuses on variances. Certain variances are acceptable, and others, usually those falling outside a particular range, are unacceptable. The actions taken by the project manager for all variances are described in the cost management plan. [Planning]

PMI®, *PMBOK® Guide*, 2004, 158–159

**13. c. −$350**

CV is calculated by $EV - AC$, or $\$1,500(2/3) - \$1,350 = -\$350$. [Monitoring and Controlling]

PMI®, *PMBOK® Guide*, 2004, 173

**14. b. Use the project schedule as an input to cost budgeting**

Accurate project performance measurement depends on accurate cost and schedule information. The project schedule includes planned start and finish dates for all activities tied to work packages and control accounts. This information is used to aggregate costs to the calendar period for which the costs are planned to be incurred. [Planning]

PMI®, *PMBOK® Guide*, 2004, 168

**15. d. The information is insufficient to make an assessment.**

The information provided tells us that, as of the fourth month, more money has been spent than was planned. However, we need to know how much work has been completed to determine how the project is performing. In earned value terms, we are missing the EV. [Monitoring and Controlling]

Frame 1995, 205–210

**16. a. Performance measurements**

The CV, SV, CPI, and SPI for WBS components for specific work packages and control accounts should be documented and communicated according to the project's communications management plan. [Monitoring and Controlling]

PMI®, *PMBOK® Guide*, 2004, 177

**17. c. Order-of-magnitude**

An order-of-magnitude estimate, which is referred to also as a ballpark estimate, has an accuracy range of –25% to +75% and is made without detailed data. [Planning]

Ward 2000, 139; PMI®, *PMBOK® Guide*, 2004, 161

**18. d. Are usually beyond the project manager's control**

Overhead includes costs such as rent, insurance, or heating, that pertain to the project as a whole and cannot be attributed to a particular work item. The amount of overhead to be added to the project is frequently decided by the performing organization and is beyond the control of the project manager. [Monitoring and Controlling]

ESI October 2004, 4-7 and 4-8; Meredith and Mantel 2006, 342–343

**19. a. $ETC = BAC - EV^c$**

This formula assumes that the estimate to complete is based on atypical variances. [Monitoring and Controlling]

PMI®, *PMBOK® Guide*, 2004, 175

**20. b. Issue a budget update**

Budget updates reflect changes to an approved cost baseline. These changes generally are made in response to an approved scope change. [Monitoring and Controlling]

PMI®, *PMBOK® Guide*, 2004, 177

### 21. d.  Value engineering

Value engineering considers possible cost trade-offs as a design evolves. The technique entails identifying the functions that are needed and analyzing the cost effectiveness of the alternatives available for providing them.  [Monitoring and Controlling]

Meredith and Mantel 2006, 246

### 22. b.  Parametric estimating

Parametric estimating involves using project characteristics (parameters) in a mathematical model to predict project costs.  The example is representative of a simple parametric model.  [Planning]

PMI®, *PMBOK® Guide*, 2004, 142, 165, 169

### 23. b.  15% to 20%

The CPI has been proven to be an accurate and reliable forecasting tool. Researchers have found that the cumulative CPI does not change by more than 10% once a project is approximately 20% complete.  The CPI provides a quick statistical forecast of final project costs.  [Monitoring and Controlling]

Fleming and Koppelman 2000, 134

### 24. a.  Code of accounts allocation provision

Three recognized earned value rules are to (1) determine the ETC calculation to be used on the project, (2) establish how EV credit will be determined (for example, 0–100, 0–50–100, and so on), and (3) define the WBS level at which the earned value analysis will be performed. [Planning]

PMI®, *PMBOK® Guide*, 2004, 159

### 25. b.  Performance measurement baseline

The undistributed budget is applied to project work that has not yet been linked to WBS elements at or below the lowest level of reporting.  It is, therefore, part of the performance measurement baseline and is expected to be used in the performance of project work.  [Monitoring and Controlling]

Fleming and Koppelman 2000, 104–108

### 26. a.  Before the budget request

Often project cost estimates are prepared after budgetary approval is provided.  However, work package cost estimates should be prepared before the budget request if at all possible, to enhance accuracy. [Planning]

PMI®, *PMBOK® Guide*, 2004, 167

### 27. d.  Approved change requests

An approved change request from the integrated change control process can include modifications to the cost terms of the contract project scope, cost baseline, or cost management plan.  [Monitoring and Controlling]

PMI®, *PMBOK® Guide*, 2004, 172

### 28. d.  Represent the basic level at which project performance is measured and reported

Control accounts represent a specific work package in the WBS and are normally tracked daily or weekly through a time card that is part of the organization's cost accounting system.  The purpose of control accounts is to monitor and report on project performance.  This objective is accomplished by collecting the results (cost, schedule, resource usage) for each work package at various points in time.  [Planning]

Cleland 2002, 327; PMI®, *PMBOK® Guide*, 2004, 158

### 29. a.  EV to date plus the remaining project budget

EAC is a forecast of the most likely total value based on project performance and risk quantification.  To calculate EAC, the AC of a project must be known and used in the calculation.  Any calculation that relies solely on the EV will not yield an accurate measure of cost performance. [Monitoring and Controlling]

PMI®, *PMBOK® Guide*, 2004, 175–176

### 30. c.  CVs

Cumulative cost curves, or S-curves, enable the project manager to monitor cost variances at a glance.  The difference in height between the planned-expenditure curve and the actual-expenditure curve represents the monetary value of variances at any given time.  [Monitoring and Controlling]

Frame 1995, 188, PMI®, *PMBOK® Guide*, 2004, 174

**31. c.  Unit costs decrease in a regular pattern as more units are produced**

Learning curve theory indicates that human performance usually improves when a task is repeated.  Specifically, each time output doubles, worker hours per unit decrease by a fixed percentage.  This percentage is called the learning rate.  [Planning]

Meredith and Mantel 2006, 342–344

**32. c.  Time reporting systems**

Performance review meetings are conducted to determine schedule, budget, and quality performance among other important issues.  Time reporting systems are a performance reporting tool and technique in project communications management used to record and provide time expended for the project.  [Monitoring and Controlling]

PMI®, *PMBOK® Guide*, 2004, 176

**33. c.  Amount of time before net cash flow becomes positive**

Payback period analysis determines the time required for a project to recover the investment in it and become profitable.  A weakness of this approach is a lack of emphasis on the magnitude of the profitability.  [Planning]

Ward 2000, 145; PMI®, *PMBOK® Guide*, 2004, 158

**34. c.  Current variances are viewed as typical of future variances**

Past performance is indicative of future performance; therefore, using a performance indicator to modify the remaining project budget yields the most accurate estimate.  [Monitoring and Controlling]

PMI®, *PMBOK® Guide*, 2004, 176

**35. a.  Tests the "official" position of the project manager against a statistically forecasted range of final possibilities based on actual project performance**

The most commonly used method of performance measurement, earned value analysis, integrates scope, cost, and schedule measures to assess project performance by calculating PV, AC, and EV for each activity.  [Monitoring and Controlling]

Fleming and Koppelman 2000, 136; PMI®, *PMBOK® Guide*, 2004, 172–173

### 36. b. Total life-cycle costs

Project life-cycle costs do not account for the cost of operations, maintenance, or in the case of a capital asset, disposition. [Planning]

PMI®, *PMBOK® Guide*, 2004, 157

### 37. a. CVs are severe, and a realistic measure of performance is needed

After the CVs exceed certain ranges, the original project budget may be questioned and changed as a result of new information. [Monitoring and Controlling]

PMI®, *PMBOK® Guide*, 2004, 177

### 38. d. Documented lessons learned

Lessons learned but not documented are "lessons lost." The lessons learned knowledge database will help current project members, as well as people on future projects, make better decisions. Accordingly, the reasons for the variance, the rationale supporting the corrective action, and other related information must be documented. [Monitoring and Controlling]

PMI®, *PMBOK® Guide*, 2004, 177

### 39. d. Cost baseline

Cost baseline is an output from the cost budgeting process. [Monitoring and Controlling]

PMI®, *PMBOK® Guide*, 2004, 177

### 40. a. Helps monitor project performance at a glance

Cost curves for planned and actual expenditures are created by adding each month's costs to the previous reporting period's expenditures. By doing so, one can quickly see how the project is performing. [Monitoring and Controlling]

Frame 1995, 188

PROJECT *Quality* MANAGEMENT

# PROJECT QUALITY MANAGEMENT

## Study Hints

The Project Quality Management questions on the PMP® certification exam are straightforward—especially if you know definitions of terms and understand statistical process control. You are not required to solve quantitative problems, but there are questions on statistical methods of measuring and controlling quality.

The exam is likely to reflect a heavy emphasis on customer satisfaction and continuous improvement through the use of quality tools such as Pareto analysis and cause-and-effect diagrams. You must also know the differences among quality planning, quality assurance, and quality control.

The *PMBOK® Guide* includes all quality-related activities under the term Project Quality Management, which comprises the three quality processes mentioned above. Review *PMBOK® Guide* Figure 8-1 for an overview of the Project Quality Management structure before taking the practice test. Know this chart thoroughly.

Following is a list of the major Project Quality Management topics. Use it to help focus your study efforts on the areas most likely to appear on the exam.

# Major Topics

*Key* **PMBOK®** **Guide** *concepts*

- Quality defined
- Quality management
- Quality planning
- Quality policy
- Quality planning tools and techniques
  - Cost/benefit analysis
  - Benchmarking
  - Design of experiments
  - Cost of quality
- Key quality planning outputs
  - Quality management plan
  - Quality metrics
  - Quality checklists
  - Process improvement plan
  - Quality baseline
- Quality assurance
  - Quality audits
  - Process analysis
  - Formative quality evaluation
  - Quality improvement
  - Ownership of quality responsibility
  - Self-inspection
- Quality control
  - Variable
  - Attribute
  - Probability
  - Standard deviation
  - Process control
  - Sampling

*Quality control tools*

- Cause-and-effect diagrams
- Control charts
- Flowcharting
- Histograms
- Pareto charts
- Run charts
- Scatter diagrams
- Statistical sampling
- Inspection
- Defect repair review

## Major Topics (continued)

*Continuous process improvement and* kaizen

*Just-in-time (JIT)*

*Impact of motivation on quality*

*Priority of quality versus cost and schedule*

*Design and quality*

# Practice Questions

INSTRUCTIONS: Note the most suitable answer for each multiple-choice question in the appropriate space on the answer sheet.

1. Quality is very important to your company. Each project has a quality statement that is consistent with the organization's vision and mission. Both internal and external quality assurance are provided on all projects to—

   a. Ensure confidence that the project will satisfy relevant quality standards
   b. Monitor specific project results to note whether they comply with relevant quality standards
   c. Identify ways to eliminate causes of unsatisfactory results
   d. Use inspection to keep errors out of the process

2. Benchmarking is a technique used in—

   a. Inspections
   b. Root cause analysis
   c. Quality planning
   d. Quality control

3. In quality management, the practice "rework" is—

   a. Acceptable under certain circumstances
   b. An adjustment made that is based on quality control measurements
   c. Action taken to bring a defective or nonconforming component into compliance
   d. Not a concern if errors are detected early

4. The quality function deployment process is used to—

   a. Provide better product definition and product development
   b. Help products succeed in the marketplace
   c. Improve the functional characteristics of a product
   d. Support production planning and the just-in-time approach

5. As it applies to quality, the law of diminishing returns says that—

   a. 100% quality is unattainable
   b. 100% inspection is not cost effective
   c. Beyond a certain point, additional investment in quality has a negative ROI
   d. Providing quality products will stop, or at least diminish, the number of returned items

6. You are leading a research project that will require between 10 and 20 aerospace engineers. Some senior-level aerospace engineers are available. They are more productive than junior-level engineers, who cost less and who are available as well. You want to determine the optimal combination of senior- and junior-level personnel. In this situation, the appropriate technique to use is to—

   a. Conduct a design of experiments
   b. Use the Ishikawa diagram to pinpoint the problem
   c. Prepare a control chart
   d. Analyze the process using a Pareto diagram

7. The purpose of the Taguchi method is to—

   a. Manage the flow of material for better visibility and control
   b. Use statistical techniques to compute a "loss function" to determine the cost of producing products that fail to achieve a target value
   c. Design, group, and manage production operations as self-contained flexible cells capable of start-to-finish processing of a family of items
   d. Regulate coordination and communication among process stages

8. Quality assurance promotes quality improvement. A "breakthrough" is the accomplishment of any improvement that takes the organization to unprecedented levels of performance by attacking—

   a. Special causes of variation
   b. Common causes of variation
   c. Inspection over prevention
   d. Specific tolerances

9. To anticipate and help develop approaches to deal with potential quality problems on your project, you want to use a variety of root-cause analysis techniques including all the following approaches *except*—

   a. Fishbone diagrams
   b. Ishikawa diagrams
   c. System or process flowcharts
   d. Checklists

10. Which of the following statements best describes attribute sampling versus variables sampling?

    a. Attribute sampling is concerned with prevention, whereas variables sampling is concerned with inspection.
    b. Attribute sampling is concerned with conformance, whereas variables sampling is concerned with the degree of conformity.
    c. Attribute sampling is concerned with special causes, whereas variables sampling is concerned with any causes.
    d. Both are the same concept.

11. Constancy of purpose is a core concept for continuous improvement. An organization displaying constancy of purpose must have all the following elements *except*—

    a. Documented and well-disseminated statements of purpose and vision
    b. A set of strategic and tactical plans
    c. An awareness by all members of the organization of the purpose, vision, goals, and objectives and their roles in achieving them
    d. Separate quality assurance and quality control departments reporting to senior management

12. Recently, your company introduced a new processing system for its products. You were the project manager for this system and now have been asked to lead a team to implement needed changes to increase efficiency and productivity. To help you analyze the process, you and your team have decided to use which of the following techniques?

    a. System flowcharts
    b. Design of experiments
    c. Pareto analysis
    d. Control charts

13. Your project scheduler has produced defective reports for the past six accounting cycles, causing customer dissatisfaction and lost productivity due to rework. You discovered that the project scheduler needs better training on using the scheduling tool. The cost of the training falls under which of the following categories?

    a. Overhead costs
    b. Failure costs
    c. Prevention costs
    d. Indirect costs

14. Project quality management was once thought to include only inspection or quality control. In recent years, the concept of project quality management has broadened. Which statement is *not* representative of the new definition of quality management?

    a. Quality is designed into the product or service, not inspected into it.
    b. Quality is the concern of the quality assurance staff.
    c. Customers require a documented and, in some cases, registered quality assurance system.
    d. National and international standards and guidelines for quality assurance systems are available.

15. The project team should have a working knowledge of statistical process control to help evaluate quality control outputs. Of all the topics involved, which of the following is the most important for the team to understand?

    a. Sampling and probability
    b. Attribute sampling and variables sampling
    c. Tolerances and control limits
    d. Special causes and random causes

16. Rank ordering of defects should be used to guide corrective action. This is the underlying principle behind—

    a. Trend analysis
    b. Inspections
    c. Control charts
    d. Pareto diagrams

17. Long-term contracting is an important aspect of project quality management because it—

    a. Provides incentives to vendors to make quality commitments
    b. Improves quality through the use of benefit-cost analysis
    c. Usually results in lower costs and increased productivity
    d. Provides for mandatory audits

18. Based on quality control measurements on your manufacturing project, management realizes that immediate corrective action is required to the material requirements planning (MRP) system to minimize rework. To implement the necessary changes you should follow—

    a. The organization's quality policy
    b. The quality management plan
    c. Established operational definitions and procedures
    d. A defined integrated change control process

19. In order to monitor the number of errors or defects that have been identified and the number that remain undetected, you should—

    a. Design an experiment
    b. Use a checklist
    c. Conduct a trend analysis
    d. Perform an audit

20. Your quality assurance department recently performed a quality audit of your project and identified a number of findings and recommendations. One recommendation seems critical and should be implemented because it affects successful delivery of the product to your customer. Your next step should be to—

    a. Call a meeting of your project team to see who is responsible for the problem
    b. Reassign the team member who had responsibility for oversight of the problem
    c. Perform product rework immediately
    d. Issue a change request to implement the needed corrective action

21. You are the project manager on a project to improve traffic flow in the company's parking garage. You decide to use flowcharting to—

    a. Help analyze how problems occur
    b. Show dependencies between tasks
    c. Show the results of a process
    d. Forecast future outcomes

22. You are managing a major international project, and your contract requires you to prepare both a project plan and a quality management plan. Your core team is preparing a project quality management plan. Your first step in developing this plan is to—

    a. Determine specific metrics to use in the quality management process
    b. Identify the quality standards for the project
    c. Develop a quality policy for the project
    d. Identify specific quality management roles and responsibilities for the project

23. Six sigma refers to the aim of setting tolerance limits at six standard deviations from the mean, whereas the normally expected deviation of a process is—

    a. One standard deviation
    b. Two standard deviations
    c. Three standard deviations
    d. Undeterminable because of the unique nature of every process

24. You recognize the importance of quality control on your project. However, you also know that quality control has costs associated with it and that the project has a limited budget. One way to reduce the cost of quality control is to—

   a. Work to ensure that the overall quality program is ISO compliant
   b. Use statistical sampling
   c. Conduct inspections throughout the process
   d. Use trend analysis

25. The continuous improvement process provides a way for an organization to create and sustain a culture of continuous improvement. As such, it should be directed by—

   a. The project manager
   b. Top management
   c. Employees participating in quality circles
   d. Stakeholders

26. Quality inspections also may be called—

   a. Control tests
   b. Walk-throughs
   c. Statistical sampling
   d. Checklists

27. Your management has prescribed that a quality audit be conducted at the end of every phase in a project. This audit is part of the organization's—

   a. Quality assurance process
   b. Quality control process
   c. Quality improvement program
   d. Process adjustment program

28. Recently your company introduced a new set of "metal woods" to its established line of golfing equipment. However, in the past weeks many of the clubs have been returned due to quality problems. You decide to conduct a failure mode and criticality analysis to—

   a. Analyze the product development cycle after product release to determine strengths and weaknesses
   b. Evaluate failure modes and causes associated with the design and manufacture of an existing product
   c. Evaluate failure modes and causes associated with the design and manufacture of a new product
   d. Help management set priorities in its existing manufacturing processes to avoid failures

29. The "rule of seven" as applied to statistical process control charts means that—

    a. Seven rejects typically occur per thousand inspections
    b. Seven consecutive measurements are ascending, descending, or the same
    c. At least seven inspectors should be in place for every thousand employees
    d. A process is not out of control even though seven measurements fall outside the lower and upper control limits

30. You are a project manager for residential construction. As a project manager, you must be especially concerned with building codes— particularly in the quality planning process. You must ensure that building codes are reflected in your project plans because—

    a. Standards and regulations are an input to quality planning
    b. Quality audits serve to ensure there is compliance with regulations
    c. They are a cost associated with quality initiatives
    d. Compliance with standards is the primary objective of quality control

31. You work as a project manager in the largest hospital in the region. Studies have shown that patients have to wait for long periods before being treated. To assist in identifying the factors contributing to this problem, you and your team have decided to use which of the following techniques?

    a. Cause-and-effect diagrams
    b. Pareto analysis
    c. Scatter diagrams
    d. Control charts

32. The ISO 9000 standards provide—

    a. A description of how products should be produced
    b. Specifics for the implementation of quality systems
    c. A framework for quality systems
    d. The maximum process requirements necessary to ensure that customers receive a good product

33. To use statistical quality control effectively, the project team should know the differences between—

    a. Prevention and quality control
    b. Special causes and random causes
    c. Attribute sampling and statistical sampling
    d. Control limits and operational definitions

34. Even though your project is vastly different from a manufacturing operation, you believe the principles of *kaizen* will work well. The *kaizen* approach to continuous improvement emphasizes—

    a. The greater importance of customer satisfaction over cost
    b. Radical changes in operating practices
    c. Incremental improvement
    d. The use of quality circles to improve morale

35. Your company is establishing a cost-of-quality approach to determine the relative importance of its quality problems. Training costs are included in which one of the following categories?

    a. Prevention costs
    b. Appraisal costs
    c. Internal failure costs
    d. External failure costs

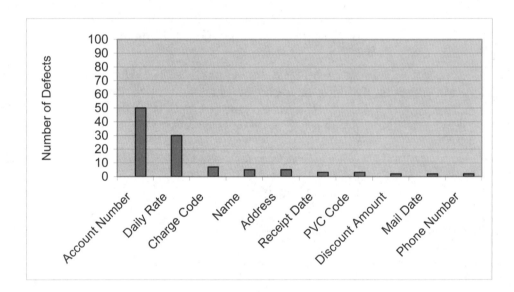

36. The above Pareto chart indicates defects in areas associated with billing a client for your project services. Based on Pareto analysis, which area(s) indicate the greatest opportunity for improvement?

    a. Account number because if this is incorrect, the invoice may be sent to the wrong client
    b. Daily rate because if this is incorrect, the total amount of the invoice will be wrong, thus impacting cash flow
    c. All areas except account number and daily rate because they account for 80% of all categories
    d. Account number and daily rate because they account for 80% of all problems

37. Results of quality control testing and measurement are used—

    a. As an input to quality planning
    b. To prepare an operational definition
    c. To prepare a control chart
    d. As an input to quality assurance

38. Statistical sampling is a method to determine the conformance to requirements for some component or product of a project. Its greatest advantage is that it—

    a. Does not require a large expenditure of resources
    b. Is accurate enough with a sampling of less than 1%
    c. Does not require 100% inspection of the components to achieve a satisfactory inference of the population
    d. Needs to be conducted only when a problem is discovered with the end product or when the customer has some rejects

39. The statistical control chart is a tool used primarily to help—

    a. Monitor process variation over time
    b. Measure the degree of conformance
    c. Determine whether results conform
    d. Determine whether results conform to requirements

40. The quality management plan describes all the following *except* the—

    a. Method for implementing the quality policy
    b. QA, QC, and continuous process improvement for the project
    c. Efforts at the front end of a project to ensure that earlier decisions are correct
    d. Procedures used to conduct trade-off analyses among cost, schedule, and quality

## Answer Sheet

1. | a | b | c | d |

2. | a | b | c | d |

3. | a | b | c | d |

4. | a | b | c | d |

5. | a | b | c | d |

6. | a | b | c | d |

7. | a | b | c | d |

8. | a | b | c | d |

9. | a | b | c | d |

10. | a | b | c | d |

11. | a | b | c | d |

12. | a | b | c | d |

13. | a | b | c | d |

14. | a | b | c | d |

15. | a | b | c | d |

16. | a | b | c | d |

17. | a | b | c | d |

18. | a | b | c | d |

19. | a | b | c | d |

20. | a | b | c | d |

21. | a | b | c | d |

22. | a | b | c | d |

23. | a | b | c | d |

24. | a | b | c | d |

25. | a | b | c | d |

26. | a | b | c | d |

27. | a | b | c | d |

28. | a | b | c | d |

29. | a | b | c | d |

30. | a | b | c | d |

31. | a | b | c | d |

32. | a | b | c | d |

33. | a | b | c | d |

34. | a | b | c | d |

35. | a | b | c | d |

36. | a | b | c | d |

37. | a | b | c | d |

38. | a | b | c | d |

39. | a | b | c | d |

40. | a | b | c | d |

# Answer Key

**1. a. Ensure confidence that the project will satisfy relevant quality standards**

Quality assurance increases project effectiveness and efficiency and provides added benefits to project stakeholders. It includes all the planned and systematic quality activities to ensure that the project uses all the processes to meet requirements. Quality assurance should be performed throughout the project. [Executing]

PMI®, *PMBOK® Guide*, 2004, 179

**2. c. Quality planning**

The other tools and techniques used in quality planning are benefit/cost analysis, flowcharting, design of experiments, cost of quality, brainstorming, force field analysis, nominal group techniques, matrix diagrams, affinity diagrams, and prioritization matrices. [Planning]

PMI®, *PMBOK® Guide*, 2004, 185–186

**3. c. Action taken to bring a defective or nonconforming component into compliance**

Rework is a frequent cause of project overruns. The project team must make every reasonable effort to control and minimize rework so that defective or nonconforming components are brought into compliance with requirements or specifications. [Monitoring and Controlling]

PMI®, *PMBOK® Guide*, 2004, 372

**4. a. Provide better product definition and product development**

Quality function deployment helps a design team to define, design, manufacture, and deliver a product or service to meet or exceed customer needs. Its main features are to capture the customer's requirements, ensure cross-functional teamwork, and link the main phases of product development—product planning, part deployment, process planning, and production planning. [Planning]

Soin 1992, 42–43; Evans and Lindsay 2001, 405–406

**5. c. Beyond a certain point, additional investment in quality has a negative ROI**

If a company has paid $100,000 to gain 98% quality and it would cost an additional $25,000 to gain the other 2%, this is known as the law of diminishing returns. [Monitoring and Controlling]

Friedman 1994, 332

**6. a. Conduct a design of experiments**

This technique is used to identify which variables have the most influence on the overall outcome. It usually is applied to a product rather than to a service. For example, roller blade designers might want to determine which combination of number of wheels and titanium ball bearings would produce the most desirable "ride" characteristics at a reasonable cost. This technique, however, can be applied to project management issues such as cost and schedule trade-offs. An appropriately designed "experiment" often will help project managers find an optimal solution from a relatively limited number of options. [Planning]

PMI®, *PMBOK® Guide*, 2004, 185

**7. b. Use statistical techniques to compute a "loss function" to determine the cost of producing products that fail to achieve a target value**

The Taguchi method is used to estimate the loss associated with controlling or failing to control process variability. It is based on the principle that by carefully selecting design parameters to produce robust designs, an organization can produce products that are more forgiving and tolerant. The tool helps determine the value or break-even point of improving a process to reduce variability. [Monitoring and Controlling]

Mansir and Schacht 1988, 4-86 through 4-95; Evans and Lindsay 2001, 77–78

**8. b. Common causes of variation**

Quality improvement includes action taken to increase project effectiveness and efficiency in order to provide added benefits to stakeholders. A breakthrough attacks chronic losses, or in Deming's terminology, common causes of variation. [Executing]

Evans and Lindsay 2001, 422; PMI®, *PMBOK® Guide*, 2004, 191

**9. d. Checklists**

Checklists are used to verify that a set of required steps has been performed in the quality planning process. [Monitoring and Controlling]

PMI®, *PMBOK® Guide*, 2004, 187

**10. b. Attribute sampling is concerned with conformance, whereas variables sampling is concerned with the degree of conformity.**

Attribute sampling determines whether a result does or does not conform. Variables sampling rates a result on a continuous scale to measure the degree of conformity. [Monitoring and Controlling]

PMI®, *PMBOK® Guide*, 2004, 191

**11. d. Separate quality assurance and quality control departments reporting to senior management**

Top management should provide constancy of purpose so that it can be infused throughout the organization. Constancy of purpose also requires a shared belief among organization members that management's behavior clearly signals its commitment to and support of achievement of the vision. Quality assurance and control are functions that must be performed by everyone, not just those assigned to specific departments. [Executing]

Mansir and Schacht 1988, 3-4 and 3-5

**12. d. Control charts**

This function of control charts is achieved through graphical display of results over time to determine whether differences in the results are created by random variations or are unusual events. In a manufacturing environment, such charts are used to track repetitive actions such as manufactured lots. In a project management environment, they can be used to monitor processes such as cost and schedule variances, number requirements, and errors in project documents. [Monitoring and Controlling]

PMI®, *PMBOK® Guide*, 2004, 192–193

**13. c. Prevention costs**

Prevention costs include any expenditure directed toward ensuring that quality is achieved the first time.

Rose 2005, 8–9

**14. b. Quality is the concern of the quality assurance staff.**

Quality concerns all levels of management and staff. Responsibilities for quality are assigned to top management as well as to all workers. [Planning]

Willborn and Cheng 1994, 13 and 17

**15. a. Sampling and probability**

Sampling and probability form the basis of statistical process control, which helps the team monitor project results for compliance with relevant quality standards so that methods can be identified to eliminate causes of unsatisfactory results. [Monitoring and Controlling]

PMI®, *PMBOK® Guide*, 2004, 190

**16. d. Pareto diagrams**

Pareto diagrams are histograms, ordered by frequency of occurrence, that show how many results were generated by type or category of identified cause. The project team should take action to fix the problems that are causing the greatest number of defects first. Pareto diagrams are based on Pareto's Law, which holds that a relatively small number of causes will typically produce a large majority of defects, also called the "solzo rule." [Monitoring and Controlling]

PMI®, *PMBOK® Guide*, 2004, 195

**17. a. Provides incentives to vendors to make quality commitments**

Vendors that have long-term relationships with buyers are generally more inclined to invest in process and quality improvement because they have a higher probability of recovering their costs. The stability provided through long-term contracts permits better planning and encourages better communication between the buyer and seller. Long-term contracting with fewer vendors also reduces buyer-related costs by simplifying accounting, collections, and other administrative tasks. [Planning]

Mansir and Schacht 1988, 4-11; Evans and Lindsay 2001, 87–88

**18. d. A defined integrated change control process**

If the recommended corrective or preventive actions require a change to any of the project's baselines, a change request should be prepared in conformance with the integrated change control process. [Monitoring and Controlling]

PMI®, *PMBOK® Guide*, 2004, 197

**19. c. Conduct a trend analysis**

Trend analysis involves using mathematical techniques to forecast future outcomes based on historical results. It is performed using run charts. It is used to monitor technical performance, as well as cost and schedule performance. [Monitoring and Controlling]

Ward 2000, 232; PMI®, *PMBOK® Guide*, 2004, 196

**20. d. Issue a change request to implement the needed corrective action**

The information obtained from a quality audit can be used to improve quality systems and performance. In most cases, implementing quality improvements requires preparation of change requests. [Executing]

PMI®, *PMBOK® Guide*, 2004, 190

**21. a. Help analyze how problems occur**

Flowcharts depict the interrelationship of a system's components. As such, they aid the team in anticipating where quality problems might occur, which helps in developing approaches for dealing with these potential problems. [Monitoring and Controlling]

PMI®, *PMBOK® Guide*, 2004, 193

**22. c. Develop a quality policy for the project**

The quality policy includes the overall intentions and direction of the organization with regard to quality, as formally expressed by top management. If the performing organization lacks a formal quality policy or if the project involves multiple performing organizations, as in a joint venture, the project management team must develop a quality policy for the project as an input to its quality planning. [Planning]

PMI®, *PMBOK® Guide*, 2004, 184

**23. c. Three standard deviations**

When the results of a sample of items measured falls within three standard deviations and that sample is representative of the entire population, you can assume that more than 99% of all items fall within that range. This generally accepted range of results has been used by quality control professionals through the years. Six sigma is a program started by Motorola that, from a statistical standpoint, indicates a quality standard of only 3.4 defects per million. [Executing]

Bicheno 1994, 57; Evans and Lindsay 2001, 42–43

### 24. b. Use statistical sampling

Statistical sampling uses part of a population to draw conclusions about the total population. It is a well-proven technique that can significantly reduce the cost of quality control. [Monitoring and Controlling]

PMI®, *PMBOK® Guide*, 2004, 196

### 25. b. Top management

Top management leads the effort to stimulate creativity, pride, teamwork, and the quest for knowledge. Top management should seek to create an integrated effort working toward improving performance at every level and in every activity. [Executing]

Mansir and Schacht 1988, 1-8

### 26. b. Walk-throughs

Inspections comprise an examination of a work product to determine if it conforms to standards. Additional names for inspections are audits, reviews, or peer reviews (in some application areas, these terms may have narrow and specific meanings). [Monitoring and Controlling]

PMI®, *PMBOK® Guide*, 2004, 196

### 27. a. Quality assurance process

Quality assurance is a managerial function that establishes processes or procedures in an organization or project to assist in determining whether quality standards are being met. It is the application of planned, systematic quality activities to ensure that the project will use all processes needed to meet requirements and is performed throughout the life of the project. [Executing]

PMI®, *PMBOK® Guide*, 2004, 187

### 28. c. Evaluate failure modes and causes associated with the design and manufacture of a new product

This technique is a method of analyzing design reliability. A list of potential failure modes is developed for each element, and then each mode is given a numeric rating for frequency of occurrence, criticality, and probability of detection. These data are used to assign a risk priority number for prioritizing problems and guiding the design effort. [Monitoring and Controlling]

Soin 1992, 157–159; Evans and Lindsay 2001, 768–769

**29. b. Seven consecutive measurements are ascending, descending, or the same**

Consecutive points on a process control chart that are ascending, descending, or the same indicate an abnormal trend in the process and must be investigated. [Monitoring and Controlling]

Ireland 1991, V-6; Evans and Lindsay 2001, 741

**30. a. Standards and regulations are an input to quality planning**

In quality planning, the project management team must consider any application-area specific standards, regulations, rules, and guidelines that may affect the project as part of the enterprise environmental factors. Building codes are an example of regulations. [Planning]

PMI®, *PMBOK® Guide*, 2004, 14 and 184

**31. a. Cause-and-effect diagrams**

Cause-and-effect diagrams, also called Ishikawa diagrams or fishbone diagrams, are used to illustrate how various causes and subcauses interact to create a special effect. It is named for its developer, Kaoru Ishikawa. [Planning]

Ward 2000, 108; PMI®, *PMBOK® Guide*, 2004, 192

**32. c. A framework for quality systems**

ISO 9000 provides a basic set of requirements for a quality system, without specifying the particulars for implementation. [Planning]

Schmauch 1994, 6–10; Evans and Lindsay 2001, 528 and 533

**33. b. Special causes and random causes**

Special causes are unusual events; random causes are normal process variations. The project team must be able to identify unusual events so that their causes can be identified and corrected. [Monitoring and Controlling]

PMI®, *PMBOK® Guide*, 2004, 191

**34. c. Incremental improvement**

Imai, a Japanese engineer, coined the word *kaizen* to describe an approach to quality that means making small improvements every time a process is repeated. [Executing]

Imai 1986, 3; Evans and Lindsay 2001, 370–371

**35. a. Prevention costs**

Cost of quality refers to the total cost of all efforts to achieve product or service quality. Prevention costs are a category of quality costs. Prevention costs are investments made to keep nonconforming products from occurring and reaching the customer. They include quality planning costs, process control costs, information systems costs, and training and general management costs. [Planning]

PMI®, *PMBOK® Guide*, 2004, 186; Evans and Lindsay 2001, 486–487

**36. d. Account number and daily rate because they account for 80% of all problems**

Pareto analysis focuses on what Joseph Juran called the "vital" few. Named after Vilfredo Pareto, an Italian economist whose studies showed that 80% of the wealth was held by 20% of the population, quality analysis typically shows that 80% of all problems (defects) are found in 20% of the items or areas studied.

Rose 2005, 86–87

**37. d. As an input to quality assurance**

Quality control activities result in measurements that are used as inputs to the QA process. Such quality control measurements are used to reevaluate and analyze the quality standards and processes of the organization. [Executing]

PMI®, *PMBOK® Guide*, 2004, 189

**38. c. Does not require 100% inspection of the components to achieve a satisfactory inference of the population**

The application of the statistical concept of probability has proven, over many years in many applications, that an entire population of products need not be inspected, if the sample selected conforms to a normal distribution of possible outcomes (the "bell" curve). [Monitoring and Controlling]

PMI®, *PMBOK® Guide*, 2004, 196

**39. a. Monitor process variation over time**

Used to monitor process variation and to detect and correct changes in process performance, the statistical control chart helps people understand and control their processes and work. [Monitoring and Controlling]

Mansir and Schacht 1988, 4-73; PMI®, *PMBOK® Guide*, 2004, 192–193

**40. d. Procedures used to conduct trade-off analyses among cost, schedule, and quality**

A part of the overall project management plan, the quality management plan should address all aspects of how quality management will be implemented on the project and how the project team will implement the quality policy. Trade-off analyses are business judgments and, as such, are not procedural steps to be included in the quality management plan. [Planning]

PMI®, *PMBOK® Guide*, 2004, 186

# PROJECT HUMAN RESOURCE MANAGEMENT

## Study Hints

The Project Human Resource Management questions on the PMP® certification exam focus heavily on organizational structures, roles and responsibilities of the project manager, team building, and conflict resolution. Many of the questions are taken from the *PMBOK® Guide* and the following PMI® handbooks, which have been consolidated into one publication available from PMI® entitled *Principles of Project Management* (1997).

- *Conflict Management for Project Managers* by John R. Adams and Nicki S. Kirchof

- *Organizing for Project Management* by Dwayne P. Cable and John R. Adams

- *Roles and Responsibilities of the Project Manager* by John R. Adams and Brian W. Campbell

- *Team Building for Project Managers* by Linn C. Stuckenbruck and David Marshall

- *The Project Manager's Work Environment: Coping with Time and Stress* by Paul C. Dinsmore, Martin Dean Martin, and Gary T. Huettel

Three other publications also are useful for questions in this area:

- *Organizing Projects for Success,* vol. 1 of *The Human Aspects of Project Management* by Vijay K. Verma

- *Human Resource Skills for the Project Manager,* vol. 2 of *The Human Aspects of Project Management* by Vijay K. Verma

- *Managing the Project Team,* vol. 3 of *The Human Aspects of Project Management* by Vijay K. Verma

In contrast to other areas of the *PMBOK® Guide* in which commonly known terms are used, much of the terminology developed for Project Human Resource Management appears to be peculiar to PMI®. (In fact, much of the terminology has been used in project management literature for many years, but that literature has not always been widely disseminated.) For example, in the area of project organizational structures, some experts with years of experience in the field have not encountered such terms or concepts as *project expeditor* or *weak matrix*. Accordingly, committing to memory PMI®'s definition and classification of the following subject areas is imperative:

- Project organizational structures
- Experience and educational requirements of the project manager
- Types of power exercised by the project manager
- Conflict management concepts

In spite of the unfamiliarity of some of the terminology, most exam takers do not find the human resource questions on the exam difficult.

PMI® views Project Human Resource Management as composed of three elements: organizational planning, staff acquisition, and team development. See *PMBOK® Guide* Figure 9-1 for an overview of this structure. Know it cold!

Following is a list of the major Project Human Resource Management topics. Use it to help focus your study efforts on the areas most likely to appear on the exam.

# Major Topics

---

*Overall* **PMBOK**® Guide *approach to project human resource management*

*Forms of organization*

- Functional
- Project expeditor
- Project coordinator
- Weak matrix
- Strong matrix
- Balanced matrix
- Projectized
- Composite

*Project interfaces*

- Organizational
- Technical
- Interpersonal

*Human resource planning constraints*

- Organizational structure of the performing organization
- Collective bargaining agreements
- Preferences of the project management team
- Expected staff assignments

*Human resource planning outputs*

- Role and responsibility assignments
- Staffing management plan
- Organization chart

*Acquire the project team*

*Project manager roles and responsibilities*

- Functions
- Roles
- Qualifications
- Experience and educational requirements
- Negotiation

*Types of power*

- Legitimate
- Coercive
- Reward
- Expert
- Referent

---

# Major Topics (continued)

*Project conflict*

- Why conflict is unavoidable on projects
- Seven sources of conflict in project environments

*Conflict and the project life cycle*

*Conflict management*

- Problem solving (or confrontation)
- Compromising
- Smoothing
- Withdrawal
- Forcing

*Team building*

- Goals and results of project team building
- Symptoms of poor teamwork
- Ground rules for project team building
- The team-building process

*Colocation and virtual teams*

*Motivation theories*

- Maslow's Hierarchy of Needs
- McGregor's Theory X and Theory Y
- Herzberg's Theory of Motivation
- Expectancy theory

*Reward and recognition systems*

*Personnel issues*

- Fringe benefits
- Perquisites
- Arbitration
- Productivity
- Human resource functions

# Practice Questions

INSTRUCTIONS:  Note the most suitable answer for each multiple-choice question in the appropriate space on the answer sheet.

1. You have been assigned as project manager on what could be a "bet the company" project.  You realize that to be successful you need to exercise maximum control over project resources.  Which form of project organization should you establish for this project?

    a.  Strong matrix
    b.  Projectized
    c.  Project coordinator
    d.  Weak matrix

2. Which of the following is a ground rule for project team building?

    a.  Perform frequent performance appraisals
    b.  Ensure that each team member reports to his or her functional manager in addition to the project manager
    c.  Start early
    d.  Try to solve team political problems

3. Project A is being administered using a matrix form of organization.  The project manager reports to a senior vice president who provides visible support to the project.  In this scenario, which of the following statements best describes the relative power of the project manager?

    a.  The project manager will probably not be challenged by project stakeholders.
    b.  In this strong matrix, the balance of power is shifted to the functional line managers.
    c.  In this tight matrix, the balance of power is shifted to the project manager.
    d.  In this strong matrix, the balance of power is shifted to the project manager.

4. You are leading a team to recommend an equitable reward and recognition system for project managers. Before finalizing the plan, you want to ensure that executives understand the basic objective of reward systems. This objective is to—

   a. Be comparable with the award system established for functional managers to indicate parity and to show the importance of project management to the company
   b. Make the link between project performance and reward clear, explicit, and achievable
   c. Motivate project managers to work toward common objectives and goals as defined by the company
   d. Attract people to join the organization's project management career path

5. Which of the following factors contributes the most to team communication?

   a. External feedback
   b. Performance appraisals
   c. Smoothing over of team conflicts by the project manager
   d. Colocation

6. You are managing a virtual team. The project has been under way for several months, and you believe your team members do not view themselves as a team or unified group. To help rectify this situation, you should—

   a. Ensure that every member of the project team uses e-mail as a form of communication
   b. Mandate that the team follow the vision and mission statement of his or her organization
   c. Create symbols and structures that solidify the unity of the dispersed work group
   d. Provide team members with the latest in communications technology and mandate its use

7. Major difficulties arise when multiple projects need to be managed in the functional organizational structure because of—

   a. The level of authority of the project manager
   b. Conflicts over the relative priorities of different projects in competition for limited resources
   c. Project team members who are focused on their functional specialty rather than on the project
   d. The need for the project manager to use interpersonal skills to resolve conflicts informally

8. The team you have organized for your new project consists of three people who will work full-time and five people who will support the project on a part-time basis. All team members know one another and have worked together in the past. To ensure a successful project start-up, your first step should be to—

   a. Meet with each team member individually to discuss assignments
   b. Prepare a responsibility assignment matrix and distribute it to each team member
   c. Distribute the project plan and WBS to the team
   d. Hold a project kickoff meeting

9. The primary result of effective team development is—

   a. Improved project performance
   b. An effective, smoothly running team
   c. An understanding by project team members that the project manager is ultimately responsible for project performance
   d. Enhancement of the ability of stakeholders to contribute as individuals and team members

10. Given that you are neighbors, you and the CEO of your company have established a friendly personal relationship. Recently, your company appointed you project manager for a new project that is crucial to achieving next year's financial targets. Which type of power available to project managers might you be able to rely on?

   a. Referent
   b. Reward
   c. Formal
   d. Expert

11. The team members on your project have been complaining that they do not have any sense of identity as a team because they are located in different areas of the building. To remedy this situation, you developed a project logo and had it printed on T-shirts to promote the project, but this action has not worked. Your next step is to—

   a. Initiate a newsletter
   b. Create an air of mystery about the project
   c. Establish a "war room"
   d. Issue guidelines on how team members should interact with other stakeholders

12. Two team members on your current construction project are engaged in a major argument concerning the selection of project management software. They refuse to listen to each other. The most appropriate conflict resolution approach for you to use in this situation is—

    a. Accommodating
    b. Compromising
    c. Collaborating
    d. Forcing

13. The project team directory is an output from which of the following processes?

    a. Develop project team
    b. Acquire project team
    c. Human resource planning
    d. Manage project team

14. Team-building activities include management and individual actions taken specifically and primarily to improve team performance. Many of these actions may enhance team performance as a secondary effect. An example of some action that may enhance team performance as a secondary effect is—

    a. Establishing team performance goals and holding off-site retreats to review ways of best achieving these goals
    b. Colocating all team members in a single physical location
    c. Establishing a team-based reward and recognition system
    d. Involving nonmanagement-level team members in the planning process

15. Your project has been under way for some time, but indicators show that it is in trouble. You have observed all the following symptoms of bad teamwork in your project team *except*—

    a. Frustration
    b. Excessive meetings
    c. Lack of trust or confidence in the project manager
    d. Unproductive meetings

16. A management style characterized by little or no information flowing up or down between the project manager and project team is called—

    a. Egocentric
    b. Democratic
    c. Participative
    d. Laissez-faire

17. As a project manager, you realize that team development is essential for project success. Therefore, you want to review the technical context within which your team operates, including areas such as quality assurance, risk management, and procurement. This information can be found in the—

    a. Team charter
    b. Project management plan
    c. Staffing management plan
    d. Organizational policies and guidelines

18. In both the weak and strong matrix organizational structures, the primary condition leading to conflict is—

    a. Communication barriers
    b. Conflicting interests
    c. Need for consensus
    d. Ambiguous jurisdictions

19. As project manager you are primarily responsible for implementing the project plan by authorizing the execution of project activities. Because you do not work in a purely projectized organization, however, you do not have direct access to human resource administrative activities. Therefore you need to—

    a. Outsource these functions
    b. Prepare a project team charter that is signed off by a member of the human resources department to delineate responsibilities
    c. Ensure that your team is sufficiently aware of administrative requirements to ensure compliance
    d. Ask the head of human resources to approve your project staffing plan personally

20. Constant bickering, absenteeism, and substandard performance have characterized the behavior of certain members of your team. You have planned an off-site retreat for the team to engage in a variety of activities. Your primary objective for investing time and money in this event is to improve—

    a. Team performance
    b. Morale
    c. Quality
    d. Individual performance

21. Two team members on your project often disagree. You need a conflict resolution method that provides a long-term resolution. You decide to use which one of the following approaches?

    a. Confronting
    b. Problem solving
    c. Collaborating
    d. Smoothing

22. A constraining factor that may affect the organization of the project team is—

    a. The organizational structure of the performing organization
    b. Poor communication among team members
    c. Ambiguous staffing requirements
    d. Team morale

23. As a project manager, you believe in using a "personal touch" to further team development. One approach that has proven effective toward this goal is—

    a. Creating a team name
    b. Providing flexible work time
    c. Issuing a project charter
    d. Celebrating special occasions

24. Team development on a project is often complicated when individual team members are accountable to both a functional manager and the project manager. Effective management of this dual reporting relationship is generally the responsibility of the—

    a. Team members involved
    b. Project manager
    c. Project owner or sponsor
    d. Functional manager

25. You are project manager for a two-year project, now beginning its second year. The mix of team members has changed. In addition, several of the completed work packages have not received the required sign-offs and three work packages are five weeks behind schedule. To gain control of this project, you need to—

    a. Rebaseline your original staffing management plan with current resource requirements
    b. Change to a projectized organizational structure for maximum control over resource assignments
    c. Work with your team to prepare a responsibility assignment matrix
    d. Create a new division of labor by assigning technical leads to the most critical activities

26. You are part of a team that is working to develop a new medical implant device. Your project manager is an expert in medical implantation devices, yet he continually seeks opinions from the team about a wide variety of project and product issues. Team members often run project meetings while he sits silently at the head of the table. Which one of the following best characterizes his leadership style?

    a. Laissez-faire
    b. Team directed
    c. Collaborative
    d. Shared leadership

27. The major difference between the project coordinator and project expeditor forms of organization is that—

    a. Strong commitment to the project usually does not exist in the project expeditor form of organization
    b. The project coordinator cannot personally make or enforce decisions
    c. The project expeditor acts only as an intermediary between management and the project team
    d. The project coordinator reports to a higher-level manager in the organization

28. Which of the following represents a constraint on the acquire project team process?

    a. Preassignment of staff to the project
    b. Recruitment practices of the organizations involved
    c. Use of outsourcing
    d. Team member training requirements

29. During a recent status review meeting for your project, one team member was critical of others and seemed to try to diminish their status on the team. This person was assuming which of the following destructive team roles?

    a. Recognition seeker
    b. Blocker
    c. Aggressor
    d. Dominator

30. Objectives for conducting performance appraisals during the course of a project can include all of the following *except*—

    a. Initial establishment of roles and responsibilities
    b. Discovery of unknown or unresolved issues
    c. Development of individual training plans
    d. Establishment of goals for future time periods

31. A project manager who generally makes decisions without considering information provided by team members is using which management style?

    a. Laissez-faire
    b. Autocratic
    c. Bureaucratic
    d. Judicious

32. Your organization is adopting a project-based approach to business, which has been difficult. Although project teams have been created, they are little more than a collection of functional and technical experts who focus on their specialties. You are managing the company's most important project. As you begin this project, you must place a high priority on—

    a. Creating an effective team
    b. Identifying the resources needed to finish the project on time
    c. The best way to communicate status to the CEO
    d. Establishing firm project requirements

33. In organizing a project, a project manager must deal with conflict. Which statement is true regarding conflict in projects?

    a. A matrix form of organization can produce a lack of clear role definitions and lead to ambiguous jurisdictions between and among functional leaders and project managers
    b. Sources of conflict include project priorities, PERT/CPM schedules, contract administrative procedures, and type of contract
    c. Conflict is to be avoided whenever possible
    d. Strong matrix project managers have few human resource conflicts, because they can dictate their needs to functional managers

34. The terms strong matrix, balanced matrix, and weak matrix when applied to the matrix structure in project organization refer to the—

    a. Ability of the organization to achieve its goals
    b. Physical proximity of project team members to one another and to the project manager
    c. Degree of the project manager's authority
    d. Degree to which team members bond together

35. The chances for successful completion of a multidisciplinary project are increased if project team members are—

    a. Problem oriented
    b. Politically sensitive to top management's needs
    c. Focused on individual project activities
    d. Focused on customer demands

36. Hierarchical-type charts are a tool and technique for use in human resource planning. Of the following, which one is helpful in tracking project costs and can be aligned with the organization's accounting system?

    a. RACI
    b. RAM
    c. RBS
    d. OBS

37. When choosing the most appropriate form of project organization, the first step is to—

    a. Create the WBS and let it determine the project organizational structure
    b. Produce an initial project plan and determine the functional areas responsible for each task
    c. Refer to the project charter developed by top management
    d. Develop a project schedule, including a top-down flowchart, and identify the functional areas to perform each task

38. The key way for a project manager to promote optimum team performance in project teams whose members are not colocated is to—

    a. Build trust
    b. Establish a reward and recognition system
    c. Obtain the support of the functional managers in the other locations
    d. Exercise his or her right to control all aspects of the project

39. Conflicts in which of the following three areas represent more than 50% of all project conflicts?

    a. Personalities, cost objectives, and schedules
    b. Cost objectives, administrative procedures, and schedules
    c. Schedules, project priorities, and personnel resources
    d. Personalities, project priorities, and cost objectives

40. Your client has requested information showing which work packages have been assigned to the marketing department. You give your client the—

    a. WBS
    b. OBS
    c. RAM
    d. RACI

# Answer Sheet

| | | | | | | | | | |
|---|---|---|---|---|---|---|---|---|---|
| 1. | a | b | c | d | 21. | a | b | c | d |
| 2. | a | b | c | d | 22. | a | b | c | d |
| 3. | a | b | c | d | 23. | a | b | c | d |
| 4. | a | b | c | d | 24. | a | b | c | d |
| 5. | a | b | c | d | 25. | a | b | c | d |
| 6. | a | b | c | d | 26. | a | b | c | d |
| 7. | a | b | c | d | 27. | a | b | c | d |
| 8. | a | b | c | d | 28. | a | b | c | d |
| 9. | a | b | c | d | 29. | a | b | c | d |
| 10. | a | b | c | d | 30. | a | b | c | d |
| 11. | a | b | c | d | 31. | a | b | c | d |
| 12. | a | b | c | d | 32. | a | b | c | d |
| 13. | a | b | c | d | 33. | a | b | c | d |
| 14. | a | b | c | d | 34. | a | b | c | d |
| 15. | a | b | c | d | 35. | a | b | c | d |
| 16. | a | b | c | d | 36. | a | b | c | d |
| 17. | a | b | c | d | 37. | a | b | c | d |
| 18. | a | b | c | d | 38. | a | b | c | d |
| 19. | a | b | c | d | 39. | a | b | c | d |
| 20. | a | b | c | d | 40. | a | b | c | d |

# Answer Key

### 1. b.  Projectized

In a projectized organizational structure, all project team members report directly and solely to the project manager.  He or she has complete control over these resources and, therefore, exercises more authority over them than in any other project organizational structure.  [Planning]

PMI®, *PMBOK® Guide*, 2004, 28–29

### 2. c.  Start early

Starting the team-building process early in the project is crucial for setting the right tone and preventing bad habits and patterns from developing. [Executing]

Stuckenbruck and Marshall 1997, 137

### 3. d.  In this strong matrix, the balance of power is shifted to the project manager.

The project manager's ability to influence project decisions increases the higher up he or she—and the person to whom he or she reports—is placed in the organization.  In the strong matrix, the project manager's authority ranges from moderate to high.  [Planning]

Stuckenbruck 1981, 89; Verma 1995, 156–157; PMI®, *PMBOK® Guide*, 2004, 28

### 4. b.  Make the link between project performance and reward clear, explicit, and achievable

Reward and recognition systems are formal management actions that provide an incentive to behave in a particular way, usually with respect to achieving certain goals.  Such systems are described in the staffing management plan.  [Executing]

PMI®, *PMBOK® Guide*, 2004, 209 and 214

### 5. d.  Colocation

Colocation is the placement of team members in the same physical location to enhance their ability to perform as a team, primarily through increased communication.  [Executing]

PMI®, *PMBOK® Guide*, 2004, 214

### 6. c. Create symbols and structures that solidify the unity of the dispersed work group

Because the dispersed project team does not share the same physical space each day, team members need symbols and structures to identify them as a unified group. As the group works together, symbols should be developed to show accomplishments as a group. These symbols should be visible throughout the organization. [Executing]

Kostner 1994, 53–54, 170; PMI®, *PMBOK® Guide*, 2004, 211

### 7. b. Conflicts over the relative priorities of different projects in competition for limited resources

When a finite group of resources must be distributed across multiple projects, conflicts in work assignments will occur. [Executing]

Cleland 2002, 230–232; PMI®, *PMBOK® Guide*, 2004, 212

### 8. d. Hold a project kickoff meeting

An indispensable tool in project management, the kickoff meeting is held at the outset of the project and is designed to get the project rolling. The meeting provides the opportunity not only to present the project charter and discuss the project's goals and objectives but also to establish rapport among team members. [Executing]

Frame 1994, 157

### 9. a. Improved project performance

Improved project performance not only increases the likelihood of meeting project objectives, it also creates a positive team experience contributing to the enhancement of team capabilities. [Executing]

PMI®, *PMBOK® Guide*, 2004, 215

### 10. a. Referent

Referent power is based on a less powerful person's identification with a more powerful person. This type of power is useful in terms of persuasion and helps the project manager exert influence over individuals from whom he or she needs support. [Planning]

Kirchof and Adams 1989, 26–27

**11. c.  Establish a "war room"**

Colocating team members, even on a temporary basis, enhances communications, thereby contributing to improved project performance. In addition, the war room provides a sense of identity to the project team and raises the visibility of the project within the organization.  [Executing]

PMI®, *PMBOK® Guide*, 2004, 214

**12. d.  Forcing**

Forcing, using power or dominance, implies the use of position power to resolve conflict.  It involves imposing one viewpoint at the expense of another.  Project managers may use it when time is of the essence, when an issue is vital to the project's well-being, or when they think they are right based on available information.  Although this approach is appropriate when quick decisions are required or when unpopular issues are an essential part of the project, it puts project managers at risk. [Executing]

Kirchof and Adams 1989, 11; Verma 1996, 118–120

**13. b.  Acquire project team**

The project team directory is part of project staff assignments, an output from the acquire project team process.  Other outputs are resource availability and updates to the staffing management plan.  [Planning]

PMI®, *PMBOK® Guide*, 2004, 212

**14. d.  Involving nonmanagement-level team members in the planning process**

Team-building activities vary from breakfast review meetings to golf outings to off-site sessions designed to improve interpersonal relationships. The purpose of all team-building activities, however, is to improve team performance.  Many actions, such as involving nonmanagement-level team members in the planning process or establishing ground rules for surfacing and dealing with conflict, may enhance team performance as a secondary effect.  [Executing]

PMI®, *PMBOK® Guide*, 2004, 199 and 214

### 15. b.  Excessive meetings

The problem is not too many meetings but unproductive ones.  The purpose of project meetings is to focus the skills and resources of the project team on project performance.  Meetings that are considered "gripe sessions" or a time for the project manager to "lay down the law" are demoralizing to the team.  [Executing]

Stuckenbruck and Marshall 1985, 7

### 16. d.  Laissez-faire

With this management style, decision-making authority is diffuse.  Because little or no information flows between the project manager and team, team members are left to make decisions for themselves.  This style may be effective for strong, self-directed work groups, but it can cause frustration and a sense of isolation in teams that need more direction.  [Planning]

Frame 1995, 77–78

### 17. b.  Project management plan

The project management plan is the ultimate "guidebook" to how the project will be managed, and includes resource requirements plus descriptions of project management activities, such as quality assurance, risk management, and procurement that will help the project management team identify required roles and responsibilities.  [Planning]

PMI®, *PMBOK® Guide*, 2004, 204

### 18. d.  Ambiguous jurisdictions

Ambiguous jurisdictions exist when two or more parties have related responsibilities, but their work boundaries and role definitions are unclear.  This situation is found frequently in weak and strong matrix organizations because of the "two-boss" concept.  [Executing]

Filley 1975, 9

**19. c. Ensure that your team is sufficiently aware of administrative requirements to ensure compliance**

A purely projectized work environment is unusual because project managers rarely have every function under their control. But compliance with administrative requirements, government regulations, union contract provisions, and other constraints is a consideration in human resource management. [Planning]

PMI®, *PMBOK® Guide*, 2004, 209

**20. a. Team performance**

Team development leads to improved team performance, which ultimately results in improved project performance. Improvements in team performance can come from many sources and can affect many areas of project performance. For example, improved individual skill levels such as enhanced technical competence may enable team members to perform their assigned activities more effectively. Team development efforts have greater benefit when conducted early but should take place throughout the project life cycle. [Executing]

PMI®, *PMBOK® Guide*, 2004, 212

**21. c. Collaborating**

Collaborating is an effective technique for managing conflict when a project is too important to be compromised. It involves incorporating multiple ideas and viewpoints from people with different perspectives and offers a good opportunity to learn from others. It provides a long-term resolution. [Executing]

Verma 1996, 119–120; PMI®, *PMBOK® Guide*, 2004, 217

**22. a. The organizational structure of the performing organization**

Constraints are factors over which the project team has no control and that limit the team's options. The organizational structure of the performing organization determines whether the project manager's role is a strong one (as in a strong matrix) or a weak one (as in a weak matrix). [Planning]

PMI®, *PMBOK® Guide*, 2004, 204

**23. d. Celebrating special occasions**

Project managers can show interest in their team members by celebrating occasions such as birthdays, anniversaries with the organization, and special achievements. Other approaches include being supportive, being clear, learning some information about each team member, and being accessible. Through observation and conversation, the project management team monitors indicators such as progress toward project deliverables, accomplishments that are a source of pride for team members, and interpersonal issues. [Executing]

Frame 1995, 104–105; PMI®, *PMBOK® Guide*, 2004, 216–217

**24. b. Project manager**

Effective management of this dual reporting relationship is critical to project success and is, therefore, generally the responsibility of the project manager. [Executing]

PMI®, *PMBOK® Guide*, 2004, 215

**25. c. Work with your team to prepare a responsibility assignment matrix**

The responsibility assignment matrix defines project roles and responsibilities in terms of the project scope definition. It can be used to show who is a participant, who is accountable, who handles review, who provides input, and who must sign off on specific work packages or project phases. [Planning]

PMI®, *PMBOK® Guide*, 2004, 206

**26. d. Shared leadership**

Shared leadership is more than participatory management or collaboration; it involves letting the project team take over as much of the leadership role as it will accept. [Executing]

Verma 1997, 159

**27. d. The project coordinator reports to a higher-level manager in the organization**

The relative position of the project coordinator in the organization is thought to lead to an increased level of authority and responsibility. [Executing]

Cable and Adams 1982, 15–17; Verma 1995, 153–156

### 28. b.  Recruitment practices of the organizations involved

Staff assignments in organizations are governed by the policies, procedures, or guidelines of individual components.  These policies will constrain the project manager's actions in acquiring a project team.  The more familiar the project manager is with such policies, the easier it will be for him/her to assemble a team.  [Planning]

PMI®, *PMBOK® Guide*, 2004, 210

### 29. c.  Aggressor

The aggressor is destructive in that he or she criticizes others and attempts to deflate their status.  Other destructive team roles are the blocker, withdrawer, recognition seeker, topic jumper, dominator, and, in some cases, devil's advocate.  Destructive behavior, if allowed to continue, can endanger a team-building effort.  [Executing]

Stuckenbruck and Marshall 1985, 48–49

### 30. a.  Initial establishment of roles and responsibilities

Project performance appraisals are a tool and technique for the manage project team process and are used, among other objectives, to reclarify roles and responsibilities.  It is critical that team members receive positive feedback in what might otherwise be a hectic environment.  [Executing]

PMI®, *PMBOK® Guide*, 2004, 217

### 31. b.  Autocratic

Autocratic managers are not concerned with processing information coming from outside themselves.  The autocratic style is sometimes appropriate because of time pressure or an emergency situation when decisions must be made quickly.  When used in other situations, this style blocks out needed input from the project team.  [Executing]

Frame 1995, 75–77

### 32. a.  Creating an effective team

An effective team is critical to project success, but such a team is not born spontaneously.  In early project phases, it is vitally important for the project manager to place a high priority on initiating and implementing the team-building process.  [Executing]

Verma 1997, 137; PMI®, *PMBOK® Guide*, 2004, 214

**33. a. A matrix form of organization can produce a lack of clear role definitions and lead to ambiguous jurisdictions between and among functional leaders and project managers**

Matrix management is useful but complex, involving difficult communication because of the use of borrowed and often part-time resources who are spread throughout the organization. [Executing]

Kirchof and Adams 1989, 15

**34. c. Degree of the project manager's authority**

In a strong matrix organization, the balance of power shifts toward the project manager. In a weak matrix organization, the balance of power shifts toward the functional or line manager. [Planning]

PMI®, *PMBOK® Guide*, 2004, 28

**35. a. Problem oriented**

Problem-oriented people tend to learn and use whatever problem-solving techniques appear helpful. Although the project manager must be politically sensitive, team members need not have developed this skill to the extent required of the project manager; and rather than focusing on individual activities, team members should take a systems approach focusing on the entire project. [Executing]

Meredith and Mantel 2006, 183–185

**36. c. RBS**

The resource breakdown structure (RBS) is a variation of the organizational breakdown structure (OBS) and is used to show which work elements are assigned to individuals and other resource categories. As an example, it can show all crane operators and cranes even though they may be scattered throughout the OBS and WBS, which can help track project costs. [Planning]

PMI®, *PMBOK® Guide*, 2004, 205

**37. b. Produce an initial project plan and determine the functional areas responsible for each task**

All effort on a project starts from the project plan, which details the work that must be accomplished. [Planning]

Meredith and Mantel 2006, 235–266

### 38. a. Build trust

Team members who are physically separate from one another tend not to know each other well. They have few opportunities to develop trust in the traditional way, and they tend to communicate poorly with one another. Trust then must become the foundation upon which all team-building activities are built. [Executing]

Kostner 1994, 169

### 39. c. Schedules, project priorities, and personnel resources

Although all the areas listed contain potential conflicts, over 50% of all conflict in a project environment is caused by schedules, priorities, and personnel resources. [Executing]

Stuckenbruck and Marshall 1985, 45–46

### 40. b. OBS

The organizational breakdown structure (OBS) is a tool used to show the work units or work packages that are assigned to specific organizational units.

Ward 2000, 140

PROJECT *Communications* MANAGEMENT

# PROJECT COMMUNICATIONS MANAGEMENT

## Study Hints

The Project Communications Management questions on the PMP® certification exam are relatively basic and are taken primarily from the *PMBOK® Guide* and other PMI®-published reference materials. Common sense and your own experience will play a large role in your ability to answer the questions on this topic. There will be questions that test your specific knowledge of *PMBOK® Guide* terms and concepts. However, there will also be many general questions that require you to choose the "best" answer. To answer these questions correctly, you must apply common sense.

The questions focus on formal and informal communication, verbal versus written communication, conflict resolution, and management styles. PMI® considers management style to be an essential component of how a project manager communicates.

The PMI® handbooks (which are now included in *Principles of Project Management*, PMI®, 1997), *Roles and Responsibilities of the Project Manager* by John R. Adams and Brian W. Campbell, *Conflict Management for Project Managers* by John R. Adams and Nicki S. Kirchof, and *Team Building for Project Managers* by Linn C. Stuckenbruck and David Marshall, should be studied thoroughly for this section of the PMP® certification exam. The PMI® publication *Human Resource Skills for the Project Manager,* which is volume 2 of *The Human Aspects of Project Management* by Vijay K. Verma, is another useful reference. PMI® considers the kickoff meeting one of the most effective mechanisms in Project Communications Management. The nature and purpose of this meeting are discussed in *Team Building for Project Managers*.

PMI® views Project Communications Management as a process consisting of four elements: communications planning, information distribution, performance reporting, and manage stakeholders. See *PMBOK® Guide* Figure 10-1 for an overview of this structure. Know this chart thoroughly.

Following is a list of the major Project Communications Management topics. Use it to help focus your study efforts on the areas most likely to appear on the exam.

# Major Topics

*Importance of project communications management*

*The communications model*

- Sender
- Message
- Medium
- Receiver

*Communication channels*

*Communications planning*

*Communications requirements*

*Communications technology*

*Stakeholder analysis*

*Communications management plan*

*Information distribution*

- Written and oral
- Internal and external
- Formal and informal
- Vertical and horizontal

*Kickoff meeting*

*Barriers to communication*

*Communications role of the project manager*

*The project manager and the customer*

*Building effective team communication*

- Effective communicator
- Communication expeditor
- Communication blockers
- Tight matrix
- Project "war room"
- Effective meetings

# Major Topics (continued)

*Management styles*

- Authoritarian
- Combative
- Conciliatory
- Disruptive
- Ethical
- Facilitating
- Intimidating
- Judicial
- Promotional
- Secretive

*Management skills*

- Leading
- Communicating
- Negotiating and managing conflicts
- Problem solving
- Influencing the organization
- Motivation

*Performance reporting*

- Status review meetings
- Information presentation tools
- Forecasts

*Documentation*

# Practice Questions

INSTRUCTIONS: Note the most suitable answer for each multiple-choice question in the appropriate space on the answer sheet.

1.  As project manager, you plan to conduct a "kickoff" meeting at which you will discuss all the following *except*—

    a.  Establishing working relationships and standard formats for global communication
    b.  Reviewing project plans
    c.  Establishing individual and group responsibilities and accountabilities
    d.  Discussing specific legal issues regarding the contract

2.  One purpose of the communications management plan is to provide information about the—

    a.  Methods that will be used to convey information
    b.  Methods that will be used for releasing team members from the project when they are no longer needed
    c.  Project organization and stakeholder responsibility relationships
    d.  Experience and skill levels of each team member

3.  Project managers for international projects should recognize key issues in cross-cultural settings and place special emphasis on—

    a.  Establishing a performance reporting system
    b.  Developing a system to manage communications
    c.  Establishing and following a production schedule for information distribution to avoid responding to requests for information between scheduled communications
    d.  Using translation services for formal, written project reports

4.  In the manage stakeholders process, lessons learned focus on—

    a.  Updated policies and procedures
    b.  Improved business skills
    c.  Knowledge management
    d.  Causes of issues and reasons corrective actions were chosen

5. You finally have been appointed project manager for a major company project. One of your first activities as project manager has been to set up an information gathering and retrieval system, which will include all the following *except*—

   a. Manual filing systems
   b. Project management software
   c. Data collection devices
   d. Electronic databases

6. An issue log or action-item log is a tool and technique used in which of the following processes?

   a. Manage project team
   b. Manage stakeholders
   c. Performance reporting
   d. Close project

7. You are managing a project with team members located at customer sites on three different continents. You have a number of stakeholders on your project, and most of them are located outside of the corporate office. Who should be responsible for stakeholder management?

   a. A specific team member in each of the three locations
   b. You, because you are the project manager
   c. The project sponsor
   d. A core team including you, as the project manager, and three representatives from the three different locations

8. Stakeholder needs and expectations are identified, analyzed, and documented in the—

   a. Stakeholder management plan
   b. Human resources management plan
   c. Communications management plan
   d. Information distribution plan

9. Which of the following qualifications is the most important for a project manager?

   a. Supervisory experience
   b. Negotiation skill
   c. Education in a technical field
   d. Ability to work well with others

10. You are responsible for a project in your organization that has multiple internal customers. Because many people in your organization are interested in this project, you decide to prepare a project communications management plan. Your first step in preparing this plan is to—

    a. Conduct a stakeholder analysis to assess information needs
    b. Determine a production schedule to show when each type of communication will be produced
    c. Describe the information you plan to distribute
    d. Set up a repository for all project documents so that they will be easily accessible

11. Project managers spend a great deal of time communicating with the team, the stakeholders, the client, and the sponsor. One can easily see the challenges involved, especially if one team member must communicate a technical concept to another team member in a different country. The first step in this process is to—

    a. Encode the message
    b. Decode the message
    c. Determine the feedback loops
    d. Determine the medium

12. The project management plan is an input to the performance reporting process. Which part of the plan is most relevant to this process?

    a. Configuration management process
    b. Communications techniques
    c. Work breakdown structure
    d. Performance measurement baseline

13. You are in the initiating phase of your project. You observe a high degree of conflict among your stakeholders. Such conflict typically centers on—

    a. The technical decisions that need to be made
    b. Enforcement of the project management methodology
    c. Establishing the project in a matrix management environment
    d. Whether a PMO is required

14. Which of the following terms describes the strong pressures within a group to conform to group norms at the expense of critical and innovative thinking?

    a. Group dynamics
    b. Groupspeak
    c. Groupthink
    d. Group pressure

15. As a project manager, you try to use empathic listening skills to help understand another person's frame of reference. In following this approach, you should—

    a. Mimic the content of the message
    b. Probe, then evaluate the content
    c. Evaluate the content, then advise
    d. Rephrase the content and reflect the feeling

16. Information received from stakeholders concerning project operations can be distributed and used to modify or improve future performance of the project. This is done as an update to organizational process assets during which of the following processes?

    a. Communications planning
    b. Information distribution
    c. Performance reporting
    d. Manage stakeholders

17. Statements of organizational policies and philosophies, position descriptions, and constraints are examples of—

    a. Downward communication
    b. Lateral communication
    c. External communication
    d. Horizontal communication

18. An example of a good team-building exercise is—

    a. Performance review meeting
    b. Phase-end lessons learned sessions
    c. Project report preparation
    d. Customer meeting on the project's progress

19. You have decided to organize a study group of other project managers in your organization to help prepare for the PMP® exam. What type of communication are you employing in your efforts to organize this group?

    a. Horizontal
    b. Vertical
    c. Formal
    d. External

20. Your company CEO just sent you an e-mail asking you to make a presentation on your project, which has been in progress for 18 months, to over 50 identified internal and external stakeholders. He scheduled the presentation for next Monday. The first step in preparing the presentation is to—

    a. Define the audience
    b. Determine the objective
    c. Decide on the general form of the presentation
    d. Plan a presentation strategy

21. On your project, scope changes, constraints, assumptions, integration and interface requirements, and overlapping roles and responsibilities pose communications challenges. The presence of communication barriers is most likely to lead to—

    a. Reduced productivity
    b. Increased hostility
    c. Low morale
    d. Increased conflict

22. General management skills relevant to the information distribution process include—

    a. Operational planning
    b. Organizational behavior
    c. Managing stakeholder requirements
    d. Influencing the organization

23. The most common communication problem that occurs during negotiation is that—

    a. Each side may misinterpret what the other side has said
    b. Each side may give up on the other side
    c. One side may try to confuse the other side
    d. One side may be too busy thinking about what to say next to hear what is being said

24. As an output from communications planning, it may be necessary to update the—

    a. WBS
    b. Corporate policies, procedures, and processes
    c. Knowledge management system
    d. Overall product improvements

25. The project manager can enhance project communications and team building by doing all the following *except*—

    a. Having a "war room"
    b. Being a good communication blocker
    c. Being a communication expeditor
    d. Holding effective meetings

26. Sample attributes of a communications management plan include which of the following?

    a. Roles
    b. Responsibilities
    c. Ethics
    d. Authority

27. In dealing with the customer, the project manager should—

    a. Be honest to the extent that the project organization is protected from litigation
    b. Strive to develop a friendly, honest, and open relationship
    c. Try to maximize profits by encouraging scope creep
    d. Do whatever it takes to satisfy the customer and win additional business

28. You have recently heard that the client calls your progress reports the "Code of Hammurabi" because they seem to be written in hieroglyphics and are completely indecipherable to all but an antiquities scholar. This situation could have been avoided by—

    a. Informing the client at the start of the project of the types of reports they will receive
    b. Using risk management techniques to identify client issues
    c. Hiring an expert report writer to prepare standard reports
    d. Engaging in communications planning

29. When communicating with an action-oriented person, a project manager should—

    a. Be as brief as possible and emphasize the practicality of his or her ideas
    b. Provide options, including the pros and cons
    c. Remain patient if the other person goes off on tangents
    d. Speak as quickly as possible to ensure that all the information is conveyed

30. You want to ensure that the information you collect showing project progress and status is meaningful to stakeholders. To determine specific metrics, you will conduct a stakeholder analysis, and then determine the level of detail stakeholders require. You will document this in the—

    a. WBS
    b. Project management methodology
    c. Project charter
    d. Communications management plan

31. The process of conferring with others to come to terms or reach an agreement is called—

    a. Win-win
    b. Negotiation
    c. Getting to "yes"
    d. Confrontation

32. At the end of each project, the project team should prepare a lessons learned summary that focuses on all the following *except*—

    a. Sharing best practices with other project teams in the organization
    b. Warning others of potential problems
    c. Suggesting methods to mitigate risks effectively to ensure success
    d. Sharing only positive aspects of the project for future replication elsewhere in the organization

33. Changes in the information distribution process should trigger changes to the—

    a. Project management plan and performance reporting system
    b. Integrated change control system and the communications management plan
    c. Monitor and control project process and the project management plan
    d. Communications management plan

34. The most important requirement for ensuring that issues get resolved is that they are—

    a. Included in the WBS
    b. Included in the project's risk register
    c. Assigned an owner and a target date for closure
    d. Brought to the project manager's attention immediately

35. As head of the PMO, you will participate in performance reviews for all major projects. To ensure these reviews are productive, you believe project managers must ensure that—

    a. Work performance information on the status of deliverables is collected
    b. Earned value analysis is used for all projects
    c. All project documents are available to meeting attendees before the meeting
    d. The focus is on cost and schedule variances rather than scope, resources, quality, and risks

36. Performance reports provide information on—

    a. Scope, schedule, cost, and quality
    b. Customer satisfaction
    c. Unacceptable variances
    d. Scope creep

37. Which of the following statements is true regarding communication within a project environment?

    a. The project manager must assume the primary burden of responsibility to ensure that messages sent have been received.
    b. Effective meetings, a "war room," and a tight matrix promote effective communication.
    c. If a project consists of 12 people, 48 potential channels of communication exist.
    d. Most project managers spend 30% of their working hours engaged in communication.

38. Communications planning often is tightly linked with enterprise environmental factors and organizational influences. This means that which of the following statements is true?

    a. The project's organizational structure has a major effect on the project's communications requirements.
    b. Standardized guidelines, work instructions, and performance measurement criteria are key items to consider.
    c. Procedures for approving and issuing work authorizations should be taken into consideration.
    d. Criteria and guidelines to tailor standard processes to the specific needs of the project should be stated explicitly.

39. In person-to-person communication, messages are sent on verbal levels and nonverbal levels simultaneously. As a general rule, what percentage of the message actually is sent through nonverbal cues?

    a. 5% to 15%
    b. 20% to 30%
    c. 40% to 50%
    d. Greater than 50%

40. Which of the following formulas calculates the number of communication channels in a project?

    a. $\dfrac{n(n-1)}{2}$

    b. $\dfrac{n^2-1}{2}$

    c. $\dfrac{n^2-1}{n}$

    d. $\dfrac{2^n-2}{1^n}$

## Answer Sheet

| | | | | | | | | | | |
|---|---|---|---|---|---|---|---|---|---|---|
| 1. | a | b | c | d | | 21. | a | b | c | d |
| 2. | a | b | c | d | | 22. | a | b | c | d |
| 3. | a | b | c | d | | 23. | a | b | c | d |
| 4. | a | b | c | d | | 24. | a | b | c | d |
| 5. | a | b | c | d | | 25. | a | b | c | d |
| 6. | a | b | c | d | | 26. | a | b | c | d |
| 7. | a | b | c | d | | 27. | a | b | c | d |
| 8. | a | b | c | d | | 28. | a | b | c | d |
| 9. | a | b | c | d | | 29. | a | b | c | d |
| 10. | a | b | c | d | | 30. | a | b | c | d |
| 11. | a | b | c | d | | 31. | a | b | c | d |
| 12. | a | b | c | d | | 32. | a | b | c | d |
| 13. | a | b | c | d | | 33. | a | b | c | d |
| 14. | a | b | c | d | | 34. | a | b | c | d |
| 15. | a | b | c | d | | 35. | a | b | c | d |
| 16. | a | b | c | d | | 36. | a | b | c | d |
| 17. | a | b | c | d | | 37. | a | b | c | d |
| 18. | a | b | c | d | | 38. | a | b | c | d |
| 19. | a | b | c | d | | 39. | a | b | c | d |
| 20. | a | b | c | d | | 40. | a | b | c | d |

# Answer Key

**1. d.   Discussing specific legal issues regarding the contract**

Conducted after contract award or approval of the project, the kickoff meeting provides an opportunity for project participants to get to know each other and review information about the project.  It is not a forum to discuss detailed project issues.  [Executing]

Stuckenbruck and Marshall 1985, 18–19

**2. a.   Methods that will be used to convey information**

The plan should also contain a distribution structure that shows the methods that will be used to distribute various types of information and the individuals or organizations to whom the information will be distributed, production schedules showing when each type of communication will be produced, and methods to access information between scheduled communications.  Also included should be a discussion of how the plan will be updated and revised as needs change.  The communication plan is a component of the project management plan.  The level of detail of its content should be commensurate with the size and complexity of the project.  [Planning]

PMI®, *PMBOK® Guide*, 2004, 227–228

**3. b.   Developing a system to manage communications**

Project stakeholders must receive information in a timely fashion.  Global communications that use standard formats through a communications management system may reduce the impact of cultural differences.  [Executing]

Verma 1997, 110; PMI®, *PMBOK® Guide*, 2004, 229

**4. d.   Causes of issues and reasons corrective actions were chosen**

As part of the updates to the organizational process assets, lessons learned should be documented about stakeholder management with a focus on the documentation of issues that were resolved and how they were resolved and closed.  [Monitoring and Controlling]

PMI®, *PMBOK® Guide*, 2004, 236

### 5. c.  Data collection devices

Information gathering and retrieval systems and information distribution methods are two of the tools and techniques for information distribution. Meetings, e-mail, and hardcopy reports are examples of information distribution methods.  [Executing]

PMI®, *PMBOK® Guide*, 2004, 229

### 6. b.  Manage stakeholders

Issue logs or action-item logs are used to document and monitor the resolution of issues.  [Monitoring and Controlling]

PMI®, *PMBOK® Guide*, 2004, 236

### 7. b.  You, because you are the project manager

Stakeholder management refers to any action taken by the project manager or project team to satisfy the needs of and resolve issues with project stakeholders.  The project manager is responsible for stakeholder management.  [Monitoring and Controlling]

PMI®, *PMBOK® Guide*, 2004, 235

### 8. c.  Communications management plan

The communications management plan describes how project information will be gathered, organized, and distributed to the project's stakeholders. As such, it is a critical component in stakeholder management.  [Planning and Monitoring and Controlling]

PMI®, *PMBOK® Guide*, 2004, 227–228 and 235

### 9. d.  Ability to work well with others

Project management requires getting things done through people who generally do not report directly to the project manager.  The ability to influence project team members, as well as other key stakeholders, is crucial for success.  [Executing]

Adams and Campbell 1982, 14

## 10. a. Conduct a stakeholder analysis to assess information needs

Stakeholder analysis is used to analyze the information needs of the stakeholders and determine the sources to meet those needs. The analysis should include consideration of appropriate methods and technologies for providing the information needed. [Planning]

PMI®, *PMBOK® Guide*, 2004, 225

## 11. a. Encode the message

It is essential to translate thoughts or ideas into a language that is understood by others; this is the first step in the basic communication model. Then, the message is sent using a variety of technologies, and the receiver decodes it or translates it back into meaningful thoughts or ideas. [Planning]

PMI®, *PMBOK® Guide*, 2004, 224

## 12. d. Performance measurement baseline

This is an approved, time-phased plan against which project scope, schedule, and cost performance are measured on a regular basis. It may also include technical and quality parameters. [Monitoring and Controlling]

PMI®, *PMBOK® Guide*, 2004, 232

## 13. c. Establishing the project in a matrix management environment

At the initiating phase, very few decisions have been made regarding project governance. It is important to establish the roles, responsibilities, and decision-making authority early so that the project can get underway as quickly as practicable. [Initiating]

Meredith and Mantel 2006, 303

## 14. c. Groupthink

Irving Janis invented this term in 1971 to alert people to a serious disadvantage that can arise when a team becomes too cohesive and too amiable. [Executing]

Stuckenbruck and Marshall 1985, 38–39

### 15. d. Rephrase the content and reflect the feeling

Empathic listening requires seeing the world the way the other person sees it, with the goal of understanding that person's views and feelings. Unlike sympathetic listening, empathic listening contains no element of value judgment. [Executing]

Covey 1989, 239–241

### 16. b. Information distribution

Information distribution involves making information available to project stakeholders in a timely manner. This is done through the communications management plan and also through responding to unexpected requests for information. Feedback from stakeholders is used to improve project performance. [Executing]

PMI®, *PMBOK® Guide*, 2004, 230

### 17. a. Downward communication

Downward communication provides direction and control for project team members and other employees. It contains job-related information, such as actions required, standards, the time activities should be performed, activities to be completed, and progress measurement. [Executing]

PMI®, *PMBOK® Guide*, 2004, 229

### 18. b. Phase-end lessons learned sessions

When conducted at the end of critical stages of project completion, phase-end lessons learned sessions promote collaboration and communication among project team members. This "coming together" to look back at accomplishments and forward to what needs to be done fosters a sense of teamwork. [Executing]

PMI®, *PMBOK® Guide*, 2004, 230

### 19. a. Horizontal

Communication skills are used to exchange information between the sender and the receiver. Horizontal communication occurs between or among peers, that is, across, rather than up and down, the organization. [Executing]

PMI®, *PMBOK® Guide*, 2004, 229

## 20.  b.   Determine the objective

Only after the objective is determined can the other issues listed be addressed effectively.  The information must be relevant to audience needs.  [Monitoring and Controlling]

Acker 1992, 29; PMI®, *PMBOK® Guide*, 2004, 231; Verma 1997, 18–19

## 21.  d.   Increased conflict

Barriers to communication lead to a poor flow of information. Accordingly, messages are misinterpreted by recipients, thereby creating different perceptions, understanding, and frames of reference.  Left unchecked, poor communication increases conflict among project stakeholders, which causes the other problems listed to arise.  [Executing]

ESI October 2004, 7-4; Verma 1997, 24–25

## 22.  c.   Managing stakeholder requirements

Communications skills are part of general management skills and include the exchange of information.  Regarding information distribution, this means that the right persons get the right information at the right time as defined in the communications management plan.  [Executing]

PMI®, *PMBOK® Guide*, 2004, 224 and 229

## 23.  a.   Each side may misinterpret what the other side has said

Effective communication is the key to successful negotiation. Misunderstanding is the most common communication problem.  A project manager should listen actively, acknowledge what is being said, and speak for a purpose.  [Executing]

Fisher et al. 1991, 32–34; Verma 1996, 165

## 24.  a.   WBS

Communications planning often entails the creation of additional deliverables that in turn require additional time and effort.  This means that it may be necessary to update the project's WBS, schedule, and budget.  [Planning]

PMI®, *PMBOK® Guide*, 2004, 228

**25. b.  Being a good communication blocker**

In addition to the other items listed, the project manager can also enhance communication by eliminating communication blocks and serving as an example of an effective communicator.  [Executing]

Stuckenbruck and Marshall 1985, 32–33

**26. b.  Responsibilities**

The team member charged with information distribution should be identified in the communications management plan.  Other attributes include the communication item, the purpose for the distribution of the information, the frequency, the time frame for the distribution of the information, the layout of the information, and the method of transmission.  [Planning]

PMI®, *PMBOK® Guide*, 2004, 227–228

**27. b.  Strive to develop a friendly, honest, and open relationship**

Relationships built on honesty can withstand adversity.  Therefore, the best approach for a project manager is to be honest in his or her dealings.  When a customer has faith in the credibility of the project manager, additional revenue-generating work will likely follow.  [Executing]

Adams and Campbell 1982, 10

**28. d.  Engaging in communications planning**

The communications management plan is prepared during communications planning.  The plan should include a description of the information to be distributed, including format, content, level of detail, and conventions and definitions to be used.  [Planning]

PMI®, *PMBOK® Guide*, 2004, 228–229

**29. a.  Be as brief as possible and emphasize the practicality of his or her ideas**

Action-oriented people tend to be pragmatic and do not like to belabor an issue.  Therefore, the best approach is to present ideas succinctly along with the benefits associated with their application.  [Executing]

Youker 1996, 799

### 30. d. Communications management plan

An analysis of stakeholder information needs must be conducted by the project team to ensure that stakeholders are receiving the information required to participate in the project. Performance reports are examples of one type of information stakeholders typically require. Such information requirements should be included in the communications management plan. [Planning]

PMI®, *PMBOK® Guide*, 2004, 233

### 31. b. Negotiation

Negotiation involves compromise so that each party feels it has received something of value, even though it has had to make certain sacrifices. [Executing]

PMI®, *PMBOK® Guide*, 2004, 15

### 32. d. Sharing only positive aspects of the project for future replication elsewhere in the organization

The lessons learned summary should document the major positive and negative aspects of the project so that future projects can benefit from the team's successes and failures, by replicating the good things about the project and avoiding the mistakes. [Executing]

Garrett 2001, 171; PMI®, *PMBOK® Guide*, 2004, 230

### 33. d. Communications management plan

Any change regarding information identification, collection, and distribution must be reflected in the communications management plan. [Executing]

PMI®, *PMBOK® Guide*, 2004, 231

### 34. c. Assigned an owner and a target date for closure

If issues are left unresolved, conflicts arise and the project may be delayed. Holding someone accountable to ensure the issue is addressed expedites resolution. [Executing]

PMI®, *PMBOK® Guide*, 2004, 236

**35. a. Work performance information on the status of deliverables is collected**

As an input to performance reporting, work performance information describes the status of the identified project deliverables. It provides detail regarding what has been accomplished to date or for a specific time period. [Monitoring and Controlling]

PMI®, *PMBOK® Guide*, 2004, 232

**36. a. Scope, schedule, cost, and quality**

Project performance focuses on the four main areas of a project: scope, schedule, cost, and quality. It does not focus on one area to the exclusion of the others. [Monitoring and Controlling]

PMI®, *PMBOK® Guide*, 2004, 231

**37. b. Effective meetings, a "war room," and a tight matrix promote effective communication.**

Effective meetings start and end on time, follow an agenda, and result in action items for people to complete. A war room provides team identity and a place to conduct project business. A tight matrix indicates that project team members are located within close physical proximity, which fosters informal communication and team building. [Executing]

Stuckenbruck and Marshall 1985, 32

**38. a. The project's organizational structure has a major effect on the project's communications requirements.**

Enterprise environmental factors will undoubtedly influence the project's success and must be considered, and organizational influences should be considered because the project is typically part of a larger organization. The maturity of the organization with respect to its project management system, culture, style, organizational structure, and project management office can also influence the project. [Planning]

PMI®, *PMBOK® Guide*, 2004, 27, 83, and 225

**39. d. Greater than 50%**

Nonverbal cues can be divided into four categories: physical, aesthetic, signs, and symbols. Many studies have demonstrated that most messages are conveyed through such nonverbal cues as facial expression, touch, and body motion, rather than through the words spoken. [Executing]

Acker 1992, 47–48; Verma 1996, 19

**40. a.** $\dfrac{n(n-1)}{2}$

Where n = the number of stakeholders. [Planning ]

PMI®, *PMBOK® Guide*, 2004, 226

# PROJECT RISK MANAGEMENT

## Study Hints

Most exam takers find the Project Risk Management questions on the PMP® certification exam demanding because they address many concepts that project managers have not been exposed to in their work or education. However, the questions correspond closely to *PMBOK® Guide* material, so you should not have much difficulty if you study the concepts and terminology found in the *PMBOK® Guide*. Although the questions included do not contain mathematically complex work problems, they do require you to know certain theories, such as expected monetary value (EMV) and decision-tree analysis. Additionally, you are likely to encounter questions related to levels of risk faced by both buyer and seller based on various types of contracts.

PMI® views risk management as a six-step process including risk management planning, risk identification, qualitative risk analysis, quantitative risk analysis, risk response planning, and risk monitoring and control. *PMBOK® Guide* Figure 11-1 provides an overview of this approach. Know this chart thoroughly.

Following is a list of the major Project Risk Management topics. Use it to help focus your study efforts on the areas most likely to appear on the exam.

# Major Topics

---

*Project risk management*

- Risk defined
- Types of risk
  - Known risks
  - Unknown risks
  - Business risk
  - Insurable risk
- Risk factors
  - Risk event
  - Probability of occurrence
  - Amount at stake (impact)

*Risk processes*

*Risk management planning*

*Risk identification*

- Definition
- Timing
- Risk categories
- Other sources for risk identification

*Risk identification tools and techniques*

- Brainstorming
- Delphi method
- Interviews
- Strengths-weaknesses-opportunities-threats (SWOT) analysis
- Checklists
- Assumption analysis
- Diagramming techniques

*Risk identification output*

*Qualitative risk analysis*

- Probability/impact risk rating matrix
- Impact analysis
- Data precision ranking

*Qualitative risk analysis output*

---

# Major Topics (continued)

*Quantitative risk analysis*

- Interviewing
- Sensitivity analysis
- Statistical independence
- Expected monetary value
- Decision-tree analysis
- Decision-tree analysis guidelines
- Monte Carlo analysis
  - Path convergence
  - Statistical distribution

*Quantitative risk analysis output*

*Risk response planning*

- Risk responses
  - Avoidance
  - Transference
  - Mitigation
  - Acceptance

*Risk response plan*

*Risk monitoring and control*

- Definition
- Major tools and techniques
- Principal output

# Practice Questions

INSTRUCTIONS: Note the most suitable answer for each multiple-choice question in the appropriate space on the answer sheet.

1. As the project manager, you have the option of proposing one of three systems to a client: a full-feature system that not only satisfies the minimum requirements but also offers numerous special functions (the "Mercedes"); a system that meets the client's minimum requirements (the "Yugo"); and a system that satisfies the minimum requirements plus has a few extra features (the "Toyota"). The on-time records and associated profits and losses are depicted on the decision tree below. What is the expected monetary value of the "Toyota" system?

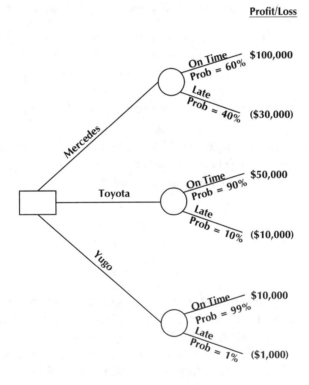

**Profit/Loss**

On Time Prob = 60% — $100,000
Late Prob = 40% — ($30,000)

Mercedes

Toyota

On Time Prob = 90% — $50,000
Late Prob = 10% — ($10,000)

Yugo

On Time Prob = 99% — $10,000
Late Prob = 1% — ($1,000)

a. $9,900
b. $44,000
c. $45,000
d. $48,000

2. A risk response strategy that can be used for both threats and opportunities is—

   a. Share
   b. Avoid
   c. Accept
   d. Transfer

3. The risk urgency assessment is a tool and technique used for—

   a. Risk response planning
   b. Risk identification
   c. Qualitative risk analysis
   d. Quantitative risk analysis

4. Projects are particularly susceptible to risk because—

   a. Murphy's law states that "if something can go wrong, it will"
   b. Each project is unique in some measure
   c. Project management tools are generally unavailable at the project team level
   d. There are never enough resources to do the job

5. As project manager, you have assembled the team to prepare a comprehensive list of project risks. Which one of the following documents would be the most helpful in this process?

   a. OBS
   b. WBS
   c. RBS
   d. CBS

6. You are working on identifying possible risks to your project to develop a nutritional supplement. You want to develop a comprehensive list of risks that can be addressed later through qualitative and quantitative risk analysis. Although a number of possible techniques can be used, risk identification is an information gathering technique used in—

   a. Documentation reviews
   b. Probability/impact analysis
   c. Checklist analysis
   d. Brainstorming

7. The Delphi technique is a particularly useful method for identifying risks to—

   a. Present a sequence of decision choices graphically to decision makers
   b. Define the probability of occurrence of specific variables
   c. Reduce bias in the analysis and keep any one person from having undue influence on the outcome
   d. Help take into account the attitude of the decision maker toward risk

8. A workaround is—

   a. An unplanned response to a negative risk event
   b. A plan of action to follow when something unexpected occurs
   c. A specific response to certain types of risk as described in the risk management plan
   d. A proactive, planned method of responding to risks

9. Most statistical simulations of budgets, schedules, and resource allocations use which of the following approaches?

   a. PERT
   b. Decision-tree analysis
   c. Present value analysis
   d. Monte Carlo analysis

10. In the path convergence example below, if the odds of completing activities 1, 2, and 3 on time are 50%, 50%, and 50%, what are the chances of starting activity 4 on day 6?

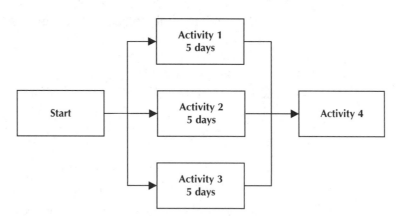

   a. 10%
   b. 13%
   c. 40%
   d. 50%

11. A project health check identified a risk that your project would not be completed on time. As a result, you are quantifying the project's risk exposure and determining what cost and schedule contingency reserves might be needed. You performed a schedule risk analysis using Monte Carlo analysis. The basis for your schedule risk analysis is the—

    a. WBS
    b. Gantt chart
    c. PDM schedule
    d. Probability/impact risk rating matrix

12. You are developing radio frequency (RF) technology that will improve overnight package delivery. You ask each stakeholder to estimate the most optimistic package delivery time using the RF technology, the most pessimistic time, and the most likely time. This shows that next you plan to—

    a. Use a triangular probability distribution
    b. Conduct a sensitivity analysis
    c. Structure a decision analysis as a decision tree
    d. Determine the strategy for risk response

13. Each of the following statements about risk avoidance is true *except* that it—

    a. Focuses on eliminating the elements that are creating the risk
    b. Includes making the decision not to bid on a project in which the risk exposure is believed to be too high
    c. Accepts the consequences of the risk event should it occur
    d. Focuses on relating the objective that is in question, such as reducing scope

14. If the probability of event 1 is 80% and of event 2 is 70% and they are independent events, how likely is it that both events will occur?

    a. 6%
    b. 15%
    c. 24%
    d. 56%

15. The project scope statement should be used in the risk identification process because it—

    a. Identifies project assumptions
    b. Identifies all the work that must be done and, therefore, includes all the risks on the project
    c. Helps organize all the work that must be done on the project
    d. Contains information on risks on prior projects

16. Your project team has identified all the risks on the project and has categorized them as high, medium, and low. The "low" risks are placed on which of the following for monitoring?

    a. Threat list
    b. Low risk list
    c. Watch list
    d. Low impact list

17. A general contingency is used for—

    a. Risks that are identified at the outset of the project
    b. Risks that are not identified at the outset of the project but are known before they occur
    c. Risks that cannot be known before they occur because they are external risks
    d. Any risks that cannot be known before they occur

18. The simplest form of quantitative risk analysis and modeling techniques is—

    a. Probability analysis
    b. Sensitivity analysis
    c. Delphi technique
    d. Utility theory

19. If a business venture has a 60% chance to earn $2 million and a 20% chance to lose $1.5 million, what is the expected monetary value of the venture?

    a. −$50,000
    b. $300,000
    c. $500,000
    d. $900,000

20. You are managing the construction of a highly sophisticated data center in Port Moresby, Papua New Guinea. Although this location offers significant economic advantages, the threat of typhoons has caused you to create a backup plan to operate in Manila in case the center is flooded. What type of risk response is this?

    a. Passive avoidance
    b. Mitigation
    c. Active acceptance
    d. Deflection

21. A recent earned value analysis shows that your project is 20% complete, the CPI is .67, and the SPI is .87. In this situation, you should—

    a. Perform additional resource planning, add resources, and use overtime as needed to accomplish the same amount of budgeted work
    b. Rebaseline the schedule, then use Monte Carlo analysis
    c. Conduct a risk response audit to help control risk
    d. Update the risk identification and qualitative and quantitative risk analyses

22. The purpose of a numeric scale in risk management is to—

    a. Avoid high-impact risks
    b. Assign a relative value to the impact on project objectives if the risk in question occurs
    c. Rank order risks in terms of very low, low, moderate, high, and very high
    d. Test project assumptions

23. Risk score measures the—

    a. Variability of the estimate
    b. Product of the probability and impact of the risk
    c. Range of schedule and cost outcomes
    d. Reduced monetary value of the risk event

24. Which of the following is an example of recommended corrective action in risk management?

    a. Conducting a risk audit
    b. Engaging in additional risk response planning
    c. Performing the contingency plan
    d. Conducting a risk review

25. The primary advantage of using decision-tree analysis in project risk management is that it—

    a. Considers the attitude of the decision maker toward risk
    b. Forces consideration of the probability of each outcome
    c. Helps identify and postulate risk scenarios for the project
    d. Shows how risks can occur in combination

26. Your project is using complex, unproven technology. Your team conducted a brainstorming session to identify risks. Poor allocation of project resources was the number one risk. Accordingly, the team recommended placing heavy emphasis on meeting the next intermediate milestone. Thus, this intermediate milestone is known as a—

    a. Risk trigger
    b. Planned risk response
    c. Known unknown
    d. Root cause

27. When managing current projects, it is important to use lessons learned from previous projects to improve the organization's project management process. Therefore, in project closing procedures, it is important to review the—

    a. Secondary risks that occurred
    b. Checklists for risk identification
    c. WBS dictionary
    d. Team members' curriculum vitae

28. Risk mitigation involves—

    a. Using performance and payment bonds
    b. Eliminating a specific threat by eliminating the cause
    c. Avoiding the schedule risk inherent in the project
    d. Reducing the probability and/or impact of an adverse risk event to an acceptable threshold

29. On a typical project, when are risks highest and impacts (amount at stake) lowest?

    a. During the concept phase
    b. At or near completion of the project
    c. During the implementation phase
    d. When the project manager is replaced

30. Two key inputs to the quantitative risk analysis process from the project management plan are the—

    a. WBS and milestone list
    b. Scope management plan and process improvement plan
    c. Schedule management plan and cost management plan
    d. Procurement management plan and quality baseline

31. The highest risk impact generally occurs during which of the following project life-cycle phases?

    a. Concept and planning
    b. Planning and implementation
    c. Implementation and closeout
    d. Concept and closeout

32. Which of the following statements best characterizes a cost or duration estimate developed with a limited amount of information?

    a. It should be part of the planning for the needed management reserve.
    b. It is an input to risk identification.
    c. It is an output from risk identification.
    d. It must be factored into the list of prioritized project risks.

33. You need to outsource a key task on your project. Which of the following contract types provides the greatest amount of risk transfer to the contractor?

    a. Cost plus
    b. Firm fixed price
    c. Labor hour
    d. They all provide the same degree of transfer because in each case, a contractor is performing the work.

34. Accurate and unbiased data are essential for qualitative risk analysis. Which of the following should you use to examine the extent of understanding of project risk?

    a. Data quality assessment
    b. Project assumptions testing
    c. Sensitivity analysis
    d. Influence diagrams

35. Assigning more talented resources to the project to reduce time to completion or to provide better quality than originally planned are examples of which one of the following strategies?

    a. Enhance
    b. Exploit
    c. Share
    d. Contingent response

36. Which of the following is *not* an objective of a risk audit?

    a. Confirming that risk management has been practiced throughout the project life cycle
    b. Confirming that the project is well managed and that the risks are being controlled
    c. Helping to identify the deterioration of the project's value potential in its early stages
    d. Ensuring that each risk identified and deemed critical has a computed expected value

37. Contingency planning involves—

    a. Defining the steps to be taken if an identified risk event should occur
    b. Establishing a management reserve to cover unplanned expenditures
    c. Preparing a stand-alone document that is separate from the overall project plan
    d. Determining needed adjustments to make during the implementation phase of a project

38. Your firm specializes in roller-coaster construction. It recently received an RFP to build the world's most "death-defying" roller coaster. You know that such a roller coaster has never been built before and that this would be a high-risk project. Accordingly, what type of contract would you want to be awarded for this project?

    a. Firm-fixed-price
    b. Time-and-materials
    c. Cost-plus-a-percentage-of-cost
    d. Cost-plus-fixed fee

39. As head of the project office, you need to focus on those items where risk responses can lead to better project outcomes. One way to help you make these decisions is to—

    a. Determine a relative ranking or priority list of project risks
    b. Assess trends in quantitative risk analysis results
    c. Prioritize risks and conditions
    d. Assess trends in qualitative risk analysis results

40. You are the project manager for the construction of an incinerator to burn refuse. Local residents and environmental groups are opposed to this project. Management agrees to move this project to a different location. This is an example of which of the following risk responses?

    a. Passive acceptance
    b. Active acceptance
    c. Mitigation
    d. Avoidance

## Answer Sheet

1. a b c d
2. a b c d
3. a b c d
4. a b c d
5. a b c d
6. a b c d
7. a b c d
8. a b c d
9. a b c d
10. a b c d
11. a b c d
12. a b c d
13. a b c d
14. a b c d
15. a b c d
16. a b c d
17. a b c d
18. a b c d
19. a b c d
20. a b c d

21. a b c d
22. a b c d
23. a b c d
24. a b c d
25. a b c d
26. a b c d
27. a b c d
28. a b c d
29. a b c d
30. a b c d
31. a b c d
32. a b c d
33. a b c d
34. a b c d
35. a b c d
36. a b c d
37. a b c d
38. a b c d
39. a b c d
40. a b c d

## Answer Key

**1. b. $44,000**

$$EMV_{\text{Toyota}} = (\$50,000 \times 90\%) + (-\$10,000 \times 10\%)$$
$$= \$45,000 + (-\$1,000)$$
$$= \$44,000$$

[Planning]

PMI®, *PMBOK® Guide*, 2004, 257

**2. c. Accept**

Risk exists on every project and it is unrealistic to think it can be completely eliminated. There are certain risks that simply must be accepted because we cannot control whether or not they will occur (for example, an earthquake). Acceptance is a strategy for dealing with risk that can be used for both threats and opportunities. [Planning]

PMI®, *PMBOK® Guide*, 2004, 263

**3. c. Qualitative risk analysis**

Risks whose occurrence may happen in the near-term need urgent attention. The purpose of the risk urgency assessment is to identify those risks that have a high likelihood of happening sooner rather than later. [Planning]

PMI®, *PMBOK® Guide*, 2004, 253

**4. b. Each project is unique in some measure**

Uniqueness means that the past is an imperfect guide to the future. [Planning]

Frame 1994, 75

**5. c. RBS**

The risk breakdown structure is one of several ways to ensure the identification of project risks. [Planning]

PMI®, *PMBOK® Guide*, 2004, 243

### 6. d. Brainstorming

Brainstorming is a frequently used information-gathering technique for risk identification because it enables the project team to develop a list of potential risks relatively quickly. Project team members, or invited experts, participate in the session. Risks are easily categorized for follow-on analysis. [Planning]

PMI®, *PMBOK® Guide*, 2004, 247

### 7. c. Reduce bias in the analysis and keep any one person from having undue influence on the outcome

The Delphi technique provides a means for arriving at a consensus using a panel of experts to determine a solution to a specific problem. Project risk experts are identified but participate anonymously. Each panelist answers a questionnaire. Then the responses, along with opinions and justifications, are evaluated, and statistical feedback is given to each panel member. The process continues until group responses converge toward a solution. [Planning]

Wideman 1992, C-2 and C-3; PMI®, *PMBOK® Guide*, 2004, 248

### 8. a. An unplanned response to a negative risk event

Used in risk monitoring and control, workarounds are risk responses that have not been defined in advance of the risk event occurring. [Monitoring and Controlling]

PMI®, *PMBOK® Guide*, 2004, 380

### 9. d. Monte Carlo analysis

Monte Carlo analysis supports various statistical distributions (normal, triangular, beta, uniform, and so on) used in estimating budgets, schedules, and resource allocations. [Planning]

Frame 1994, 90; PMI®, *PMBOK® Guide*, 2004, 258 and 364

### 10. b. 13%

Probability (starting activity 4 on day 6) = $(0.5)^3$ = 0.125 or 13% [Planning]

PMI®, *PMBOK® Guide*, 2004, 259

**11. c. PDM schedule**

When determining the likelihood of meeting the project's schedule end date through Monte Carlo, the PDM schedule data is used as input to the simulation program. Cost risk, on the other hand, uses cost estimates from the WBS. [Planning]

PMI®, *PMBOK® Guide*, 2004, 258

**12. a. Use a triangular probability distribution**

Interviews often are used to help quantify the probability and consequences of risks on project objectives. The type of information collected during the interview depends on the type of probability distribution that is used. A triangular distribution is used if information is gathered on the optimistic (low), pessimistic (high), and most likely scenarios. [Planning]

PMI®, *PMBOK® Guide*, 2004, 255–256

**13. c. Accepts the consequences of the risk event should it occur**

Accepting the consequences of the risk event is categorized as risk acceptance. With this risk response approach, the project team takes no action to reduce the probability of the risk's occurring. [Planning]

Carter et al. 1994, 113–114; PMI®, *PMBOK® Guide*, 2004, 263

**14. d. 56%**

The likelihood is determined by multiplying the probability of event 1 by the probability of event 2. [Planning]

Wideman 1992, IV-7

**15. a. Identifies project assumptions**

Project assumptions, which should be enumerated in the project scope statement, are areas of uncertainty, and as such are potential causes of project risk. [Planning]

PMI®, *PMBOK® Guide*, 2004, 247

**16. c. Watch list**

Even low-priority risks must be monitored. A watch list is used to ensure such risks are tracked. [Planning]

PMI®, *PMBOK® Guide*, 2004, 253

### 17. d.  Any risks that cannot be known before they occur

There is a category of risks that is sometimes called unknown-unknowns, meaning that the risk is not knowable and, therefore, the probability of the risk is also not knowable.  Your lead technical advisor becoming seriously ill, your offices being ransacked by persons engaged in industrial espionage, or one of your subcontractors winning the lottery and running off to the Cayman Islands are all examples of risks that are not known before they occur.  However, such risks must be expected and a general contingency can be set aside to address the impact they leave in their wake.  [Monitoring and Controlling]

Pritchard 2001, 317

### 18. b.  Sensitivity analysis

Sensitivity analysis, as a quantitative risk analysis and modeling technique, places a value on the impact to the project plan of changing a single project variable.  Uncertainty and risk are reflected by defining a likely range of variation for each element of the baseline estimate.  Such an analysis is done only for those variables that greatly affect cost, time, or economic return and to which the project will be the most sensitive.  The effect of changing each of these variables is then assessed across the assumed ranges.  [Planning]

Wideman 1992, C-1 and C-2; PMI®, *PMBOK® Guide*, 2004, 257

### 19. d.  $900,000

$EMV = (\$2M \times 60\%) + (-\$1.5M \times 20\%) =$

$(\$1.2M) + (-\$300,000) = \$900,000$

[Planning]

Frame 1994, 82–83

### 20. c.  Active acceptance

Active acceptance means not only accepting the consequences of a risk, but also establishing a plan for dealing with the risk, should it occur.  Organizations typically establish a contingency plan funded by a contingency reserve (of time, money, or resources) to handle known, or even sometimes potential unknown, threats or opportunities.  [Planning]

PMI®, *PMBOK® Guide*, 2004, 263

**21. d. Update the risk identification and qualitative and quantitative risk analyses**

Earned value is used for monitoring overall project performance against a baseline plan. When a project deviates significantly from the baseline, you should update the risk identification and qualitative and quantitative risk analyses. [Monitoring and Controlling]

PMI®, *PMBOK® Guide*, 2004, 266

**22. b. Assign a relative value to the impact on project objectives if the risk in question occurs**

Relative or numeric, well-defined scales can be developed using agreed-upon definitions by the stakeholders. When using a numeric scale, each level of impact has a specific number assigned to it. A more unconventional approach is a nonlinear scale, which reflects the organization's desire to avoid high-impact threats or exploit high-impact opportunities. [Planning]

PMI®, *PMBOK® Guide*, 2004, 244–245

**23. b. Product of the probability and impact of the risk**

The risk score provides a convenient way to compare risks because comparing impacts or probabilities alone is meaningless. [Planning]

Carter et al. 1994, 54; PMI®, *PMBOK® Guide*, 2004, 252

**24. c. Performing the contingency plan**

Corrective action in risk management is the process of making changes to bring expected performance in line with the risk management plan. Such action consists of performing either the planned risk response, such as implementing contingency plans, or a workaround. [Monitoring and Controlling]

PMI®, *PMBOK® Guide*, 2004, 267

**25. b. Forces consideration of the probability of each outcome**

A graphical way to bring together information, decision-tree analysis quantifies the likelihood of failure and places a value on each decision. Usually applied to cost and time considerations, this form of risk analysis may be linked to a sensitivity analysis. [Planning]

Wideman 1992, C-3 and C-4; PMI®, *PMBOK® Guide*, 2004, 257

**26. a. Risk trigger**

A risk trigger is an indicator that alerts the project team to the potential that the risk may, or is about to, occur. Risk triggers are identified in the risk identification process and watched in the risk monitoring and control process. [Planning]

PMI®, *PMBOK® Guide*, 2004, 378

**27. b. Checklists for risk identification**

Checklists are a tool and a technique for risk identification and include risks encountered on similar, previous projects identified through the lessons learned process. The project team should review the checklist as part of the risk identification process as well as during closeout, adding to the list as necessary, based on its experience, to help others in the future. [Planning]

PMI®, *PMBOK® Guide*, 2004, 248

**28. d. Reducing the probability and/or impact of an adverse risk event to an acceptable threshold**

It is often more effective to take early action to reduce probability and/or impact of a risk occurring on a project than implementing a contingency after the risk has occurred. [Planning]

PMI®, *PMBOK® Guide*, 2004, 262

**29. a. During the concept phase**

Risks are highest at the beginning of a project because the project faces an uncertain future, and impacts are lowest then because investments in human and material resources are minimal. [Planning]

Frame 1994, 84; Wideman 1992, II-1 and II-5; PMI®, *PMBOK® Guide*, 2004, 21

**30. c. Schedule management plan and cost management plan**

The cost and schedule of a project are two areas impacted significantly by risk occurrences. Information on these two areas, because of their quantitative nature, makes excellent input to the risk quantification process to help determine overall impact. [Planning]

PMI®, *PMBOK® Guide*, 2004, 255

### 31. c.  Implementation and closeout

Opportunity and risk generally remain high during the concept and planning phases.  However, the amount at stake remains low because of the relatively low level of investment up to that point.  During project implementation and closeout, however, risk falls to lower levels as remaining unknowns are translated into knowns.  At the same time, the amount at stake rises steadily as the necessary resources are invested to complete the project.  [Planning]

Wideman 1992, II-5 and II-6

### 32. b.  It is an input to risk identification.

Much of the output from planning in other knowledge areas, such as cost and duration estimates, may entail risk and is reviewed during the risk identification process.  This process requires an understanding of the schedule, cost, and quality management plans found in the project management plan.  Estimates that are aggressive or developed with a limited amount of information are even more likely to entail risk and, therefore, must also be an input to risk identification.  [Planning]

PMI®, *PMBOK® Guide*, 2004, 246

### 33. b.  Firm fixed price

In a firm-fixed-price contract, contractors assume the greatest amount of risk because they are legally obligated to perform the work for the negotiated price.

Verzuh 2005, 102

### 34. a.  Data quality assessment

Qualitative risk analysis requires accurate and unbiased data.  The use of low-quality data may result in a qualitative risk analysis that is of little use to the project manager regarding understanding of the risk, data available about the risk, data quality, and data reliability and integrity.  [Planning]

PMI®, *PMBOK® Guide*, 2004, 252

### 35. b.  Exploit

Although it might have a negative connotation, exploitation is a strategy used for risks with positive impacts.  [Planning]

PMI®, *PMBOK® Guide*, 2004, 262

**36. d. Ensuring that each risk identified and deemed critical has a computed expected value**

It is not feasible or necessary to quantify every risk. Therefore, a risk audit should never have as an objective to ensure that each project risk has a computed expected value. [Monitoring and Controlling]

Carter et al. 1994, 132; PMI®, *PMBOK® Guide*, 2004, 266

**37. a. Defining the steps to be taken if an identified risk event should occur**

For some risks it is appropriate for the project team to make a response plan that will be executed only under certain predefined conditions if it is believed that there will be sufficient warning to implement the plan. [Monitoring and Controlling]

PMI®, *PMBOK® Guide*, 2004, 265

**38. c. Cost-plus-a-percentage-of-cost**

This contract type reimburses an allowable cost of services performed plus an agreed-upon percentage of the estimated cost as profit. It provides the least risk to the seller. [Planning]

Ward 2000, 56

**39. a. Determine a relative ranking or priority list of project risks**

The probability and impact matrix can be used to classify risks according to their level of impact. [Planning]

PMI®, *PMBOK® Guide*, 2004, 253

**40. d. Avoidance**

Risk avoidance is taking an action to eliminate the threat posed by an adverse risk. [Planning]

PMI®, *PMBOK® Guide*, 2004, 261

# PROJECT PROCUREMENT MANAGEMENT

## Study Hints

The Project Procurement Management questions on the PMP® certification exam tend to be more process oriented than legally focused. You do not need to know any country's specific legal code; however, some non-U.S. exam takers complain that the nature of many of the questions requires an understanding of U.S. contract law. Although an occasional question relating to the U.S. system may appear on the exam, such questions do not seem to be problematic for most exam takers. A firm understanding of the procurement process usually will help you find the correct answer.

The exam requires you to know the basic differences between the three broad categories of contracts (fixed-price, cost-reimbursement, and time-and-materials) and the risks inherent in specific contract types for both the buyer and the seller. Several questions will also test your knowledge of the various types of contracts within each category (for example, firm-fixed-price versus fixed-price level-of-effort contract). A question or two may also be included on international contracting, such as the timing of foreign currency exchange and duty on goods delivered to a foreign country.

In addition to the *PMBOK® Guide*, you may want to peruse the following two PMI® handbooks: *Contract Administration for the Project Manager* by Martin D. Martin et al. and *Negotiating & Contracting for Project Management* by Penny Cavendish and Martin D. Martin.[1] You will most certainly want to review the text and your notes for any courses you have taken in contracting or procurement.

PMI® views Project Procurement Management as a six-step process comprising plan purchases and acquisitions, plan contracting, request seller responses, select sellers, contract administration, and contract closure. See *PMBOK® Guide* Figure 12-1 for an overview of this structure. Know this chart thoroughly.

Following is a list of the major Project Procurement Management topics. Use it to help focus your study efforts on the areas most likely to appear on the exam.

---

[1]Note that the procurement process is described as a five-cycle process in *Negotiating and Contracting for Project Management,* whereas the *PMBOK® Guide* identifies six process steps. For exam study purposes, concentrate on the six *PMBOK® Guide* process steps; however, the content of the rest of this monograph should be helpful.

# Major Topics

*Project procurement management overview*

*Step 1: Plan purchases and acquisitions*

- Make-or-buy analysis
- Procurement management plan
- Contract statement of work
- Contract categories and risks
  Fixed-price or lump-sum
  Cost-reimbursement
  Time-and-materials
- Contract types and risks
  Cost-plus-a-percentage-of-cost
  Cost-plus-fixed fee
  Cost-plus-incentive fee
  Fixed-price-plus-incentive fee
  Firm-fixed-price
- Contract incentives

*Step 2: Plan contracting*

- Contract origination
- Evaluation criteria
- Procurement documents

*Step 3: Request seller responses*

- Proposals

*Step 4: Select sellers*

- Evaluating prospective sellers
  Contract negotiation
  Weighting system
  Screening system
  Independent estimates
  Seller rating systems
  Proposal evaluation techniques
  Expert judgment
- Contract negotiation stages and tactics
  Five stages
  Negotiation tactics
  Source selection output

## Major Topics (continued)

*Step 5:* **Contract administration**

- Contract documentation
- Standard clauses
- Elements of a legally enforceable contract
- Changes and change control
- Undefined work
- Contract management plan

*Step 6:* **Contract closure**

- Records management system
- Contract closure procedure
- Procurement audit
- Closed contracts

**Organizing for contract management**

- Centralized contracting
- Decentralized contracting

**Privity of contract**

**Foreign currency exchange**

# Practice Questions

INSTRUCTIONS: Note the most suitable answer for each multiple-choice question in the appropriate space on the answer sheet.

1. What doctrine causes a party to relinquish rights under a contract because it knowingly fails to execute those rights?

   a. Assignment of claims
   b. Material breach
   c. Waiver
   d. Warranties

2. Contract closure is a process that involves—

   a. Customer satisfaction analysis and final payment
   b. Administrative closure and archiving records
   c. Final contractor payment and lessons learned
   d. Product verification and acceptance of deliverables

3. You are managing a project that has five subcontractors. You must monitor contract performance, make payments, and manage provider interface. One subcontractor submitted a change request to expand the scope of its work. You decided to award a contract modification based on a review of this request. All these activities are part of—

   a. Contract administration
   b. Contract execution
   c. Contract formation
   d. Contract resolution

4. All the following are processes in project procurement management *except*—

   a. Contract termination
   b. Contract administration
   c. Solicitation planning
   d. Source selection

5. Which term describes those costs in a contract that are associated with two or more projects but are not traceable to either of them individually?

   a. Variable
   b. Direct
   c. Indirect
   d. Semivariable

6. Contract type selection is dependent on the degree of risk or uncertainty facing the project manager. From the perspective of the buyer, the preferred contract type in a low-risk situation is—

   a. Firm-fixed-price
   b. Fixed-price incentive
   c. Cost-plus-fixed fee
   d. Cost-plus-a-percentage-of-cost

7. The buyer has negotiated a cost-plus-incentive fee contract with the seller. The contract has a target cost of $300,000, a target fee of $40,000, a share ratio of 80/20, a maximum fee of $60,000, and a minimum fee of $10,000. If the seller has actual costs of $380,000, how much fee will the buyer pay?

   a. $104,000
   b. $56,000
   c. $30,000
   d. $24,000

8. Which term describes the failure by either the buyer or the seller to perform part or all of the duties of a contract?

   a. Termination of contract
   b. Partial performance
   c. Breach of contract
   d. Contract waiver

9. Working in the systems integration field, you are primarily responsible for coordinating the work of numerous subcontractors. Your current project is coming to an end. You have 15 major subcontractors as well as a variety of other sellers. Now that you are in contract closure, you should—

   a. Conduct a trend analysis
   b. Use earned value to assess lessons learned
   c. Ask each contractor to meet with you individually at its own expense
   d. Conduct a procurement audit

10. In some cases, contract termination refers to—

    a. Contract closeout by mutual agreement
    b. Contract closeout by delivery of goods or services
    c. Contract closeout by successful performance
    d. Certification of receipt of final payment

11. Significant differences between the seller's price and your independent estimate may indicate all the following *except* the—

    a. SOW was not adequate
    b. Seller misunderstood the SOW
    c. Marketplace has drastically changed
    d. Project team chose the wrong contract type

12. You are a contractor for a state agency. Your company recently completed a water resource management project for the state and received payment on its final invoice today. A procurement audit has been conducted. Formal notification that the contract has been closed should be provided to your company by the—

    a. State's project manager
    b. Person responsible for contract administration
    c. Project control officer
    d. Project sponsor or owner

13. Which term describes contract costs that are traceable to or caused by a specific project work effort?

    a. Variable
    b. Fixed
    c. Indirect
    d. Direct

14. When a seller breaches a contract, the buyer *cannot* receive—

    a. Compensatory damages
    b. Punitive damages
    c. Liquidated damages
    d. Consequential damages

15. Market conditions is an input to which one of the following processes?

    a. Plan contracting
    b. Select sellers
    c. Plan purchases and acquisitions
    d. Contract closure

16. Which term is *not* a common name for a procurement document that solicits an offer from prospective sellers?

    a. Contractor initial response
    b. Request for information
    c. Request for quotation
    d. Invitation for negotiation

17. Because you are working under a firm-fixed-price contract, management wants you to submit the final invoice and close out the contract as soon as possible. Before final payment on the contract can be authorized, you must—

    a. Prepare a contract completion statement
    b. Audit the procurement process
    c. Update and archive contract records
    d. Settle subcontracts

18. Recent data indicate that more than 10,000 airline passengers are injured each year from baggage that falls from overhead bins. You performed a make-or-buy analysis and decided to outsource an improved bin design and manufacture. The project team needs to develop a list of qualified sources. As a general rule, which method would the project team find especially helpful?

    a. Advertising
    b. Internet
    c. Trade catalogs
    d. Relevant local associations

19. As you prepare to close out contracts on your project, you should review all the following types of documentation *except* the—

    a. Contract document for the contract being closed out
    b. Procurement audit report
    c. Invoice and payment records
    d. Seller performance reports

20. You are working on a new project in your organization. You need to decide how best to staff the project and handle all its resource requirements. Your first step should be to—

    a. Conduct a make-or-buy analysis
    b. Conduct a market survey
    c. Solicit proposals from sellers via an RFP to determine whether you should outsource the project
    d. Review your procurement department's qualified-seller lists and send an RFP to selected sellers

21. Your company decided to award a contract for project management services on a pharmaceutical research project. Because your company is new to project management and does not understand the full scope of services that may be needed under the contract, it is most appropriate to award a—

    a. Lump-sum contract
    b. Fixed-price incentive contract
    c. Cost-plus-a-percentage-of-cost contract
    d. Time-and-materials contract

22. Requirements for formal contract acceptance and closure usually are defined in the—

    a. Proposal
    b. Statement of work
    c. Contract terms and conditions
    d. Procurement audit report

23. You plan to award a contract to provide project management training for your company. You decide it is important that any prospective contractor have an association with a major university that awards master's certificates in project management. This is an example of—

    a. Setting up an independent evaluation
    b. Preparing requirements for your statement of work
    c. Establishing a weighting system
    d. Establishing a screening system

24. All the following elements must be evident in a written contract for it to be legally enforceable *except*—

    a. Legal capacity
    b. Mutual assent
    c. Appropriate form
    d. Pricing structure

25. A purchase order is a good example of which form of contracting?

    a. Unilateral
    b. Bilateral
    c. Trilateral
    d. Severable

26. You are responsible for ensuring that your seller's performance meets contractual requirements. For effective contract administration, you should—

    a. Hold a bidders' conference
    b. Establish the appropriate contract type
    c. Implement the contract change control system
    d. Develop a statement of work

27. The primary purpose of contract administration is to ensure that—

    a. The buyer fulfills his or her contractual obligations
    b. Payment is made in a timely fashion
    c. Disagreements are handled quickly and to everyone's satisfaction
    d. The seller's performance meets contractual requirements

28. Buyers use a variety of methods to provide incentives to a seller to complete work early or within certain contractually specified time frames. One such incentive is the use of liquidated damages. From the seller's perspective, liquidated damages are what form of incentive?

    a. Positive
    b. Negative
    c. Nominal
    d. Risk-prone

29. The principal function of a warranty is to—

    a. Provide assurance of the level of quality to be provided
    b. Provide a way to assert claims for late payment
    c. Provide a way to allow additional time following acceptance to correct deficiencies, without additional costs
    d. Ensure that goods purchased fit the purposes for which they are to be used

30. Contract closure and close project are similar in that they both require—

    a. That someone other than the project manager manage the activities involved
    b. Verification that no errors occurred at any time while the work was being performed
    c. That a WBS be prepared
    d. Verification that the work and deliverables were acceptable

31. You have decided to award a contract to a seller that has provided quality services to your company frequently in the past. Your current project, although somewhat different from previous projects, is similar to other work the seller has performed. In this situation, to minimize your risk you should award what type of contract?

    a. Fixed-price with economic price adjustment
    b. Fixed-price incentive (firm target)
    c. Firm-fixed-price
    d. Cost-plus-award fee

32. As project manager, you need a relatively fast and informal method addressing disagreements with contractors. One such method is to submit the issue in question to an impartial third party for resolution. This process is known as—

    a. Alternative dispute resolution
    b. Problem processing
    c. Steering resolution
    d. Mediation litigation

33. A no-cost settlement sometimes is used—

    a. To close out a successful contract
    b. In lieu of formal termination procedures
    c. When buyer property has been furnished under the contract
    d. When such an arrangement is acceptable to one of the parties involved

34. When writing payment terms in your lump-sum subcontracts it is especially important to—

    a. Include incentives for outstanding performance
    b. Describe the payment process in detail to avoid confusion
    c. Link progress made to compensation paid
    d. Associate the payment to a specific time period for more efficient accounting

35. You need to outsource the testing function of your project. Your subcontracts department informed you that the following document must be prepared before starting the procurement:

    a. Statement of work
    b. Procurement management plan
    c. Evaluation methodology
    d. Contract terms and conditions

36. A buyer has negotiated a fixed-price incentive contract with the seller. The contract has a target cost of $200,000, a target profit of $30,000, and a target price of $230,000. The buyer also has negotiated a ceiling price of $270,000 and a share ratio of 70/30. If the seller completes the contract with actual costs of $170,000, how much profit will the buyer pay the seller?

    a. $21,000
    b. $35,000
    c. $39,000
    d. $51,000

37. Requirements for formal deliverable acceptance are defined in the—

    a. Contract
    b. Procurement management plan
    c. Overall project management plan
    d. Specifications

38. Payment bonds are often required by the contract and require specific actions under the stated conditions. Payment bonds are specifically designed to ensure that the prime contractor provides payment of—

    a. Insurance premiums
    b. Weekly payrolls
    c. Subcontractors, laborers, and sellers of material
    d. Damages for accidents caused

39. During plan contracting, the project team is responsible for—

    a. Determining the make-or-buy decision
    b. Developing the procurement documents
    c. Specifying schedule parameters in the form of delivery dates
    d. Developing the specifications and drawings to accompany the solicitation

40. You are working on a contract in a remote location. The contract requires you to be on site at the office on a daily basis. You were unable to get to the office for three days last month because of severe blizzard conditions. Your failure to appear at the office was excused because of a clause in the contract entitled—

    a. Non compos mentis
    b. Forjurer royalme
    c. Force majeure
    d. Force minoris dictus

## Answer Sheet

1. a b c d    21. a b c d
2. a b c d    22. a b c d
3. a b c d    23. a b c d
4. a b c d    24. a b c d
5. a b c d    25. a b c d
6. a b c d    26. a b c d
7. a b c d    27. a b c d
8. a b c d    28. a b c d
9. a b c d    29. a b c d
10. a b c d    30. a b c d
11. a b c d    31. a b c d
12. a b c d    32. a b c d
13. a b c d    33. a b c d
14. a b c d    34. a b c d
15. a b c d    35. a b c d
16. a b c d    36. a b c d
17. a b c d    37. a b c d
18. a b c d    38. a b c d
19. a b c d    39. a b c d
20. a b c d    40. a b c d

# Answer Key

### 1. c. Waiver

Under the doctrine of waiver, a party can relinquish rights that it otherwise has under the contract. If the seller offers incomplete, defective, or late performance and the buyer's project manager knowingly accepts that performance, the buyer has waived its right to strict performance. In some circumstances, the party at fault may remain liable for provable damages, but the waiver will prevent the buyer from claiming a material breach and, thus, from terminating the contract. [Executing]

Martin et al. 1990, 34

### 2. d. Product verification and acceptance of deliverables

This process supports the close project process. It involves completing and settling each contract, including resolving open items, and closing each contract. It involves verifying that all work and deliverables were acceptable. [Closing]

PMI®, *PMBOK® Guide*, 2004, 295

### 3. a. Contract administration

The purpose of contract administration is to ensure that the contractual requirements are met by the seller. This objective is accomplished by monitoring contract performance and performing associated activities. [Monitoring and Controlling]

PMI®, *PMBOK® Guide*, 2004, 290–291

### 4. a. Contract termination

Termination is a word used to define a contract ending through mutual agreement or breach. [Closing]

Garrett 2001, 181; PMI®, *PMBOK® Guide*, 2004, 295

### 5. c. Indirect

The nature of an indirect cost is such that it is neither possible nor practical to measure how much of the cost is attributable to a single project. These costs are allocated to the project by the performing organization as a cost of doing business. [Planning]

Dobler and Burt 1996, 303; PMI®, *PMBOK® Guide*, 2004, 278

### 6. a.  Firm-fixed-price

Buyers prefer the firm-fixed-price contract because it places more risk on the seller.  Although the seller bears the greatest degree of risk, it also has the maximum potential for profit.  Because the seller receives an agreed-upon amount regardless of its costs, it is motivated to decrease costs by efficient production.  [Planning]

Cavendish and Martin 1987, 18–21; PMI®, *PMBOK® Guide*, 2004, 262

### 7. d.  $24,000

Comparing actual costs with the target cost shows an $80,000 overrun.  The overrun is shared 80/20 (with the buyer's share always listed first).  In this case 20% of $80,000 is $16,000, the seller's share, which is deducted from the $40,000 target fee.  The remaining $24,000 is the fee paid to the seller.  [Closing]

Hirsch 1986, 50

### 8. c.  Breach of contract

A breach of contract is a failure to perform either express or implied duties of the contract.  Either the buyer or the seller can be responsible for a breach of contract.  [Executing]

Jentz et al. 1984, 203; Martin et al. 1990, 37–38

### 9. d.  Conduct a procurement audit

The procurement audit attempts to identify successes and failures relative to the procurement process.  Uncovering and reporting both successes and failures can contribute to the project management knowledge base and improve the quality of project management services.  A procurement audit should be conducted as part of the contract closure process.  [Closing]

PMI®, *PMBOK® Guide*, 2004, 296

### 10. a.  Contract closeout by mutual agreement

A contract can end in successful performance, mutual agreement, or breach of contract.  Contract closeout by mutual agreement or breach of contract is called contract termination.  [Closing]

Garrett 2001, 185

**11. d.  Project team chose the wrong contract type**

The contract type is typically dictated by the SOW and chosen by the contracting officer.  [Planning]

PMI®, *PMBOK® Guide*, 2004, 288

**12. b.  Person responsible for contract administration**

The person responsible for contract administration should provide, in writing, formal notification that the contract has been completed. Requirements for formal acceptance and closeout should be defined in the contract.  [Closing]

PMI®, *PMBOK® Guide*, 2004, 297

**13. d.  Direct**

Direct costs are always identified with the cost objectives of a specific project and include salaries, travel and living expenses, and supplies in direct support of the project.  [Planning]

Dobler and Burt 1996, 302–303; PMI®, *PMBOK® Guide*, 2004, 278

**14. b.  Punitive damages**

Punitive damages are designed to punish a guilty party and, as such, are considered penalties.  Because a breach of contract is not unlawful, punitive damages are not awarded.  The other remedies listed are available to compensate the buyer's loss.  [Closing]

Jentz et al. 1984, 207

**15. c.  Plan purchases and acquisitions**

Enterprise environmental factors, which includes marketplace conditions that the team needs to be aware of as it develops its plans for purchases and acquisition, is an input to the purchases and acquisition process. [Planning]

PMI®, *PMBOK® Guide*, 2004, 275

**16. b.  Request for information**

Procurement documents are used to solicit proposals from prospective sellers.  A request for information is generally a tool to obtain source information.  [Planning]

PMI®, *PMBOK® Guide*, 2004, 282

**17. d.  Settle subcontracts**

All payments due must be settled by the seller before the contract can be closed out.  The other items listed are activities performed by the buyer.  [Closing]

Garrett 2001, 160

**18. a.  Advertising**

Advertising in newspapers or professional journals is an excellent way to identify qualified bidders.  Detailed information about specific sources may require more extensive effort, such as site visits or contact with previous customers.  [Executing]

PMI®, *PMBOK® Guide*, 2004, 285

**19. b.  Procurement audit report**

In most organizations, a procurement audit is conducted after the contract has been closed out.  Therefore, the project manager would not have a procurement audit report to review.  Answers a, c, and d are examples of the documents that should be available to the project manager and should be reviewed at closeout.  [Closing]

PMI®, *PMBOK® Guide*, 2004, 294 and 296

**20. a.  Conduct a make-or-buy analysis**

A make-or-buy analysis is a plan purchases and acquisitions tool and technique used to determine whether a particular product or service can be produced or performed cost effectively by the performing organization, or should be contracted out to another organization.  The analysis includes both direct and indirect costs and any administrative costs incurred to manage the contractor.  [Planning]

PMI®, *PMBOK® Guide*, 2004, 276

**21. d.  Time-and-materials contract**

A time-and-materials contract is a type of contract that provides for the acquisition of supplies or services on the basis of direct labor hours, at specified fixed hourly rates for wages, overhead, general and administrative expenses, and profit; and materials at cost, including materials-handling costs.  [Planning]

PMI®, *PMBOK® Guide*, 2004, 278

**22. c.  Contract terms and conditions**

The contract terms and conditions typically describe the procedure the buyer will employ to close the contract.  [Closing]

PMI®, *PMBOK® Guide*, 2004, 295

**23. d.  Establishing a screening system**

The screening system sets forth minimum requirements of performance for one or more of the evaluation criteria.  [Executing]

PMI®, *PMBOK® Guide*, 2004, 288

**24. d.  Pricing structure**

The following elements must be present for a contract to be legally enforceable:  legal capacity, mutual assent, consideration, legality, and an appropriate contract form that follows applicable laws governing businesses.  [Executing]

Cavendish and Martin 1987, 33

**25. a.  Unilateral**

The purchase order is a unilateral (one signature) offer that includes a promise to pay upon delivery.  [Planning]

ESI May 2004, 3-14; Cavendish and Martin 1987, 22

**26. c.  Implement the contract change control system**

Contract change control entails ensuring that contract changes are properly approved and that everyone who needs to know is made aware of such changes.  [Monitoring and Controlling]

PMI®, *PMBOK® Guide*, 2004, 292

**27. d.  The seller's performance meets contractual requirements**

Contracts are awarded to obtain goods and services in accordance with the buyer's stated requirements.  While there are multiple purposes in contract administration, ensuring that the seller delivers what is stated in the contract is of paramount importance.  [Monitoring and Controlling]

PMI®, *PMBOK® Guide*, 2004, 290

### 28. b.  Negative

Liquidated damages are considered negative incentives because they result in a loss of revenue for the seller if it fails to perform rather than a gain in revenue if it performs well.  [Closing]

Dobler and Burt 1996, 708–709

### 29. a.  Provide assurance of the level of quality to be provided

A warranty is one party's assurance to the other that goods will meet certain standards of quality, including condition, reliability, description, function, or performance.  This assurance may be express or implied.  [Executing]

Martin et al. 1990, 29–30

### 30. d.  Verification that the work and deliverables were acceptable

The processes of closing out a contract and closing out a project or project phase both involve verifying and documenting that the results are accepted as satisfactory.  Archiving relevant documents is also an important element in both processes.  [Closing]

PMI®, *PMBOK® Guide*, 2004, 295

### 31. c.  Firm-fixed-price

In a firm-fixed-price contract, the seller receives a fixed sum of money for the work performed regardless of costs.  This arrangement places the greatest financial risk on the seller and encourages it to control costs.  [Planning]

Dobler and Burt 1996, 342; Cavendish and Martin 1987, 19

### 32. a.  Alternative dispute resolution

Alternative dispute resolution, or dispute resolution, is a relatively informal way to address differences of opinion on contracts.  Its purpose is to address such issues without having to seek formal legal redress through the courts.  [Executing]

Bockrath 1986, 465

### 33. b.  In lieu of formal termination procedures

A no-cost settlement can be used in lieu of formal termination procedures when the seller has indicated that such an arrangement is acceptable, no buyer property has been furnished under the contract, no payments are due the seller, no other obligations are outstanding, and the product or service can be readily obtained elsewhere.  [Closing]

Garrett 2001, 187

### 34. c.  Link progress made to compensation paid

A buyer under a lump-sum contract should pay a seller for work delivered rather than time expended.  Linking payment with progress ensures that the seller will focus on results and not on effort expended.  [Planning]

Garrett 2001, Chapter 8

### 35. b.  Procurement management plan

The procurement management plan describes how all aspects of the procurement process—from developing the contract SOW to describing closeout procedures—will be managed.  This includes the type of contracts to be used, preparation of independent estimates, actions to be taken by the procurement department and the project management team, location of standardized procurement documents, management of multiple providers, and coordination of the procurement with other aspects of the project.  [Planning]

PMI®, *PMBOK® Guide*, 2004, 279

### 36. c.  $39,000

To calculate the fee that the buyer must pay, actual costs are compared with the target cost.  If actual costs are less than the target cost, the seller will earn profit that is additional to the target profit.  If actual costs are more than the target cost, the seller will lose profit from the target profit.  The amount of profit is determined by the share ratio (with the buyer's share listed first).  In this example, the seller is under target cost by $30,000.  That amount will be split 70/30.  So the buyer keeps $21,000, and the seller receives an additional $9,000 added to the target profit, which is the incentive.  Total fee is $39,000.  [Closing]

Hirsch 1986, 55–56

### 37. a. Contract

Two important components of any contract include what the buyer wants to buy and how the buyer defines acceptance of the products or services delivered. For contract closure to occur, deliverable acceptance must be completed. [Closing]

PMI®, *PMBOK® Guide*, 2004, 297

### 38. c. Subcontractors, laborers, and sellers of material

Payment bonds, which are required by the buyer, are issued by guarantors to prime contractors. The buyer wants to ensure that subcontractors of the prime contractor receive payment so that work is not disrupted. [Closing]

Martin et al. 1990, 36

### 39. b. Developing the procurement documents

This activity is the only one of those listed that takes place during plan contracting, which is the process of preparing the documents needed to support the request seller process. All the other activities occur in other phases of project procurement management. [Planning]

PMI®, *PMBOK® Guide*, 2004, 281

### 40. c. Force majeure

Force majeure clauses can be used to protect either party from events that are outside their control and not a result of their negligence, such as acts of nature, war, civil disobedience, or labor disruption. [Executing]

Garrett 2001, 54

*Professional and Social Responsibility*

# PROFESSIONAL AND SOCIAL RESPONSIBILITY

## Study Hints

Professional and Social Responsibility covers the legal, ethical, and professional behaviors of the profession.

The Professional and Social Responsibility questions on the PMP® certification exam relate directly to project managers' responsibilities to PMI®, to themselves, to the profession, *and* to their organizations. They cover the legal, ethical, and professional behaviors of the profession.

You should anticipate a host of situational questions in this area, yet most exam takers do not find these questions difficult. When considering ethical issues, always select the answer that represents the most ethical choice, even if another answer would be deemed acceptable in your experience.

Professional and Social Responsibility is not covered as a specific knowledge area in the *PMBOK® Guide*; therefore, you must refer to publications such as the following:

- *Doing Business Internationally: The Guide to Cross-Cultural Success* by Terence Brake et al.

- *Global Literacies: Lesson on Business Leadership and National Cultures* by Robert Rosen et al.

- *The Cultural Dimension of International Business* by Gary P. Ferraro

PMI® publications that address professional and social responsibility include—

- PMI® Member Ethical Standards: Member Code of Ethics and Member Standards of Conduct

- PMI® Member Ethics Case Procedures

- *Project Management Experience and Knowledge Self-Assessment Manual*

- Project Management Professional (PMP®) Code of Professional Conduct

See the next page for a list of the major Professional and Social Responsibility topics you will see on the exam. Use it to help focus your study efforts on the areas most likely to appear on the exam.

# Major Topics

*Ensuring individual integrity and professionalism*

- Legal requirements
- Ethical standards
- Community and stakeholder values

*Contributing to the project management knowledge base*

- Knowledge base in project management
- Appropriate communities
- Media
- Research strategies
- Effective communication techniques

*Enhancing individual competence*

- Personal strengths and weaknesses
- Instructional methods and tools
- Appropriate professional competencies
- Personal learning style
- Training options

*Balancing stakeholders' interests*

- Stakeholder interests
- Competing needs and objectives
- Conflict resolution techniques

*Interacting in a professional and cooperative manner*

- Standards for professional communication
- Ethnic and cultural norms of team members and stakeholders
- Stakeholders' and team members' communication preferences

# Practice Questions

INSTRUCTIONS: Note the most suitable answer for each multiple-choice question in the appropriate space on the answer sheet.

1. You just learned that the European Union has issued a new regulation for handling toxic waste. You recommend to management that your company undertake a project to develop guidelines in response to this regulation. This recommendation demonstrates the importance of—

   a. Adhering to legal requirements and ethical standards
   b. Continually searching for new and more effective methods of doing your work
   c. Using legal requirements as the basis for all project selection decisions
   d. The limited time frame in which projects must be completed

2. Your company is bidding on an international project with a requirement to perform an environmental impact study before beginning construction. The requirement to perform such a study represents—

   a. The impact that demonstrations can have on international affairs
   b. A project constraint
   c. A factor that needs to be taken into consideration as part of the bid-no bid decision
   d. An example of complying with international law

3. Your contract requires you to submit a final report in one month. The project sponsor has asked you to complete the project with incomplete data. The final report must be submitted to receive the monies due. In this situation, you should—

   a. Prepare a rough estimate based on your knowledge of the subject, and complete the project
   b. Explain in writing and in your oral presentation that you cannot complete the project because of the incomplete data
   c. Use the results of research prepared by another organization as the basis for your effort data
   d. Inform management that you need additional time, and ask for a formal extension

4. You are managing a project team that is preparing a comprehensive set of food processing regulations. At a recent industry meeting, one of the manufacturers presented you with a free gift. In this situation, you should probably—

   a. Not accept this gift because it could be interpreted as being for personal gain
   b. Determine whether the manufacturer gave the certificate to everyone else attending the meeting and, if so, accept it
   c. Accept the gift, and then inform your project sponsor when you return to your job
   d. Accept the gift to avoid embarrassing the provider

5. You are managing an international construction project. You know the city expects some form of "unofficial" compensation for approving the issuance of licenses and permits. Your best approach is to—

   a. Follow local customs explicitly, even if this means that you must make "payments" to local officials
   b. Abide by the laws, regulations, and requirements of your own country and follow them explicitly in this situation
   c. Refrain from knowingly engaging in professional misconduct
   d. Recognize the need for government involvement in the project and do whatever is required for success

6. Your manager allegedly violated PMI®'s intellectual property policy guidelines when he reproduced and distributed portions of the *PMBOK® Guide* without first requesting permission from PMI®. Yesterday, a PMI® Ethics Review Committee member asked you a series of questions related to your manager's alleged misdeeds. In this situation, you have—

   a. No involvement because you are not a party to the ethics proceedings
   b. A responsibility to cooperate with PMI® concerning ethics violations and the collection of related information
   c. No responsibility because you were not a PMI® member at the time this alleged misuse took place
   d. No obligation to provide PMI® with any information because you have no firsthand knowledge of the extant case

7. Your company is submitting a proposal for a government contract, and you are the proposal manager. One of the requirements is that the project manager must be a PMP®. Your proposed project manager, Katrina, is not a PMP®, but will be taking the exam soon. Another PMP®, Rikard, works for the company, but he is managing another project. In preparing your proposal you should—

   a. Submit Rikard's resume as the project manager; after the contract award, replace him with Katrina, provided the client agrees to the substitution
   b. Submit Katrina's resume and state she is a PMP® because you know she will pass the exam and obtain the certification
   c. Disclose Katrina's status concerning PMP® certification in your proposal and submit her resume as the project manager
   d. Request that the government change its requirement for PMP® status

8. You need to build another facility for your company and have prepared an invitation for bid (IFB) package. You probably will not conduct negotiations with the sellers; however, you may or may not award the contract to the lowest-bidding seller, which has been made clear in the IFB. In this situation, you should be prepared to—

   a. Prohibit sellers from attending the bid opening because you will need time to decide to whom to award the contract
   b. Document your award decision as completely as possible to all sellers
   c. Inform the seller who won the bid and indicate to the others that no further discussion will take place on this issue
   d. Limit the sellers who will receive the IFB to reduce conflict

9. As part of your proposal to provide project management services to Arktic Research Laboratories, you must provide information about previous experience. Your firm recently completed a contract for one of Arktic's key competitors, Polar Investigations, Ltd., for similar services. The contract requires you to keep the client information confidential for one year. Arktic has discovered that you worked with Polar and is asking for a reference at Polar with whom it can discuss your work. In this case you should—

   a. Give Arktic the Polar reference. After all, Arktic learned of your Polar work from an outside source; therefore, you are released from the terms of the contract's confidentiality clause.
   b. Include Polar as a reference, assuming that the confidentiality agreement is unnecessarily restrictive of trade
   c. Contact Polar and let it know that if you can use it as a reference you will let it know the type of work you will be doing for Arktic so that no one is at a competitive disadvantage
   d. Contact Polar and ask for permission to list it as a reference in your proposal

10. You were part of a team that worked with one of the company's most successful project managers who left to work for a competitor. Several months after he left he asked you to send him a copy of the charter he used on the MCCAW project to compare to his current assignment. In this situation you should—

    a. Send him the update because he developed the original charter and basically knows what it includes
    b. Not send him the update; invite him to the office where he can review it in your cubicle
    c. Send him the update along with a confidentiality agreement to sign
    d. Not send him the update; he does not have a legitimate need to know the contents of the document

11. You are submitting a proposal on a contract but are concerned that your labor rates may be too high based on industry standards. You have been asked to look for ways to reduce costs. Which one of the following recommendations should you make to management?

    a. Reduce existing labor rates so that they are similar to those of the competition, and, if selected, pay each person on the project extra money out of another project's account
    b. Use your existing labor rates combined with a value engineering approach as a way to lower overall cost
    c. Put resumes from the existing staff in the proposal, but plan to hire new people at a lower labor rate
    d. Use a parametric model, and submit a different type of cost proposal using lump sum pricing

12. To support the future use and improvement of your organization's risk management process, you establish a lessons learned program. The basis of a risk lessons learned program is to—

    a. Document the results of risk response audits
    b. Capture meeting minutes from project risk reviews
    c. Provide updates to risk identification checklists
    d. Establish a risk register

13. On your last project, one client wanted you to use a different material than you normally use for laying a foundation, which reduced the actual construction time by 20%. At the end of the project, you realized that its continued use would lead to significant improvement in your construction practices. Your next step should be to—

    a. Document the lessons learned and share them within the company
    b. Adjust the schedule baseline to note the reduction in time
    c. Calculate the savings based on the schedule reduction and pass the savings on to the client
    d. Issue a new methodology and mandate that it be followed

14. During the past four years, you have awarded 10 different contracts of various types and the project is finally coming to an end. As you close out these contracts, you should—

    a. Provide each contractor with formal written notice that the project is complete
    b. Prepare a complete set of indexed records and contractual files for future reference
    c. Conduct a variance analysis
    d. Conduct a procurement audit

15. Yesterday, you called a team meeting and explained your new project's objectives to the team, which included a description of the project's quality management plan. You explained that the objective of any quality management plan is to—

    a. Ensure that all regulations governing the use of biological agents will be followed
    b. Ensure that process adjustments are made in a timely fashion
    c. Improve quality in every aspect of project performance
    d. Ensure that the scope management plan is followed

16. You have a practice of conducting not one, but multiple, quality audits on a project to ensure adherence to the quality management plan. Which one of the following types of audits is *not* an example of a quality audit?

    a. Internal
    b. System
    c. Baseline
    d. Prospective

17. Your organization has a miserable project completion rate. In reviewing the lessons learned database to determine the root cause of these problems, you should be looking at all the following information *except*—

    a. New or revised activity duration estimates
    b. Modified activity sequences
    c. Analysis of alternative schedules
    d. Schedule updates

18. You recently completed a major environmental remediation project for which your company has been paid. In working on a new project that happens to be located at the same site, you have discovered a possible flaw in the disposal system that was delivered for the earlier project. The drawings for the project are incomplete. In this situation, you should—

    a. Do nothing because the project is complete and the customer accepted the work based on its own independent inspection
    b. Alert your management to the situation, both orally and in writing, and request that someone else confirm your findings
    c. Contact the customer directly and inform it of the potential problem so that it can modify your contract to correct the problem
    d. Enhance your quality assurance and project review system immediately for future projects

19. After completing a systems upgrade, you and your team performed a lessons learned review that uncovered the uneven use of resources causing a 25% cost overrun. Now you are moving on to the next company project. When starting this new project, you should—

    a. Have an outside audit team periodically review your project to provide ideas and insight for midcourse correction
    b. Use automated software cost estimating techniques
    c. Implement a structured approach to risk management
    d. Read the qualifications of the people joining your team

20. Your recent project required extensive overtime by the project team to meet a demanding schedule. You are managing the company's next project and want to avoid a similar situation. Therefore, you should—

    a. Ensure that all work efforts are traced back to the scope statement for scope verification
    b. Use project management software that includes resource histograms and resource leveling
    c. Ensure that the WBS is detailed enough and that all the activities are defined in sufficient detail
    d. Use critical chain scheduling to account for possible unplanned events with its emphasis on buffers

21. A project management maturity review revealed that no one shares information, and that people are managing projects the same way they were managed three generations ago. To promote better sharing of information, a consultant suggests that the company support which one of the following?

    a. Project team meetings
    b. In-progress customer review sessions
    c. Kickoff meetings
    d. Benchmarking forums

22. You recently were assigned to a project in Australia. Coming from Japan, you are excited about the opportunity to visit the Outback, tour Sydney Harbor, and travel to the Great Barrier Reef. To make the transition as easy as possible, your company should do which of the following first?

    a. Hire a consultant who knows the country to brief you on what to expect in Australia
    b. Give you a tourist's guide to Australia to read on the plane to your new assignment
    c. Send you to Australia for a couple of weeks before the assignment so that you get to know the place and to meet your new teammates
    d. Arrange a meeting at the Australian embassy in Tokyo so that you can meet Australian nationals and they can explain what it is like for a Japanese person to live there

23. You have been selected to manage an international project headquartered overseas. As you list the pros and cons of accepting the assignment, there is one question that you must answer honestly before saying "yes" or "no." That question is—

    a. What common ground exists between the people with whom I will be working and me?
    b. How do I translate my cultural awareness and knowledge into functional skills that I can use on the project?
    c. How can I continue to refine my skills and to develop my level of cultural competence and adaptability?
    d. How adaptable am I?

24. You are working on a joint venture with a Korean firm. During a conversation with the company president, you mention that you know how to spell several words in Hangul. Which one of the following traits best identifies the disclosure of your knowledge of his language?

    a. Confident humility
    b. Authentic flexibility
    c. Aggressive insight
    d. Positive aggrandizement

25. A person's negotiating behavior is influenced by his or her culture. Over time, an individual who is living in a culture that is different from his or her own may take on characteristics of the new culture and may behave from a new frame of reference. With respect to negotiation, this illustrates the importance of—

    a. Always looking at those with whom you are negotiating as members of a particular cultural group
    b. Moving beyond cultural stereotyping and seeing people as individuals with unique personality traits and experiences
    c. Recognizing that cultural stereotyping should be used as a starting point for all international negotiations
    d. Becoming overly dependent on cultural knowledge as the cornerstone for all negotiations

26. You are ready to enter a negotiating session with people from another country who have earned a reputation as tough negotiators. To earn your yearly bonus, you must *not* be at a disadvantage in your negotiations with them. Therefore, you must concentrate on—

    a. Seating arrangements in the negotiating room
    b. Ingratiating yourself to the most powerful negotiator on the other side of the negotiating table to earn his or her trust
    c. Active listening
    d. Setting and following strict time limits at each step of the negotiating process

27. You are meeting with several project stakeholders, including the customer. Everyone is irritated, hot, and in violent disagreement regarding the best way to proceed with the project. In general, disagreements among stakeholders should be resolved in favor of the—

    a. Sponsor
    b. Senior management
    c. Performing organization
    d. Customer

28. You are managing the construction of luxury condominiums. The client is focused on timely performance and has provided contract incentives if the job is completed early. An environmental group is concerned about adverse impacts on water drainage and is considering suing. You need to—

    a. Find appropriate resolutions to resolve differences between or among stakeholders
    b. Put the owner's requirements at the top of the list as you resolve stakeholder differences
    c. Carefully manage all communication and make status information available only on a need-to-know basis
    d. Build the condominiums according to the specifications and not worry about any other stakeholder

29. Certain members have been arguing about which project management software will work best for the project. You conduct a meeting to see whether they can reach consensus by identifying common points of agreement and striving for fair resolution. Which style of conflict resolution will you employ?

    a. Withdrawal
    b. Smoothing
    c. Problem solving
    d. Compromise

30. None of the people on your 15-person project team have worked together before, and it really shows. Each meeting is characterized by disagreements and debates. You need to get this situation under control quickly. Therefore, the first action you should take is to—

    a. Hold periodic group meetings
    b. Use a group facilitator at the next meeting
    c. Perform careful project planning
    d. Enforce strict rules about meeting behavior

31. Conflict can slow project completion. Although each conflict situation is unique, the project manager's goal remains the same: to achieve a win-win solution for everyone involved. The method most often used by project managers to resolve conflict is—

    a. Compromise
    b. Confrontation
    c. Smoothing
    d. Negotiation

32. You are managing a project whose team members are located in eight different countries. English is the lingua franca of your company. The single best way to be an effective communicator in this situation is to—

    a. Learn and use the local language
    b. Rely on interpreters
    c. Focus primarily on formal, written communication
    d. Use gestures and other forms of nonverbal communication to make your point

33. Metacommunication, paralinguistics, second-order messages, and the hidden dimension of communication all refer to—

    a. Communication skills
    b. Communication requirements
    c. Ways to exercise tolerance and compromise
    d. Nonverbal communication

34. Some people believe that to have an effective conversation, a distance of about 20 inches (51 centimeters) between the two parties involved is required. In certain cultural groups, however, the normal conversational distance is in the range of 14 to 15 inches (36 to 38 centimeters); and some groups say 9 to 10 inches (23 to 25 centimeters) is ideal. This area of nonverbal communication is important for cross-cultural communication. It is known as—

    a. Proxemics
    b. Personal space dynamics
    c. Posturing
    d. Linguistics

35. A person who believes in the inherent superiority and naturalness of his or her own culture is defined as being—

    a. Racist
    b. Ethnocentric
    c. Imperialistic
    d. Jingoistic

36. After working on various projects around the world, you have come to expect people, at times, to put other people into categories. You know that many people categorize those from your country as "brash" and "boorish." In fact, you think your current project team has categorized you as a brash person. Therefore, you should—

    a. Treat the other team members according to their country stereotypes
    b. Focus on the personalities involved
    c. Take a passive view and ignore the situation
    d. Behave in a manner that contradicts their expectations

37. Maximizing one's influence facilitates communication. This involves building and sustaining credibility. Which of the following is *not* a behavior that can help in this regard?

    a. Being flexible and open to differences
    b. Being respectful
    c. Exhibiting expertise by the answers you give
    d. Being reliable and committed

38. You have been sent abroad to conduct negotiations for a large telecommunications project. You arrive at the office promptly at 8:00 a.m.; however, at least 45 minutes of talk about families and weekend adventures goes by before anyone mentions business. Given their business approach, your hosts' culture is noted for which one of the following characteristics?

    a. High context
    b. Low context
    c. Friendliness
    d. Expressiveness

39. You are meeting with your diverse project team, represented by different nationalities, levels of experience, and positions in the company hierarchy. Everyone is encouraged to state their opinion, which is considered by the group. This team exhibits which of the following characteristics?

    a. Integrate others' worlds into your own
    b. Look globally for new ideas
    c. Be open to change
    d. Understand and value others

40. You work for a company that hires only left-handed people. A new manager suggested that it would be nice to have a few right-handed people in the company to get a different point of view on things. Such diversity would have which of the following impacts on this company?

    a. Have no impact
    b. Cause only problems
    c. Either cause problems or lead to benefits
    d. Can simultaneously cause problems and lead to benefits

## Answer Sheet

1.  a  b  c  d       21.  a  b  c  d
2.  a  b  c  d       22.  a  b  c  d
3.  a  b  c  d       23.  a  b  c  d
4.  a  b  c  d       24.  a  b  c  d
5.  a  b  c  d       25.  a  b  c  d
6.  a  b  c  d       26.  a  b  c  d
7.  a  b  c  d       27.  a  b  c  d
8.  a  b  c  d       28.  a  b  c  d
9.  a  b  c  d       29.  a  b  c  d
10.  a  b  c  d       30.  a  b  c  d
11.  a  b  c  d       31.  a  b  c  d
12.  a  b  c  d       32.  a  b  c  d
13.  a  b  c  d       33.  a  b  c  d
14.  a  b  c  d       34.  a  b  c  d
15.  a  b  c  d       35.  a  b  c  d
16.  a  b  c  d       36.  a  b  c  d
17.  a  b  c  d       37.  a  b  c  d
18.  a  b  c  d       38.  a  b  c  d
19.  a  b  c  d       39.  a  b  c  d
20.  a  b  c  d       40.  a  b  c  d

# Answer Key

**1. a. Adhering to legal requirements and ethical standards**

As part of one's professional and social responsibility in project management, legal requirements and ethical standards must be adhered to in order to protect the community and all project stakeholders.

PMI®, *PMP® Role Delineation Study,* 2000, 59

**2. b. A project constraint**

Constraints are factors that limit the project management team's options. A requirement that the product of the project be socially, economically, and environmentally sustainable also will have an effect on the project scope, staffing, and schedule.

PMI®, *PMBOK® Guide,* 2004, 355

**3. b. Explain in writing and in your oral presentation that you cannot complete the project because of the incomplete data**

Deliverables are an output from the direct and manage project execution process. In this situation, however, you cannot complete the assigned deliverable because of the incomplete data. You must ensure individual integrity and professionalism by explaining the situation both in writing and orally—even though it means you cannot complete the assigned tasks.

PMI®, *PMBOK® Guide,* 2004, 93; PMI®, Member Ethical Standards, 1

**4. a. Not accept this gift because it could be interpreted as being for personal gain**

As a project management professional, you have a responsibility to refrain from offering or accepting inappropriate payments, gifts, or other forms of compensation for personal gain unless the giving or receiving of those things conforms with applicable laws and customs of the country where project management services are being provided.

PMI®, PMP® Code of Professional Conduct

**5. c. Refrain from knowingly engaging in professional misconduct**

Although it is important to understand politics, bribing local officials to resolve problems regarding constraints and requisite business contacts raises a question of ethics. As a project management professional, you should abide by the laws, regulations, and requirements of communities and nations and not knowingly engage or assist in any activities that have negative implications.

Verma 1997, 90–91; PMI®, Member Ethical Standards, 2

**6. b. A responsibility to cooperate with PMI® concerning ethics violations and the collection of related information**

According to PMI®'s Member Ethical Standards document, PMI® members must cooperate with the Institute concerning the review of possible ethics violations and other PMI® matters.

PMI®, Member Ethical Standards, 2

**7. c. Disclose Katrina's status concerning PMP® certification in your proposal and submit her resume as the project manager**

As a PMI® member, you must provide customers, clients, and employers with fair, honest, complete, and accurate information concerning qualifications, professional services, and the preparation of estimates concerning costs, services, and expected results.

PMI®, Member Ethical Standards, 2

**8. b. Document your award decision as completely as possible to all sellers**

In an IFB, all bids are open at a specific time, and sellers are allowed to attend the bid opening. Most of the time bids are open and read aloud for those who are present. Usually the contract award goes to the lowest-bidding seller that also is financially responsible and capable of doing the work. On occasion, however, the buyer also will consider quality and time when selecting a seller. Professional judgment is critical. If the contract is not awarded to the lowest seller, it is important to document the reasons carefully. This type of contracting method is open to fraud, collusion, and other dishonest conduct. Therefore, project managers and contracting personnel must practice carefully defined, ethical business procedures.

Cavendish and Martin 1987, 24

**9. d. Contact Polar and ask for permission to list it as a reference in your proposal**

PMI® members must honor and maintain the confidentiality and privacy of customers, clients, and employers with regard to identities, assignments undertaken, product knowledge, and other information obtained throughout the course of a professional relationship unless the customer, client, or employer grants you permission to do otherwise.

PMI®, Member Ethical Standards, 2

**10. d. Not send him the update; he does not have a legitimate need to know the contents of the document**

As part of PMI®'s Code of Professional Conduct and its Member Ethical Standards, you are responsible for maintaining and respecting the confidentiality of sensitive information obtained in the course of professional activities.

PMI®, PMP® Code of Professional Conduct, 2; PMI®, Member Ethical Standards, 2

**11. b. Use your existing labor rates combined with a value engineering approach as a way to lower overall cost**

PMI® members are responsible for providing accurate and truthful representations to the public when preparing estimates concerning costs, services, and expected results. Use value engineering when there is a more effective and less expensive way to achieve the same result.

PMI®, PMP® Code of Professional Conduct, 2; PMI®, Member Ethical Standards, 2; Ward 2000, 236

**12. d. Establish a risk register**

The risk register enumerates the project's key risks and the plan for dealing with them. The risk register is produced based on the results of the qualitative and quantitative risk analyses, as well as the risk response planning process. Use of the risk register will assist in managing risk throughout the organization and, over time, will form the basis of a risk lessons learned program. This will contribute to the project management knowledge base.

PMI®, *PMBOK® Guide*, 2004, 373; PMI®, *PMP® Role Delineation Study*, 2000, 59

**13. a. Document the lessons learned and share them within the company**

It is important to contribute to the project management knowledge base by sharing lessons learned and best practices for improving the quality of project management services. Lessons learned from scope control should be shared so that they become part of the database for the current project and other projects in the organization.

PMI®, *PMBOK® Guide*, 2004, 122 and 363

**14. d. Conduct a procurement audit**

The procurement audit is a structured review of the procurement processes on a project to identify successes and failures. Each insight gained can be transferred to other procurements on the project or other projects in the performing organization. This can contribute to the project management knowledge base and improve the quality of project management services. A procurement audit should be conducted as part of the contract closure process.

PMI®, *PMBOK® Guide*, 2004, 296

**15. c. Improve quality in every aspect of project performance**

The quality management plan increases the effectiveness and efficiency of the project and provides added benefits to the project stakeholders. Improving the quality of project management services also is a key aspect of a project manager's professional responsibilities.

PMI®, *PMBOK® Guide*, 2004, 186; PMI®, *PMP® Role Delineation Study,* 2000, 59

**16. d. Prospective**

*Prospective* is not a term used in the quality discipline to describe an audit. Quality audits should be viewed as a system of audits. Types of quality audits include internal and external; system, product, process, location, and organization; baseline and regular; and special and comprehensive. Quality audits also are one way to improve the quality of project management services because their results will contribute to the project management knowledge base and the sharing of best practices.

Willborn and Cheng 1994, 143; PMI®, *PMBOK® Guide*, 2004, 189; PMI®, *PMP® Role Delineation Study,* 2000, 101

**17. d. Schedule updates**

An output from schedule control, schedule updates occur after the prospective changes have been analyzed and the appropriate changes have been selected and processed through the change control system. Reviewing lessons learned and analyzing prospective changes can help improve the quality of project management services.

PMI®, *PMBOK® Guide*, 2004, 154; PMI®, *PMP® Role Delineation Study,* 2000, 59

**18. b. Alert your management to the situation, both orally and in writing, and request that someone else confirm your findings**

In this situation, there is a potential, yet unconfirmed, problem with a deliverable that has been completed and accepted by the customer. The project is closed; however, further action is required. Personal and professional conduct, work-related conduct, community responsibility, and client relations are issues that must be considered when working as a professional in the project management business.

PMI®, Project Management Experience and Knowledge Self-Assessment Manual, 2000, 20 and 22

**19. c. Implement a structured approach to risk management**

This situation shows the possibility of poor scheduling and inadequate risk identification and response planning. Delays in using these programmers could have been identified early as a possible project management risk. Typically, project management risks include items such as poor allocation of time and resources, inadequate quality of the project plan, and poor use of project management disciplines.

PMI®, Project Management Experience and Knowledge Self-Assessment Manual, 2000, 20 and 22

**20. c. Ensure that the WBS is detailed enough and that all the activities are defined in sufficient detail**

The purpose of the WBS is to organize and define the total scope of the project. Work not described in the WBS is outside the scope of the project. Therefore, it is important to develop a WBS that is complete and that defines all activities with appropriate detail to facilitate clear responsibility assignments.

PMI®, Project Management Experience and Knowledge Self-Assessment Manual, 2000, 20 and 22

**21. d. Benchmarking forums**

Benchmarking is one way to foster learning about best practices and opportunities for process improvements. Forums in which companies meet and discuss best practices provide a standard by which to measure performance and enable experiences to be shared.

Brake et al. 2002, 156–157

22. a. **Hire a consultant who knows the country to brief you on what to expect in Australia**

Cultural competence is no longer a nice skill to have; it is an economic necessity. It begins with open attitudes, which facilitate self-development and an awareness of others' differences. One must be grounded in cultural knowledge to be able to develop cross-cultural skills.

Brake et al. 2002, 74–75

23. d. **How adaptable am I?**

Other self-awareness questions include the following: What are my primary cultural orientations? How do they affect the way I do business? How do I differ from my mainstream culture and mainstream business culture?

Brake et al. 2002, 33–34

24. c. **Aggressive insight**

Response to this situation demonstrates aggressive insight because it is proactive. Leaders who understand their strengths and their weaknesses will question assumptions and ask for feedback from others. This constant self-examination allows a person to improve his or her work performance.

Rosen et al. 2000, 62–63

25. b. **Moving beyond cultural stereotyping and seeing people as individuals with unique personality traits and experiences**

Never assume that all members of a particular cultural group will act the same way. Although success in any aspect of international business is related directly to one's knowledge of the cultural environment in which one is operating, it is inadvisable to depend on this knowledge too much.

Ferraro 1998, 121

26. c. **Active listening**

The best negotiator is a well-informed negotiator. Active listening is absolutely essential for understanding the other side's positions and interests. The understanding that comes from your active listening can have a positive persuasive effect on your negotiating partners because it can convince them that you are knowledgeable and also that you have made the effort to really hear what they are saying. This can enhance both rapport and trust.

Ferraro 1998, 125

## 27. d.  Customer

Customer requirements must be satisfied.  However, because the needs and expectations of other stakeholders cannot be disregarded, finding appropriate resolutions to disagreements among stakeholders can be a major project management challenge and is part of one's responsibility as a project management professional.

PMI®, *PMBOK® Guide,* 2004, 26–27; PMI®, *PMP® Role Delineation Study,* 2000, 60

## 28. a.  Find appropriate resolutions to resolve differences between or among stakeholders

The project manager must balance stakeholder interests by recommending approaches that strive for fair resolution to satisfy competing needs and objectives.  Stakeholders often have different, conflicting objectives.  The first step is to identify the stakeholders, determine their requirements, and then manage and influence those requirements.  Finding appropriate solutions to differences can be one of the major challenges of project management.

PMI®, *PMBOK® Guide,* 2004, 26–27; PMI®, *PMP® Role Delineation Study,* 2000, 60

## 29. b.  Smoothing

Smoothing is a style of conflict resolution that deemphasizes differences and emphasizes commonalities regarding conflict issues.  It keeps the atmosphere friendly.  As a project management professional, you should recommend approaches that strive for fair resolution to satisfy competing needs and objectives.

Kirchof and Adams 1989, 10; Verma 1996, 118 and 120; PMI®, *PMP® Role Delineation Study,* 2000, 60

## 30. c.  Perform careful project planning

Careful and early project planning can reduce conflict later in the project life cycle.  Skill in resolving conflicts and striving for fair resolution to satisfy competing needs and objectives is part of one's professional and social responsibility as a project professional.

Thamhain and Wilemon 1975, 44; PMI®, *PMP® Role Delineation Study,* 2000, 60

### 31. b. Confrontation

Although all the methods listed are useful in resolving conflict, the one project managers use most often is confrontation (also called problem solving), in which two parties work together toward a win-win solution. This type of conflict resolution is particularly effective in project management because problems are solved as they surface, preventing any accumulation of problems during the project life cycle.

Stuckenbruck and Marshall 1985, 46–47; Verma 1996, 125

### 32. a. Learn and use the local language

Communication skills must be assessed in terms of language competency, motivation to learn another language, and willingness to use it in professional and personal situations.

Ferraro 1998, 147

### 33. d. Nonverbal communication

Nonverbal communication is as important as the language used to send and receive messages because it helps us interpret the linguistic messages being sent. In the international business environment, successful communication requires not only an understanding of other languages but also an understanding of the nonverbal aspects of those languages. In cross-cultural situations, people will rely more heavily on nonverbal cues when they are not from the same speech community.

Ferraro 1998, 65

### 34. a. Proxemics

How people use personal space in their interactions with others is another "silent language" that must be understood to achieve clear communication across cultures. How close a person gets to another in normal conversation depends on the nature of the social interaction and cultural norms.

Ferraro 1998, 78–80

### 35. b. Ethnocentric

Ethnocentrism is a basic human response, and through it we rate others according to our standards and ways of doing things. It can be highly destructive because it closes off our ability to relate to others and leads to hasty evaluations and derogatory remarks. It is important to recognize this tendency and try to avoid it.

Brake et al. 2002, 169–170

**36. d.  Behave in a manner that contradicts their expectations**

If you believe you are being stereotyped, behave in a manner that contradicts the expectations and, if necessary, allude to the differences between yourself and the stereotype.  Try not to become defensive because that will only cause the situation to degenerate.  Focus on the problem, not on the personalities.

Brake et al. 2002, 171

**37. c.  Exhibiting expertise by the answers you give**

Establishing credibility is an important task—one that requires you to be knowledgeable about your business and the current developments in your field.  Ask questions that show the level of your understanding.  Demonstrate credibility by the questions you ask, rather than by the answers you give.

Brake et al. 2002, 179

**38. a.  High context**

High-context cultures are relationship centered, that is, a great deal of broad contextual information is needed about an individual or company before the specific business at hand can be transacted.  A significant amount of time may be spent on "small talk," and information may not be communicated in a linear form.

Brake et al. 2002, 54–55

**39. d.  Understand and value others**

You must be confident and clear about your own identity and express the best of your country.  The natural next step is to understand and value others.  By developing the capacity to see the world from another perspective, you open yourself to learning what the other country has to offer.

Rosen et al. 2000, 174

**40. b.  Cause only problems**

In this situation, homogeneity is viewed as natural, desirable, and good.  Diversity is considered to be a source of conflict, inconvenience, and inefficiency instead of a force for generating new patterns of mutually beneficial relations that lead to company-wide benefits.

Brake et al. 2002, 226–227

# Practice Test

This practice test is designed to simulate PMI®'s 200-question PMP® certification exam.

INSTRUCTIONS: Note the most suitable answer for each multiple-choice question in the appropriate space on the answer sheet.

1. The progressive detailing of the project management plan is known as—

   a. Replanning
   b. Rebaselining
   c. Progressive elaboration
   d. Rolling wave planning

2. Documented, authorized directions to reduce the probability of negative consequences associated with project risks are—

   a. Approved preventive actions
   b. Approved corrective actions
   c. Implemented change requests
   d. Work performance information

3. All professional organizations and their members have a code of ethics by which individuals may be guided to the correct behavior in professional dealings with others. This means that the code of ethics—

   a. Cannot overlap with the law of the country in which the professional organization is located
   b. Can never conflict with the law
   c. Can never conflict with the accepted norm of professional conduct when applied to individuals in different countries
   d. Cannot overlap with the law of the community

4. Individual components of a system should achieve desired performance. Component performance specifications, though, should not be required unless they are needed to meet a system requirement. Cost in system integration is considered to be a design parameter. However, added design costs can lead to decreased component costs with performance even though performance and effectiveness are not changed. Further, added design costs may yield decreased production costs, and the production costs can be traded off against unit costs for materials. Assume that the above is the case on your project. Your management has asked that all cost trade-offs be examined. You need to perform—

   a. Value engineering
   b. Product breakdown
   c. Requirements management
   d. Alternatives identification

5. The project management information system (PMIS) is used by the project management team to support the development on the project management plan, facilitate feedback on it, control changes to it, and release the approved changes. This means that—

   a. The change control system should be established during the Integrated change control process
   b. The configuration management system (CMS) is a subsystem of the overall PMIS
   c. The configuration management system (CMS) is a subsystem of the change control system
   d. Each project should establish a change control board to review all proposed changes and determine their disposition

6. All of the following are examples of good contract administration skills that project managers need to exercise except—

   a. Approving invoices as the work is completed
   b. Supervising the work to be done under the terms of the contract
   c. Developing contract clauses
   d. Preparing and processing change orders

7. All of the following are acceptable forms of change requests except—

   a. Direct or indirect
   b. Externally or internally initiated
   c. Vertical or horizontal
   d. Optional or legally/contractually mandated

8. In an information technology project, the specifications for each software component, such as scripts, source code, and the data definition language, should be part of the—

   a. Scope statement
   b. Scope management plan
   c. Change management plan
   d. Change control system

9. Project scope management processes ensure that the project includes all the work required to complete the project successfully. This means that—

   a. The project should meet the requirements of every stakeholder
   b. Only the work required should be completed
   c. Technical specialists on the project should ensure that the most sophisticated solution is provided
   d. The project team should first complete the detailed scope statement and then begin work on the scope management plan

10. In addition to providing support to the project, quality assurance also provides an umbrella for—

    a. Plan-do-check-act
    b. Continuous process improvement
    c. Project management maturity
    d. Work performance information

11. When dealing with customers, a code of ethics can be used to—

    a. Describe project roles and responsibilities
    b. Establish relationships
    c. Serve as a statement as to what can be expected
    d. Describe what is to be done in all situations

12. The first step in managing stakeholders is to prepare a stakeholder analysis. Assume that you are responsible for the stakeholder analysis on your multimillion-dollar, three-year project that involves two other firms in a joint venture. As you prepare your stakeholder analysis, the first step is to—

    a. Identify the items to be used in evaluating the project outcome
    b. Identify each of the stakeholders
    c. Categorize stakeholders according to their interest and influence
    d. Determine the major interfaces on the project to assess the level of stakeholder involvement

13. Change is inevitable in the project environment. It therefore is important to learn to identify, analyze, and overcome resistance to change and to become effective change agents. One tool to help in this process is force field analysis. It was developed by—

    a. Chris Argyris
    b. Kurt Lewin
    c. Warren Bennis
    d. Larry Greiner

14. While your organization has an enterprise project management office and a detailed project management methodology that each project must follow, typically your company works only on large, complex projects. You do not feel that you need to follow these rigorous procedures as you are working on a small, routine project that will be completed in two months and only has three team members. Accordingly, you should document your decisions in your—

    a. Project management information system
    b. Project scope statement
    c. Scope management plan
    d. Process improvement plan

15. An approach to use to provide insight into the health of the project and to identify any areas that require special attention is to—

    a. Conduct periodic status reviews
    b. Prepare regular status and progress reports
    c. Prepare forecasts of the project's future
    d. Continuously monitor the project

16. A number of capital budgeting approaches often are used as decisions are made to select various projects to be part of the organization's portfolio of projects. Assume that you are part of a team that is recommending a capital budgeting approach to use as part of your project selection criteria. Of the following, which one is the least precise?

    a. Payback period
    b. Internal rate of return
    c. Net present value
    d. Discounted cash flow

17. In order to identify inefficient and ineffective policies, processes, and procedures in use on a project, you should conduct—

    a. An inspection
    b. A process analysis
    c. Benchmarking
    d. A quality audit

18. Capturing, storing, and accessing configuration information needed to manage products and product information effectively is done by using—

    a. Configuration status accounting
    b. Configuration verification and auditing
    c. Project management methodology
    d. A project management information system

19. If you apply the configuration management system along with change control processes project wide, you will achieve all but which one of the following objectives?

    a. Establish an evolutionary method to continuously identify and request changes to established baselines and to assess the value and effectiveness of those changes.
    b. Provide an opportunity to continuously validate and improve the project by considering the impact of each change.
    c. Document the specific responsibilities of each stakeholder in the integrated change control process.
    d. Provide the mechanism for the project team to consistently communicate all changes to the stakeholders.

20. Assume that your organization is a contractor for a government agency on a multiyear, complex project. As the project manager, you established a change control board to serve as a review authority regarding possible changes on your project. On this project, some of the proposed changes will need approval by the—

    a. Project sponsor
    b. Customer
    c. Project manager
    d. Configuration manager

21. The process that specifies how formal verification and acceptance of the completed project deliverables will be obtained should be included in the—

    a. Change control procedures
    b. Change management plan
    c. Scope management plan
    d. Quality management plan

22. The administrative closure procedure is an input to which of the following processes?

    a. Direct and manage project execution
    b. Monitor and control project work
    c. Close project
    d. Contract closure

23. Changes to your project can be expensive. Configuration management, therefore, should be implemented correctly. Of the following, which is the first thing you should do as you set up configuration management on your project?

    a. Define the starting point or "baseline" configuration.
    b. Set up classes of changes.
    c. Identify policies and procedures.
    d. Define controls or limitations that exist for the customer and the contractor.

24. Which one of the following is a tool used in process analysis to determine the underlying causes of defects?

    a. Root cause analysis
    b. Assumptions analysis
    c. Cost-benefit analysis
    d. Quality metrics

25. The scope change control system defines the procedures by which the project scope and product scope can be changed. Accordingly, it should be documented in the—

    a. Scope change control plan
    b. Project management methodology
    c. Scope management plan
    d. Configuration management system

26. Oftentimes when a project is terminated, senior managers will replace the project manager with an individual who is skilled at closing out projects. If this is done, the first step for the termination manager should be to—

    a. Notify all relevant stakeholders of the termination
    b. Complete the lessons learned report
    c. Conduct an immediate review of the work packages
    d. Review the status of all contracts

27. The area where the project manager can have the greatest impact on the quality of his or her project is in—

    a. Quality planning
    b. Quality assurance
    c. Quality control
    d. Quality improvement

28. Assume that you are managing a project in an electronics firm. In your firm, you realize that the executives have different views of project success. The R&D vice president defines success as deploying state-of-the-art technology, the manufacturing vice president defines success as using world-class best practices, and the marketing vice president is most interested with the number of new features that the product offers. You are preparing your project management plan and you have decided to hold a meeting to kick off this project. You have invited representatives from each of these three functional areas as well as other stakeholders who may be involved. In this meeting, you and your team need to—

    a. Create an environment in which each stakeholder contributes appropriately
    b. Explain your view of success to this group and then proceed to work on the actual contents of the plan
    c. Use the view of success of the most influential stakeholder in your company and let the others know that this is how progress will be measured
    d. Follow a detailed agenda in which you ensure all items are covered in a timely manner even if you overlook the need for in-depth discussion of some issues

29. During the planning processes on a project, stakeholder analysis is a tool and technique that should be first used during—

    a. Scope planning
    b. Communications planning
    c. Scope definition
    d. Risk identification

30. All of the following will assure that a good quality audit has been completed except—

    a. Products are safe and fit for use
    b. Improvement opportunities are identified
    c. Proper preventive action is taken when required
    d. Project team members are adequately trained for their jobs

31. On your project you want to avoid bureaucracy, so you adopt an informal approach to change control. The main problem with this approach is—

    a. There is no "paper trail" of change activity
    b. Regular disagreements between the project manager and the functional manager
    c. There are misunderstandings regarding what was agreed to
    d. Lack of sound cost estimating to assess the change's impact

32. Assume that your organization is evaluating two possible projects to pursue. Although both are ones that your company's customers have suggested, because of resource limitations, your company can initiate only one new project at this time. Project A is expected to generate $100,000 in returns two years from now, while Project B is expected to generate $110,000 three years from now. If the cost of capital is 15%, which project should you recommend?

    a. Project B because its present value is $172,327
    b. Project A because its present value is $75,614
    c. Project A because its payback period is exactly four years
    d. Project B because its net present value is $72,278

33. Leadership has been portrayed as a relationship with four major variables: the characteristics of the leader; the attitudes, needs, and other personal characteristics of the followers; the characteristics of the organization; and the social, economic, and political milieu. This view is attributable to—

    a. Peter Drucker
    b. Douglas McGregor
    c. Chris Argyris
    d. Rensis Likert

34. One way to evaluate the project schedule performance is to—

    a. Use the project management information system
    b. Determine the percent complete of in-progress schedule activities
    c. Establish a schedule change control system
    d. Determine the total float variance

35. If any of the ingredients or elements of the communications process are defective in any way, clarity of meaning and understanding will be reduced. An example of a communication macro barrier is—

    a. Cultural differences
    b. Perceptions
    c. Message competition
    d. Project jargon and terminology

36. The purpose of using root cause analysis in schedule control is to—

    a. Recommend corrective action
    b. Document requested changes
    c. Provide additional details as to when the schedule baseline should be updated
    d. Update the activity attributes

37. In performing your stakeholder analysis, 90% of your stakeholders indicated that customer satisfaction was their major expectation. As a result, you should—

    a. Be concerned because it entails a high risk
    b. List customer satisfaction as a major constraint in your scope management plan
    c. Explicitly define the process and criteria to accept completed products as part of your change management plan
    d. Document this expectation as part of the product scope description

38. Projects are supposed to succeed, not fail. However, termination is an option to consider when all but which one of the following conditions exist?

    a. The customer's strategy has changed.
    b. There are new stakeholders.
    c. Competition may make the project results obsolete.
    d. The original purposes for the project have changed.

39. In developing the WBS, you first need to identify the deliverables and related resources required to produce those deliverables. This means that you should analyze the—

    a. WBS template that you will follow
    b. Scope management plan
    c. Organizational structure and available resources
    d. Detailed project scope statement

40. The reason that the schedule performance index (SPI) is shown as a ratio is to—

    a. Enable a detailed analysis of the schedule regardless of the value of the schedule variance
    b. Distinguish between critical path and noncritical path work packages
    c. Provide the ability to show performance for a specified time period for trend analysis
    d. Measure the actual time to complete the project

41. One of the reasons why it is challenging to work on a virtual team is that e-mail is the primary form of communications. However, words alone typically comprise what percent of the total impact of any message?

    a. 7%
    b. 15%
    c. 38%
    d. 55%

42. Assume that your actual costs are $800; your planned value is $1,200; and your earned value is $1,000. Based on these data, what can be determined regarding your schedule variance?

    a. At +$200, the situation is favorable as physical progress is being accomplished ahead of your plan.
    b. At -$200, the physical progress is being accomplished at a slower rate than is planned, indicating an unfavorable situation.
    c. At +400, the situation is favorable as physical progress is being accomplished at a lower cost than was forecasted.
    d. At -$200, you have a behind-schedule condition, and your critical path has slipped.

43. The CPI on your project is .84. This means that you should—

    a. Place emphasis on improving the timeliness of the physical progress
    b. Reassess the life-cycle costs of your product, including the length of the life-cycle phase
    c. Recognize that your original estimates were fundamentally flawed and your project is in an atypical situation
    d. Place emphasis on improving the productivity by which work was being performed

44. The internal rate of return is the discount rate where NPV = 0. This means that it is the discount rate—

    a. Where the discounted cash flows are greater than the initial investment
    b. That shows whether the sum of the net present values of all estimated cash flows over the life of the project is positive
    c. That shows whether the present value of inflows is greater than the present value of outflows
    d. Where the present value of the cash inflows exactly equals the initial investment

45. Research has shown that there are seven major cultural elements that affect projects. In terms of the impact on the project, the cultural element that determines technical and personnel constraints is—

    a. Social organization
    b. Material culture
    c. Political life
    d. Language

46. If a negotiator is away from the known and familiar and is faced with differing customs and ways of doing things, the result may be—

    a. Culture shock
    b. Ethnocentrism
    c. High probability of project failure
    d. Duplicity

47. A challenge of earned value management is predicting percent complete. The simplest formula to use to calculate EV is—

    a. 0/100 rule
    b. 50/50 rule
    c. (Percent complete)(budget at completion)
    d. Milestone method

48. As you prepare the WBS, you subdivide each of the deliverables into fundamental components. Each component then should be defined and assigned to a specific organizational unit, resulting in—

    a. A product breakdown structure
    b. An organizational breakdown structure
    c. A project team directory
    d. A project team organizational chart

49. In project communications, the first step in a written communication is to—

    a. Analyze the facts and assumptions that have a bearing on the purpose of the message
    b. Collect needed materials
    c. Develop a logical sequence of the topics to be addressed
    d. Establish the basic purpose of the message

50. Assume that on your project, you are using earned value management. Your project is one that has extremely long work packages. Therefore, the method you should use to calculate EV is—

    a. 0/100 rule
    b. Milestone method
    c. Equivalent effort
    d. Apportioned effort

51. Motivation is dynamic and complex. The statement, "Motivation is an intrinsic phenomenon. Extrinsic satisfaction only leads to movements, not motivation" is attributed to which of the leading theories of motivation?

    a. Maslow's Hierarchy of Needs Theory
    b. Herzberg's Motivator-Hygiene Theory
    c. Morse and Lorsch's Contingency Theory
    d. McGregor's Theory X/Theory Y

52. Review the WBS. It is an example of a WBS organized by—

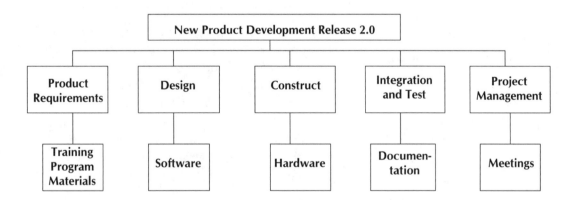

    a. Deliverables
    b. Organizations
    c. Phases
    d. Subprojects

53. During postnegotiation analysis, a negotiation agreement is prepared in the form of a—

    a. Purchase order
    b. Bill of lading
    c. Contract or memorandum of understanding
    d. Revised SOW

54. The WBS shown below indicates that—

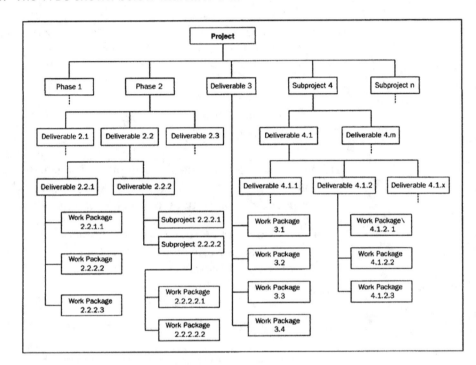

    a. Each component has the same number of managerial levels
    b. The number of levels for each component need not be the same
    c. The lowest level of the WBS is the specific task or activity
    d. The WBS is inappropriately designed as the second level contains phases, deliverables, and subprojects

55. Which of the following theorists stated that people generally are motivated according to the strength of their desire either to achieve high levels of performance or to exceed in competitive situations?

    a. David McGregor
    b. David McClelland
    c. Victor Vroom
    d. B.F. Skinner

56. Your project sponsor has asked you, "What do we now expect the total job to cost?" Given that you are using earned value, you should calculate the—

   a. To complete performance index
   b. Estimate to complete
   c. Estimate at completion
   d. Budget at completion

57. Consider the data in this table:

| Activity | % Complete | PV | EV | AC |
|----------|-----------|-------|-------|-------|
| A | 100 | 2,000 | 2,000 | 2,200 |
| B | 50 | 1,000 | 500 | 700 |
| C | 0 | 1,000 | 0 | 0 |

   Assume that your project consists only of these three activities. Your estimate at completion is $4,400.00. This means you are calculating your EAC by using which of the following formulas?

   a. EAC = AC/EV x BAC
   b. EAC = AC/EV x [work completed and in progress] + [actual (or revised) cost of work packages that have not started]
   c. EAC = [Actual to date] + [all remaining work to be done at the planned cost including remaining work in progress]
   d. EAC = % complete x BAC

58. A capital budgeting method that is often mistaken as the reciprocal of the payback period is the—

   a. Average rate of return
   b. Internal rate of return
   c. Discounted cash flow
   d. Profitability index

59. Certain types of communications styles are more effective in different phases of the project life cycle. For example, during the closing phase of the project, ideally, the project manager should use a(n)—

   a. Abstract/sequential style
   b. Concrete/random style
   c. Concrete/sequential style
   d. Abstract/random

60. Work packages are natural subdivisions of—

   a. Level one elements of the WBS
   b. Activities
   c. Objective indicators
   d. Cost accounts

61. If a team member, when facing schedule delays and cost overruns, develops several alternatives for completing the project successfully on schedule and within budget and asks questions such as Can we do it? If we do it what are the consequences? and Is it really worth the effort involved? he or she is primarily motivated by the—

    a. Contingency Theory
    b. Expectancy Theory
    c. Reinforcement Theory
    d. Equity Theory

62. In the decomposition process, identification codes should be developed and assigned to the WBS components. This is done—

    a. As soon as the WBS is baselined
    b. Prior to verification that the degree of decomposition of the work is necessary and sufficient
    c. Before the cost or control accounts have been determined
    d. Immediately after the deliverables and related work have been identified

63. You have calculated the estimate to complete based on a new estimate of the remaining work. To ensure that this completion estimate is more accurate and comprehensive than the original estimate, you should—

    a. Make sure it is an independent, noncalculated estimate for the remaining work that considers resource performance or productivity
    b. Have the estimate prepared by the project team and calculated based on the fact that similar variances are not expected in the future
    c. Use the BAC, actual cost ($AC^c$) to date, and the cumulative CPI ($CPI^c$)
    d. Realize that while you have had some variances to date, these are atypical and are not expected in the future

64. The scope baseline on the project consists of all but which of the following?

    a. WBS dictionary
    b. WBS
    c. Scope statement
    d. Scope management plan

65. Research has shown that during the execution phase of the project, the majority of conflicts involve—

    a. Personalities
    b. Project priorities
    c. Cost
    d. Schedule

66. A planning package is—

    a. An input to the activity definition process
    b. A management control point that is used as a basis for planning for work that has detailed schedule activities
    c. A WBS component below the control account but above the work package
    d. A hammock activity

67. Performance review meetings typically are used in conjunction with all but which one of the following?

    a. Variance analysis
    b. Earned value technique
    c. Project management software
    d. Trend analysis

68. One output of the cost control process is performance measurements. This is where—

    a. Modifications are made to the cost information used to manage the project
    b. The project team needs to prepare a change request and process it through the Integrated change control process
    c. A budget update is required and communicated to all stakeholders
    d. The calculated CV, SV, CPI, and SPI values for WBS components are documented and communicated to stakeholders

69. One work package on your project involves writing and editing technical documentation. Assume that you can write the text in four days and edit the text in four days. However, although editing can begin two days after the writing begins, no editorial resources are available. The latest the editor can start and still finish the project on time is Day 4. What precedence relationship is involved with these two tasks, and what is the latest day in which the documentation can be completed?

    a. Finish to start, 8 days
    b. Start to start, 6 days
    c. Start to finish, 14 days
    d. Finish to finish, 8 days

70. A network scheduling model that uses logical nodes and directed arcs that may represent time, cost, and reliability is—

    a. PERT
    b. Critical chain
    c. AOA
    d. GERT

Use the chart below to answer questions 71 and 72.

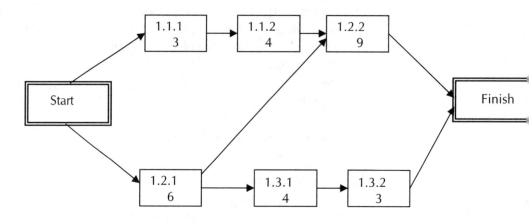

71. Which tasks have total float?

    a. 1.2.1 and 1.3.2
    b. 1.2.1, 1.3.1, 1.3.2
    c. 1.1.1, 1.1.2, 1.2.2
    d. 1.2.1 and 1.2.2

72. Which task has free float?

    a. 1.3.2
    b. 1.2.2
    c. 1.2.1
    d. 1.1.1

73. Project execution must be compared and deviations must be measured for management control according to the—

    a. Scope baseline
    b. Performance measurement baseline (PMB)
    c. Schedule baseline
    d. Cost baseline

74. In which of the following methods of resolving conflict will the conflict typically reappear again in another form?

    a. Smoothing
    b. Compromising
    c. Collaborating
    d. Confronting

75. You are a goal-oriented project manager who is more interested in work accomplishment than relationship building. This indicates that you tend to resolve conflicts primarily through the use of—

    a. Smoothing
    b. Compromising
    c. Collaborating
    d. Forcing

76. During the closing phase of the project, the top-ranked source of conflict is—

    a. Schedule
    b. Administrative procedures
    c. Cost
    d. Human resources

77. The nature of project work is such that it inevitably causes stress. Project managers thus need to learn how to cope with and manage stress and understand what stress is and why it is created. Project managers need to note that it can be a positive experience depending on how people perceive stress and should work to mentor team members accordingly. As you strive to become more aware of stress, which one of the following is not considered a stress-creating factor that is related to the project environment?

    a. Role ambiguity
    b. Corporate politics
    c. Career development
    d. Selection of team members

78. The hurdle rate is used in calculating—

    a. Life-cycle costs
    b. The average rate of return
    c. Discounted cash flow
    d. Payback period

79. Your project sponsor wants to know whether process variables are within acceptable limits. To answer this question, you should—

    a. Conduct a process analysis
    b. Conduct a root cause analysis
    c. Use a control chart
    d. Use a run chart

80. A conflict resolution approach that is not considered to be very effective when more than a few players are involved and their viewpoints are mutually exclusive is—

    a. Forcing
    b. Avoiding
    c. Compromising
    d. Collaborating

81. Assume that you want to identify the cause of problems in a process by the shape and width of the distribution of the process variables. You should use a—

    a. Histogram
    b. Pareto chart
    c. Scatter diagram
    d. Trend analysis

82. Which of the following can be used to plan for conflict in your project?

    a. Company-wide conflict resolution policies
    b. Linear responsibility charts
    c. Hierarchical referral
    d. Conflict is often spontaneous and therefore cannot be planned.

83. If you wish to use rank ordering to guide corrective actions on your project, you should use a(n):

    a. Cause-and-effect diagram
    b. Pareto chart
    c. Scatter diagram
    d. Inspection

84. Assume that on your project you want to know how many activities in the previous month were completed with significant variances. You should use a(n)—

    a. Control chart
    b. Inspection
    c. Scatter diagram
    d. Run chart

85. You have a conflict on your team but have enough time to resolve it, and you want to maintain future relationships. Thankfully, there is mutual trust, respect, and confidence among the parties involved. You decide to use confronting to resolve this conflict. In using this approach, your first step should be to—

    a. Separate people from the problem
    b. Acknowledge that conflict exists
    c. Establish ground rules
    d. Explore alternatives

86. All the following are true statements concerning scope verification and quality control except—

    a. The processes can be performed in parallel
    b. Both processes use inspection as a tool and technique
    c. Scope verification is concerned with acceptance of deliverables, while quality control is concerned with meeting quality requirements for the deliverables
    d. Scope verification typically precedes quality control

87. The key to successfully managing an international project is to build an effective project team in spite of different cultural backgrounds. This is accomplished by—

    a. Recognizing that people are different
    b. Aligning the personal inputs of different project participants
    c. Establishing the project culture during the executing stage of the project
    d. Identifying basic cultural characteristics and selecting one to follow

88. Assume you are evaluating two projects and have been asked by your management to determine the return on sales. Project A has projected revenues of $3.5 million; the total costs for this project are $3.3 million. Project B has projected revenues of $105 million; the costs are estimated to be $98 million. Based on the return on sales, what can you conclude about these two projects?

    a. Project B has a 7.1 ROS, which is higher than that of Project A.
    b. Project A has a 6.1 ROS, which is more favorable than that of Project B.
    c. Project B has a 9.3 ROS, which is more favorable than that of Project A.
    d. Project A has a 5.7 ROS, which is more favorable than that of Project B.

89. You are trying to minimize conflict with your project team members. In this situation, a tactic to follow is to—

    a. Establish a cooperative climate
    b. Conduct regular project status meetings
    c. Clarify your expectations
    d. Avoid giving surprises

90. There are three uses and types of Pareto analysis. If you wish to provide a measure of significance to factors that at first may not appear to be significant at all, you should use a—

    a. Basic Pareto analysis
    b. Comparative Pareto analysis
    c. Weighted Pareto analysis
    d. Trend Pareto analysis

91. You have decided to use a fishbone diagram to identify the relationship between an effect and its causes. To begin, you should first—

    a. Select an interdisciplinary team who has used the technique before to help brainstorm the problem
    b. Determine the major categories of defects
    c. Set up a process analysis using HIPO charts
    d. Identify the problem

92. All but which one of the following is true about the grassroots estimate?

    a. It has an accuracy rate of from -%5 to +10%.
    b. It is also called an engineering estimate.
    c. It is used primarily for Level 1 of the WBS.
    d. It may take months to prepare.

93. In order to develop a detailed project estimate, one approach is to consider the direct, indirect, fixed, variable, and semi-variable costs that are involved. Of the following, which one is an example of an indirect cost?

    a. Office power consumption
    b. Renting a construction crane for one-time project use
    c. A project team member's daily salary
    d. Material costs

94. Although there is no single best method for dealing with conflict, research has shown that the least effective style is—

    a. Competing
    b. Smoothing
    c. Forcing
    d. Withdrawal

95. The key management skills required during the adjourning stage of team development include all but which one of the following?

    a. Evaluating
    b. Reviewing
    c. Celebrating
    d. Improving

96. Assume that your project in the food service industry involves the need for the presence of the required food label as specified by the Food and Drug Administration. In this situation, you plan to use control charts as a quality control tool, so you should prepare a(n)—

    a. Variables chart
    b. Attribute chart
    c. Trend chart
    d. Run chart

97. In addition to the WBS, the resource breakdown structure (RBS) also should be prepared to show the type of resources to be used on the project. The RBS is—

    a. An output of human resource planning
    b. A tool and technique for schedule development
    c. An output of activity resource estimating
    d. A tool and technique for activity resource planning

98. In negotiating, knowing your points and issues and addressing them with confidence and assertiveness is known as—

    a. Attitudinal structuring
    b. Firm competition
    c. Soft competition
    d. Rough bargaining

99. All the following are examples of lessons learned except—

    a. Position descriptions
    b. Ground rules
    c. Recognition events
    d. Project performance appraisals

100. Unfortunately, your project has produced less-than-expected results. To ensure this doesn't happen again, you conducted a thorough lessons-learned session. You did so because—

    a. You considered it to be a good idea
    b. It is a professional obligation of every project manager to do so
    c. Your organization's project management methodology requires you to do one
    d. It is a best practice used by many organizations

101. Accuracy of estimates can be improved by considering the amount of risk in the original estimates. Assume that on your project, you have decided to use the PERT technique. For one task, your optimistic estimate of its completion is 3 days, your most pessimistic estimate is 9 days, and your most likely estimate is 5 days. If you use PERT, the expected duration of this activity is—

    a. 4.999 days
    b. 5.333 days
    c. 6.54 days
    d. 7.25 days

102. Continuing with the same example, assume that you wish to establish deviations from the mean to provide a range of estimates on task duration. In this example, assume you want to show a 95% standard deviation. What is the range for this estimate, and what type of distribution are you using?

    a. Between 4.3 and 6.3 days with a normal distribution
    b. Between 4.5 and 7.5 days with a beta distribution
    c. Between 3.3 and 7.3 days with a normal distribution
    d. Between 2.5 and 8.5 days with a beta distribution

103. The most effective means for communicating and resolving issues with stakeholders are—

    a. Video conferences
    b. Portals
    c. Face-to-face meetings
    d. E-mail

104. If you decide to follow an open subordination approach to resolving conflict, you are using which style of conflict resolution?

    a. Avoiding
    b. Accommodating
    c. Compromising
    d. Collaborating

105. The purpose of economic value added is to—

    a. Determine the opportunity costs associated with the project
    b. Determine a noontime-dependent measure of profit or return
    c. Assess the net operating profit after taxes
    d. Evaluate the return on capital percent versus the cost of capital percent

106. A watch list of low priority risks is documented in the—

    a. Work performance information
    b. Risk register
    c. Fallback plans
    d. Risk response plan

107. Assume that you are working in an organization that is moving into management by projects. In the past, your R&D organization made technical decisions based entirely on its portion of the plan, without taking into account any decisions made by production. You are managing the transition to management by projects in your company and realize that this silo approach is not acceptable. Therefore, you have decided that the company should implement life-cycle costing. A limitation of this approach is that—

    a. It does not support downstream strategic budgeting
    b. There is a high sensitivity to changing requirements
    c. It cannot influence R&D decision making
    d. It does not provide downstream, resource-impact visibility

108. All of the following are included as a tool and technique used in the close project process except—

    a. Project management methodology
    b. Work performance information
    c. Expert judgment
    d. Project management information system

109. Review the network diagram and the following table.

Letter = Activity

Number = Duration

| | Time Required, Weeks | | Cost $ | | Crashing Cost |
|---|---|---|---|---|---|
| Activity | Normal | Crash | Normal | Crash | Per Week, $ |
| A | 4 | 2 | 10,000 | 14,000 | 2,000 |
| B | 6 | 5 | 30,000 | 42,500 | 12,500 |
| C | 2 | 1 | 8,000 | 9,500 | 1,500 |
| D | 2 | 1 | 12,000 | 18,000 | 6,000 |
| E | 7 | 5 | 40,000 | 52,000 | 6,000 |
| F | 12 | 3 | 20,000 | 29,000 | 3,000 |
| G | 6 | 2 | 5,000 | 30,000 | 6,000 |

Of the various activities, which ones would you crash and in what order?

a. A, C, E, and F
b. A, B, D, and F
c. A, B, E, and F
d. C, A, F, and G

110. All of the following are examples of ways to generate options for mutual gain during negotiations except—

a. Separating inventing from deciding
b. Options broadening
c. Zero-sum game analysis
d. Multiplying options by shuttling between the specific and the general

111. Lessons learned need to be documented to be part of the historical database not only for the project but also for the performing organization. Lessons learned documentation is an output of—

a. The project plan execution process
b. The monitor and control project process
c. The perform quality assurance process
d. The information distribution process

112. Consider a company that sells products to consumers. As one product begins the deterioration and death phases of its life cycle (or the divestment phase of a system), new products or projects must be established. This means that—

    a. The company requires a continuous stream of projects to survive
    b. The company is not at a high level of maturity
    c. The company is in a period of overall decline
    d. The company definitely lacks a balanced portfolio

113. Life-cycle phase definitions are different in different industries. For example, all of the following are terms that could be used in the closing phase of a project except—

    a. Testing and commissioning
    b. Conversion
    c. Implementation
    d. Final audit

114. When developing the project charter, the organization's enterprise environmental factors and systems should be considered. They include all but which one of the following?

    a. Organizational or company culture and structure
    b. Project management information systems
    c. Company work authorization system
    d. Organizational standard processes

115. Effective leadership is one key to successful project management. There are several theories of leadership. One model is Hershey and Blanchard's situational leadership model that describes directive behavior and supportive behavior. Of the following, which one is not a key word for supportive behavior?

    a. Listen
    b. Structure
    c. Praise
    d. Facilitate

116. Successful project management involves both project leadership as well as project management skills. Several different leadership styles are appropriate in different phases of the project life cycle. Assume that you are working on a project, and it is in the execution phase. The leadership style that is most appropriate should consist of a blend of all but which one of the following?

    a. Change master
    b. Decision maker
    c. Team and synergy
    d. Trustworthiness

117. Assume that you are managing a project team. Your team is one in which its members confront issues rather than people, establish procedures collectively, and is team oriented. As the project manager, which of the following represents your team's stage of development and the approach you should use during this time?

    a. Storming; high directive and supportive approach
    b. Norming; high directive and low supportive approach
    c. Norming; high supportive and low directive approach
    d. Performing; low directive and supportive approach

118. As part of your project, you are conducting a major conference. You need to find the most appropriate conference facility. You visit five sites. The most expensive location has said that if you chose them, they will give you free vouchers for your family at one of their resorts. The next lowest-priced site has not offered you any extras; however, the location is fine for your conference. You find yourself in a situation that is an example of—

    a. An inappropriate connection
    b. A conflict of interest
    c. An opportunity to take advantage of a good deal
    d. An illegal action

119. Recognizing the increasing importance of portfolio management to organizations, your training company has decided to offer a new course in project portfolio management to increase its revenues. The project resulted from a—

    a. Customer request
    b. Business need
    c. Market demand
    d. Societal demand

120. Assume that since risk management is relatively new on projects in your company you decide to examine and document the effectiveness of risk responses in dealing with identified risks and their root causes. You should therefore—

    a. Conduct a risk audit
    b. Hold a risk status meeting
    c. Ensure that risk is an agenda item at regularly scheduled staff meetings
    d. Reassess identified risks on a periodic basis

121. The framework of the project can be clarified by documenting—

    a. The project's selection processes
    b. The organization's management responsibilities
    c. The preparation process for the organization's strategic plan
    d. The project manager's authority

122. On your systems development project, you noted during a review that the system had less functionality than planned at the critical design review. This means that in monitoring and controlling project risks, you used which of the following tools and techniques?

    a.  Risk reassessment
    b.  Variance analysis
    c.  Technical performance measurement
    d.  Reserve analysis

123. The work-around you used to deal with a risk that occurred should be documented and included in which of the following processes?

    a.  Performance reporting and monitor and control project work
    b.  Scope verification and quality assurance
    c.  Direct and manage project execution and integrated change control
    d.  Direct and manage project execution and risk monitoring and control

124. Contested changes are requested changes when the buyer and seller cannot agree on compensation for the change. They are also known as all but which one of the following?

    a.  Disputes
    b.  Demands
    c.  Appeals
    d.  Claims

125. A structured review of the seller's progress to deliver project scope and quality within cost and schedule is known as a(n)—

    a.  Buyer-conducted performance review
    b.  Procurement audit
    c.  Inspection
    d.  Status review meeting

126. You require a subject matter expert, Carl, to be available at a certain point on your project. As he is in demand by other project managers, to be sure he is available as needed on your project you decide to schedule his availability in reverse from the project end dates. This reverse resource allocation scheduling approach produces a—

    a.  Critical chain schedule
    b.  Fast-tracked schedule
    c.  Resource-loaded schedule
    d.  Resource-limited schedule

127. Ideally, the project charter is prepared by someone external to the project. In practice, the project management team actually helps to write the charter. Which of the following is a true statement concerning the charter?

    a. Only the project sponsor can issue the charter.
    b. The project manager should be selected before the develop project charter process.
    c. Approval and funding for the project are handled external to the project boundaries.
    d. The product scope description is an output of this process.

128. Assume that you were the first person in your company to be PMP® certified and also that you earned a doctorate in project management. People throughout the organization admired your achievements. Based on your success in managing projects, your company now has adopted a management-by-projects philosophy. You have been appointed head of your company's project management office to lead the organization as it transitions to this new way of working. So far, people seem to willingly comply with your demands and requests. In this situation, you are using which type of power?

    a. Legitimate
    b. Expert
    c. Contacts
    d. Referent

129. A key member of your project has deep technical skills and many years of experience in the company. Although she is not a manager, people respect her and do what she suggests. Of the following types of power, which one does she have?

    a. Legitimate
    b. Reward
    c. Referent
    d. Expert

130. Throughout the duration of a project, the product scope description is—

    a. Subject to frequent modifications by change requests
    b. Progressively elaborated
    c. Part of the organizational corporate knowledge base
    d. Frequently altered through change requests

131. You are managing a new product development project for a leading pharmaceutical company. Even though he had a nondisclosure agreement in place for two years, your brother recently left a rival firm and just told you that his company had to abandon a similar product development project, as it lacked the ability to obtain a key compound. You realize that your company will need this compound to proceed further in its development initiatives. You also realize that, if you are successful in the development of this new product in a timely manner, and if it then is approved quickly by the Food and Drug Administration, then you will be assured of a vice president position in your firm. It is very important to you to be successful on this project. You should therefore—

    a. Use your brother's information and obtain the needed compound immediately
    b. Recognize that this is an example of an inappropriate connection and disclose it immediately to your company's executive management
    c. Suggest that your company hire your brother so that he can make this critical information known to everyone on the team
    d. Realize that while your company does have a code of ethics that it can be interpreted broadly and has no affect on your actual behavior

132. As a project manager, not only must you be a leader, but you also must be responsible for the management, administrative, and technical aspects of the project. Of the following, which one is not representative of skills needed for project leadership/interpersonal relations?

    a. Sensitivity to personal goals, professional needs, and growth opportunities
    b. Understanding of the organization
    c. Ability to achieve higher visibility and priority
    d. Understanding of policies, operating procedures, and regulations of external stakeholder organizations

133. To derive the critical chain solution, the first step in the process is to—

    a. Identify the longest chain of dependent events where the dependency is either task or resource related
    b. Protect projects from task time variations by using buffers
    c. Identify the system's constraints
    d. Add duration buffers to nonwork schedule activities

134. Functional managers play a vital role in ensuring project success. Since most projects operate in a matrix environment, there is shared authority between project managers and functional managers. Functional managers tend to focus on—

    a. Who will do the task
    b. Why the project manager needs resources
    c. How much time and money is available for the task
    d. Why will the task be done

135. An example of information that is part of the organizational corporate knowledge base is—

    a. Standardized cost estimating data
    b. Industry risk study information
    c. Project management information systems
    d. Project files

136. Today, the cause of why projects are not completed on time and within cost and are terminated early is due to—

    a. Contractual issues
    b. Complexity of the project
    c. An increase in the allocated time
    d. Behavioral-oriented reasons

137. Vendor bid analysis is—

    a. A cost estimating tool and technique used to examine the price of individual deliverables when a project is won under competitive processes
    b. A plan purchases and acquisitions tool and technique used to determine the most appropriate type of contract to award given the results of the make-or-buy analysis
    c. A select sellers technique used in evaluating individual proposals
    d. A process used to evaluate a vendor's past performance on contracts of a similar nature

138. It often is advantageous to appoint a termination manager in the closing phase of the project and release the project manager so that he or she is available to work on another project. If this is the case, the termination manager should focus attention on all but which one of the following?

    a. Ensuring that documentation is complete
    b. Ascertaining any product support requirements
    c. Receiving formal acceptance of the project from the client
    d. Preparing personnel performance evaluations

139. During the stages of team development, your team is in which stage when there is problem solving and interdependence along with achievement and synergy?

    a. Storming
    b. Forming
    c. Norming
    d. Performing

140. Assume that your company has a cost-plus-fixed-fee contract. The contract value is $110,000, which consists of $100,000 of estimated costs with a 10% fixed fee. Assume that your company completes the work but only incurs $80,000 in actual cost. What is the total cost to the project?

    a. $80,000
    b. $90,000
    c. $100,000
    d. $125,000

141. Assume that your company is working under a fixed-price-incentive contract. It has a target cost of $100,000, a target profit of 10%, a price ceiling of $120,000, and a share formula of 80/20. Assume that your company completes all of the work but has actual costs of $110,000. What is the final value of this procurement?

    a. $120,000
    b. $132,000
    c. $118,000
    d. $110,000

142. Behavior roles of team members influence the team's process, behavior, and effectiveness. An example of a task-oriented role to perform is that of a(n)—

    a. Harmonizer
    b. Initiator
    c. Devil's advocate
    d. Group observer

143. You are managing a project in which your team members all work in the same geographic location and have worked together previously on many projects. Everyone is aware of the various strengths and weaknesses of the individual team members and their key areas of expertise. As a result—

    a. A kickoff meeting is recommended
    b. Team-building activities will not be needed on your project
    c. You should expect minimal conflicts and changes to occur
    d. Rewards and recognition will be handled smoothly throughout the project

144. The project management information system should first be used on a project during which of the following processes?

    a. Scope planning
    b. Develop project management plan
    c. Develop project charter
    d. Scope definition

145. Your organization has decided to use project management for all of its endeavors. It has established a Center of Excellence for Project Management to support the movement into management by projects and has appointed you as its director. Since you work in a matrix environment, which of the following types of communications is the most essential for success?

    a. Upward
    b. Lateral
    c. Downward
    d. Diagonal

146. Team building should be ongoing throughout the project life cycle. However, it is hard to maintain momentum and morale, especially on large, complex projects that span several years. One guideline to follow to promote team building is to—

    a. Consider every meeting a team meeting, not the project manager's meeting
    b. Conduct team building at specific times during the project through off-site meetings
    c. Engage the services of a full-time facilitator before any team-building initiatives are conducted
    d. Develop the project schedule using the services of a project control officer and then issue it immediately to the team

147. The preliminary project scope statement addresses and documents all but which one of the following?

    a. Characteristics and boundaries of the project
    b. Methods of acceptance
    c. Methods of scope control
    d. Project management methodology (PMM)

148. A team-building approach that facilitates concurrent engineering is—

    a. Matrix management
    b. Fast tracking
    c. Tight matrix
    d. Task force

149. Of the following, which one is not a cost estimating tool and technique?

    a.  Reserve analysis
    b.  Cost aggregation
    c.  Project management software
    d.  Cost of quality

150. You have been assigned as the project manager for a major project in your company where the customer and key supplier are located in another country.  Recently, you traveled to this country, and at the conclusion of a critical design review meeting, which was highly successful, your customer's point of contact gave you an upgrade to a first-class ticket for your trip home since it is a 17-hour flight.  Although your company's code of ethics states that gifts cannot be accepted, you know it is common practice in this country to give and to accept gifts, and you do not wish to offend your customer.  Furthermore, your supplier also was rewarded for her company's outstanding performance to date at this meeting, and your customer's representative gave her an envelope that contained some extra cash.  In this situation—

    a.  You can accept the upgrade to first class since it is a common practice to give and accept gifts in this country
    b.  It is acceptable for the supplier to accept the gift since she also lives in the same country
    c.  You and your supplier should decline the gifts since gifts are not permitted by your organization's code of ethics, and your company is the prime contractor
    d.  You should explain to the customer that your company does not allow you to accept the gift, but you will do so this one time as you are building a relationship, but cannot accept gifts in the future

151. A project final report is a recommended best practice.  While this report can be organized in a variety of ways, for each item that is covered in the report—

    a.  A recommendation for changing current practice should be made and defended
    b.  The focus should be solely on items that did not work well on the project
    c.  Individuals who did not contribute successfully as team members should be noted
    d.  An earned value discussion is warranted

152. On large contracts, the contract administrator typically has a need to resolve ambiguity in the clauses that govern work performance and other issues. Assume that on your contract there is an order of precedence clause. This means that—

   a. Inconsistencies in the solicitation of the contract shall be resolved in a given order of procedure
   b. An alternative dispute resolution process is in place that shall be followed to resolve any conflicts
   c. Any ambiguities are generally interpreted against the party who drafted the document
   d. Undefinitized contractual actions cannot be authorized

153. A member of PMI® is obligated to follow the association's Member Code of Ethics, the purpose of which is to—

   a. Earn and maintain the confidence of team members, colleagues, employees, employers, customers/clients, the public, and the global community
   b. Describe the obligations and expectations associated with membership in the Project Management Institute
   c. Set forth one's professional obligations and also one's obligations to PMI®
   d. Describe responsibilities to the profession, to customers, and the public, along with administration of the Code of Conduct for all those who are certified as project management professionals

154. Since your project spans several years and includes a number of organizations in a joint venture to develop a new product using unproven technology, your organization has decided to hold phase-end reviews. During subsequent phases of this multiphase project, this means that the develop project charter process—

   a. Authorizes each project phase
   b. Does not need further review once it is approved and issued
   c. Is only relevant to authorize the project initially
   d. Is complete once the project manager has been assigned

155. The preliminary project scope statement is developed from information provided by the—

   a. Project sponsor
   b. Project manager
   c. Project team members
   d. End user

156. A number of different decision-making styles can be used in a team environment. When quality and acceptance are both important, which of the following styles should be used?

   a. Command
   b. Consultation
   c. Consensus
   d. Coin flip

157. A management contingency reserve is—

   a. A known unknown
   b. Used for planned, but potentially required, changes to project scope and cost
   c. Not part of the project cost baseline but included in the project budget
   d. Used at the discretion of the project manager and is part of the project scope and cost baseline

158. You have been studying for the PMP® certification exam for some time and are scheduled to take the exam in one month. You further plan to attend a boot camp the week before the exam. You feel you definitely will pass because of your extensive preparations. Your company is bidding on a government contract, which has required that the project manager must be PMP® certified. You know the technical area and the prospective client well and really want to manage this project. Today, your company learned that it is on the "short list" of possible contractors. The government has asked for the resume of the person who will be your company's project manager. Your manager wants to give them your name as the contract will not be awarded, at the earliest, until two weeks after you take the exam, and because he knows you want the job. You should tell your manager—

   a. To submit your resume even though you do not have your certification because you are sure you will pass the exam
   b. To submit your resume now; if for some reason you do not pass the exam, your manager can then substitute someone who is PMP® certified
   c. That while you want to manage this project, your resume cannot be submitted at this time
   d. That he can submit your resume because you are not yet a member of PMI® so you have no conflicts at this time

159. Some organizations supplement the project charter with a—

   a. List of project constraints
   b. Contract or agreement between the project and line organizations
   c. Project statement of work
   d. Description of stakeholder influences

160. There are a number of different methods that can be used to classify the costs of quality. Your organization has decided to classify them in terms of prevention costs, appraisal costs, internal failure costs, and external failure costs. Of the following types of cost, attention to which one will provide the greatest overall savings?

    a. External failure costs
    b. Internal failure costs
    c. Appraisal costs
    d. Prevention costs

161. Which of the following quality "gurus" noted that when the per-unit costs for prevention and appraisal were less expensive than the costs of nonconformance, resources should be assigned to prevention and appraisal; however, when these costs begin to increase the per unit cost of quality, then a policy should be to maintain quality?

    a. Deming
    b. Shewhart
    c. Juran
    d. Taguchi

162. Which of the following is a tool and technique that is a statistical framework that can be used to systematically change all of the variables rather than changing them one at a time in order to provide optimal conditions for the product or process?

    a. Influence diagrams
    b. Control charts
    c. Defect repair review
    d. Design of experiments

163. During contract negotiations on large contracts, the negotiation process focuses on many key issues, with price being one of them. Separate negotiations can be made on price, quantity, quality, and timing, which can significantly lengthen the process. The negotiation process can be shortened, however, provided that—

    a. Planning is done for negotiations
    b. Expertise of the project management staff in the procurement process is at a high level
    c. A request for proposal is used rather than a request for quotation
    d. There is integrity in the relationship and prior history with the vendor

164. Contract negotiations are not required when—

    a. A company uses sealed bids
    b. There is a sole source procurement
    c. A competitive range is established
    d. A two-step process is used

165. It is critical during the proposal preparation stage that—

    a. The negotiation strategy is determined
    b. A change management strategy is developed
    c. Roles and responsibilities for the ultimate project are determined
    d. Contract terms and conditions are reviewed before the proposal is submitted to the client

166. Assume that you were recently elected to be on the board of your local PMI® chapter. You are friends with the vice president of membership for the chapter, Kim, as you both worked for the same manufacturing company in project management. Kim, a PMP®, left the manufacturing company six months ago and now works for a project management training and consulting company in your city. Today at work, another member of the local chapter showed you some unsolicited mail she had received from Kim's company concerning their services. She was surprised this company had her name and address. In this situation, you should—

    a. Tell her you have no idea how Kim's company received her name and address and take no further action.
    b. Confront Kim and ask her whether she provided her management with the local chapter's membership list.
    c. Report Kim to PMI® because this is obviously a conflict of interest.
    d. Convene a meeting of the PMI® Board to discuss this potential conflict of interest with them before taking further action.

167. Similar in concept to a responsibility matrix, a practical approach that helps design a project organization and that assists people in understanding how they relate to the organizational work package is the—

    a. Organizational breakdown structure
    b. Linear responsibility chart
    c. Resource breakdown structure
    d. Traditional organizational chart

168. Your role in the project includes helping to resolve problems; making recommendations regarding priorities; accelerating activities to meet the target schedule; promoting communications among project team members; and helping management monitor the project's progress on a regular basis. Most of the people working on your project are scientists or technical experts. You are working in which of the following types of organizational structures?

    a. Task force
    b. Balanced matrix
    c. Project expeditor
    d. Project coordinator

169. In order for a matrix organizational approach to be successful, the two-boss situation should be resolved. To overcome the two-boss problem, it is important to—

    a. Have the project manager and the functional manager work together to complete performance evaluations
    b. Prepare a responsibility chart to define responsibilities
    c. Guarantee a balance of power between the functional manager and the project manager
    d. Promote interface relationship management

170. Virtual teams are increasing in use especially with the availability of electronic communications. They are—

    a. A tool and technique in the acquire project team process
    b. An input to the communications planning process
    c. An input to the information distribution process
    d. A tool and technique in the human resource planning process

171. You are working on a project that management has decided to terminate early because the product was rendered obsolete by the introduction of new technology by a competitor. You have awarded a contract for part of the project that will be terminated, and fortunately have a clause that enables you to terminate it for convenience at any time. This means that—

    a. Your contractual obligations are complete once you issue the termination for convenience
    b. You may need to compensate the seller for seller preparations and for any completed or accepted work
    c. You need to compensate the seller only for accepted work that was completed prior to the termination order
    d. Specific rights and responsibilities are determined once the termination order is issued

172. Assume that you are managing a large project in your organization. You realize that since you will be awarding several major subcontracts, your project team requires training in contract administration. You decided that a one-week class in contract administration would be needed when you analyzed your project requirements and assessed the expertise of your team members. This training should—

    a. Commence as scheduled as stated in the staffing management plan
    b. Commence as scheduled as stated as part of the procurement management plan
    c. Be scheduled if necessary after performance assessments are prepared and each team member has had an opportunity to serve in the contract administrator role
    d. Commence as scheduled as stated in the team development plan

173. All of the following are outputs to the acquire project team process except—

    a. Resource availability
    b. Project staff assignments
    c. Updates to organizational process assets
    d. Updates to the staffing management plan

174. Assume that you are working on a project with 15 stakeholders. The number of communications channels on this project is—

    a. 15
    b. 105
    c. 210
    d. 225

175. In the initial stage of the project life cycle, the project's technical objectives are apt to be understood only in a general sense. A major component of project conflict during this stage of the project is—

    a. Concerns over priorities and procedures
    b. Concerns about technical issues
    c. Schedules
    d. Confusion of establishing a project in the matrix management environment

176. You are part of a group of project managers in your company who meets one hour after work each day to study for the PMP® exam. You are scheduled to take the exam in two weeks. Today, one of your colleagues told you he passed the exam that morning. He then proceeded to tell you the key earned value questions that were on the exam. You had really been struggling with earned value because you do not use earned value reporting in your company. Which one of the following is the most appropriate action you should take?

    a. You should continue your efforts to study for this exam
    b. Although you realize that he should not have told you these specific questions, you realize it probably is OK since there are several different versions of the exam, and the version you will take probably will be different
    c. You need to tell your colleague that he has violated the PMP® Code of Professional Conduct and you now must report him to PMI®
    d. Tell your friend not to tell anyone that he has shared this information with you and not to tell anyone any information about the exam

177. One way to decrease possible misunderstandings among team members and increase productivity is to—

    a. Use a war room
    b. Conduct scheduled team-building activities
    c. Establish a process to document all issues that are raised
    d. Establish ground rules

178. Although the project charter serves to state the project manager's authority and responsibility on the project, the project manager further requires which type of power in order to be an effective leader?

    a. Expert
    b. Legitimate
    c. Position
    e. Referent

179. At the time the risk register is first prepared, it should contain all but which one of the following?

    a. Root causes of risk
    b. Updated risk categories
    c. List of risks requiring near-term responses
    d. List of potential responses

180. All of the following indicators are used to evaluate a team's effectiveness except—

    a. Reduced staff turnover rate
    b. Increased staff availability
    c. Improvements in skills so a person can perform assigned activities more effectively
    d. Improvements in competencies and sentiments so the team can perform better as a group

181. Of the following, which one is not true concerning a contract?

    a. It is a legal relationship subject to remedy in the courts.
    b. It can take the form of a complex document or a simple purchase order.
    c. It is a mutually binding legal relationship that obligates the seller to provide specific products, services, or results and obligates the buyer to pay the seller.
    d. It includes a specific contract management plan.

182. The lessons learned process is a tool and technique used in—

    a. The close project process
    b. The project plan development process
    c. The information distribution process
    d. The communications planning process

183. Assume that you are trying to determine whether or not to conduct 100% final system tests of 500 ground-based radar units at the factory. The historical radar field failure rate is 4%; the cost to test each unit in the factory is $10,000; the cost to reassemble each passed unit after the factory test is $2,000; the cost to repair and reassemble each failed unit after factory test is $23,000; and the cost to repair and reinstall each failed unit in the field is $350,000. Using decision tree analysis, what is the expected value should you decide to conduct these tests?

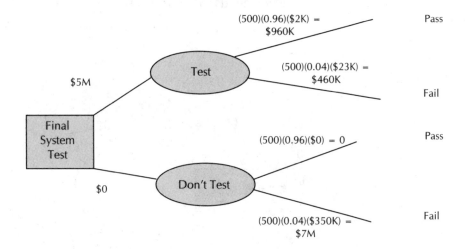

    a. $5.5 million
    b. $5.96 million
    c. $6.42 million
    d. $7 million

184. To improve the quality of procurement contracts on your project or on other projects in your organization, you should—

    a. Conduct a procurement audit
    b. Establish a records management system
    c. Use the quality audit in your quality assurance process
    d. Use lessons learned documentation

185. Typically, the seller receives formal written notice that the contract has been completed by the—

    a. Project manager
    b. Authorized contracts administrator
    c. Member of the project management team responsible for daily contract administration
    d. Purchasing Department head

186. Assume that you are trying to determine which airline to take on an upcoming trip for a face-to-face team meeting of your virtual project team. The ticket price on Airline A is $750, while the ticket price to take Airline B is $1,000. If you arrive on time, there are no extra costs. If you arrive late, you incur a per diem charge of $250.00 as well as the cost of your time, at a daily rate of $800/day. Airline A has an on-time arrival record of 60%; Airline B's arrival record is 90%. Which approach is financially advantageous for your project?

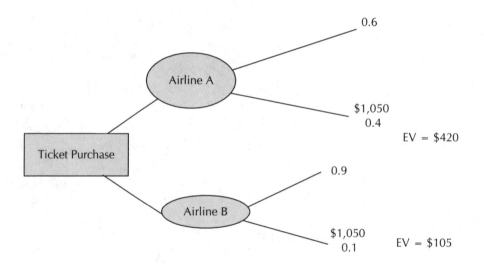

    a. Airline A at $750.00
    b. Airline A at $1,170.00
    c. Airline B at $105.00
    d. Airline B at $1,105.00

187. The most common active risk acceptance strategy is to—

    a. Transfer the risk through a cost-plus contract
    b. Establish a management reserve
    c. Establish a contingency reserve
    d. Adopt a more conservative approach should the risk occur

188. In the close project process, closure includes the development of the index of project records and the location of project documentation using the—

    a. Project management information system
    b. Records management system
    c. Work authorization system
    d. Configuration management system

189. All of the following can be used in lieu of the term "bidders conferences" except—

    a. Contractor conferences
    b. Prebid conferences
    c. Vendor conferences
    d. Project review meetings

190. Your company is in the project management training business. In addition, the company publishes several exam study aids for the PMP® and CAPM™ exam. You are fairly new to the organization and lack the experience to actually qualify to take the PMP®, but you had the required experience for the CAPM™ and took and passed it three months ago. Today, you were contacted by someone at PMI® headquarters to see if you would like to be part of a CAPM™ Exam item writing session. You should—

    a. Accept the invitation so you can contribute to the profession
    b. Ask your supervisor if it is acceptable to be on this committee
    c. Decline the invitation since it is a conflict of interest
    d. Decline the invitation because you are not PMP® certified

191. Your contractor is working under a fixed-price-incentive-fee contract that has a point of assumption. In this contract, there is a price ceiling of $11,500, which is the maximum price the contractor will be paid. The sharing ratio is 70/30, with the contractor's share at 30% and the buyer's share at 70%. The target cost is $10,000; the target profit is $850, and the target price is $10,850. For example, if the contractor performs the work for $9,000, the contractor will receive a profit of $1,150, the target profit of $850 plus $300 for 30% of the underrun. What is the point of total assumption?

    a. $10,150
    b. $10,928
    c. $11,500
    d. $11,728

192. The administrative closure procedure provides a step-by-step methodology that addresses all but which one of the following actions and activities?

    a. Definition of stakeholder approval requirements for changes and all levels of deliverables
    b. Confirmation that the project has met requirements
    c. Definition of required product verification and administrative closure of contract records
    d. Confirmation that the completion or exit criteria for the project are satisfied

193. During a bidders conference, it is important that—

    a. Only qualified sellers participate
    b. All potential sellers are given equal standing
    c. The evaluation criteria for the proposal is used to determine participation
    d. Responses to questions be provided solely to the prospective seller that asked the question

194. A weighting system can be used for all but which one of the following reasons?

    a. To select a single seller that will be asked to sign a standard contract
    b. To establish a negotiating sequence by ranking all proposals by the weighted evaluation scores that have been assigned
    c. To quantify qualitative data to minimize possible bias
    d. To establish minimum requirements of performance for one or more of the evaluation criteria

195. Which of the following types of contracts has the least risk to the seller?

    a. Firm-fixed price
    b. Cost-plus-fixed fee
    c. Cost-plus-award fee
    d. Fixed-price-incentive fee

196. Expert judgment is helpful in terms of preparing which of the following components of the preliminary project scope statement?

    a. Summary budget
    b. Technical and management details to be included
    c. Summary milestone schedule
    d. Project's business needed

197. One source of relevant information in the select seller process is seller performance evaluation documentation. This is generated in the—

    a. Close contract process
    b. Contract administration process
    c. Request seller responses process
    d. Plan contracting process

198. For complex procurement items, often contract negotiation can be an independent process. An example of an input if such a process is used is—

    a. Open items list
    b. Approved changes
    c. Documented decisions
    d. Expert judgment

199. While many different techniques can be used to rate or score proposals, all will use—

    a. A screening system
    b. A weighting system in conjunction with a screening system
    c. Expert judgment and some form of evaluation criteria
    d. Quality ratings and contractual compliance

200. Your company is preparing a proposal for project management consulting services for the government. You are a member of the proposal writing team and are PMP® certified. Both a technical and a financial proposal must be submitted, but your company realizes that low cost will win the job, and it needs a win to achieve its profit targets for the year. Although your company has won several government contracts in the past, and has had its rates audited, the chief financial officer has decided that if it uses nonaudited overhead rates, the firm can submit a competitive bid. You learned of this decision today. Your next step should be to—

    a. Continue to prepare your part of the proposal
    b. Tell your CEO that this action by your company constitutes a violation of the PMP® Code of Professional Conduct in the section titled: "Conflict of Interest Situations and Other Prohibited Professional Conduct"
    c. Tell your CEO that this action by your company constitutes a violation of the PMP® Code of Professional Conduct in the section titled: "Qualifications, Experience, and Performance of Professional Services"
    d. Tell your CEO that this action by your company constitutes a violation of the PMP® Code of Professional Conduct in the section titled: "Candidate/Certificant Practice"

# Answer Sheet

1. a b c d
2. a b c d
3. a b c d
4. a b c d
5. a b c d
6. a b c d
7. a b c d
8. a b c d
9. a b c d
10. a b c d
11. a b c d
12. a b c d
13. a b c d
14. a b c d
15. a b c d
16. a b c d
17. a b c d
18. a b c d
19. a b c d
20. a b c d
21. a b c d
22. a b c d
23. a b c d
24. a b c d
25. a b c d

26. a b c d
27. a b c d
28. a b c d
29. a b c d
30. a b c d
31. a b c d
32. a b c d
33. a b c d
34. a b c d
35. a b c d
36. a b c d
37. a b c d
38. a b c d
39. a b c d
40. a b c d
41. a b c d
42. a b c d
43. a b c d
44. a b c d
45. a b c d
46. a b c d
47. a b c d
48. a b c d
49. a b c d
50. a b c d

| | | | | | | | | |
|---|---|---|---|---|---|---|---|---|
| 51. | a | b | c | d | 76. | a | b | c | d |
| 52. | a | b | c | d | 77. | a | b | c | d |
| 53. | a | b | c | d | 78. | a | b | c | d |
| 54. | a | b | c | d | 79. | a | b | c | d |
| 55. | a | b | c | d | 80. | a | b | c | d |
| 56. | a | b | c | d | 81. | a | b | c | d |
| 57. | a | b | c | d | 82. | a | b | c | d |
| 58. | a | b | c | d | 83. | a | b | c | d |
| 59. | a | b | c | d | 84. | a | b | c | d |
| 60. | a | b | c | d | 85. | a | b | c | d |
| 61. | a | b | c | d | 86. | a | b | c | d |
| 62. | a | b | c | d | 87. | a | b | c | d |
| 63. | a | b | c | d | 88. | a | b | c | d |
| 64. | a | b | c | d | 89. | a | b | c | d |
| 65. | a | b | c | d | 90. | a | b | c | d |
| 66. | a | b | c | d | 91. | a | b | c | d |
| 67. | a | b | c | d | 92. | a | b | c | d |
| 68. | a | b | c | d | 93. | a | b | c | d |
| 69. | a | b | c | d | 94. | a | b | c | d |
| 70. | a | b | c | d | 95. | a | b | c | d |
| 71. | a | b | c | d | 96. | a | b | c | d |
| 72. | a | b | c | d | 97. | a | b | c | d |
| 73. | a | b | c | d | 98. | a | b | c | d |
| 74. | a | b | c | d | 99. | a | b | c | d |
| 75. | a | b | c | d | 100. | a | b | c | d |

101. a b c d    126. a b c d
102. a b c d    127. a b c d
103. a b c d    128. a b c d
104. a b c d    129. a b c d
105. a b c d    130. a b c d
106. a b c d    131. a b c d
107. a b c d    132. a b c d
108. a b c d    133. a b c d
109. a b c d    134. a b c d
110. a b c d    135. a b c d
111. a b c d    136. a b c d
112. a b c d    137. a b c d
113. a b c d    138. a b c d
114. a b c d    139. a b c d
115. a b c d    140. a b c d
116. a b c d    141. a b c d
117. a b c d    142. a b c d
118. a b c d    143. a b c d
119. a b c d    144. a b c d
120. a b c d    145. a b c d
121. a b c d    146. a b c d
122. a b c d    147. a b c d
123. a b c d    148. a b c d
124. a b c d    149. a b c d
125. a b c d    150. a b c d

| | | | | | | | | |
|---|---|---|---|---|---|---|---|---|
| 151. | a | b | c | d | 176. | a | b | c | d |
| 152. | a | b | c | d | 177. | a | b | c | d |
| 153. | a | b | c | d | 178. | a | b | c | d |
| 154. | a | b | c | d | 179. | a | b | c | d |
| 155. | a | b | c | d | 180. | a | b | c | d |
| 156. | a | b | c | d | 181. | a | b | c | d |
| 157. | a | b | c | d | 182. | a | b | c | d |
| 158. | a | b | c | d | 183. | a | b | c | d |
| 159. | a | b | c | d | 184. | a | b | c | d |
| 160. | a | b | c | d | 185. | a | b | c | d |
| 161. | a | b | c | d | 186. | a | b | c | d |
| 162. | a | b | c | d | 187. | a | b | c | d |
| 163. | a | b | c | d | 188. | a | b | c | d |
| 164. | a | b | c | d | 189. | a | b | c | d |
| 165. | a | b | c | d | 190. | a | b | c | d |
| 166. | a | b | c | d | 191. | a | b | c | d |
| 167. | a | b | c | d | 192. | a | b | c | d |
| 168. | a | b | c | d | 193. | a | b | c | d |
| 169. | a | b | c | d | 194. | a | b | c | d |
| 170. | a | b | c | d | 195. | a | b | c | d |
| 171. | a | b | c | d | 196. | a | b | c | d |
| 172. | a | b | c | d | 197. | a | b | c | d |
| 173. | a | b | c | d | 198. | a | b | c | d |
| 174. | a | b | c | d | 199. | a | b | c | d |
| 175. | a | b | c | d | 200. | a | b | c | d |

# Answer Key

**1. d.  Rolling wave planning**

The project plan is updated on a regular basis as more detailed information becomes known by the project team.  Adding detail is known as progressive elaboration, and the entire process is called rolling wave planning.

PMI®, *PMBOK® Guide,* 2004, 46

**2. a.  Approved preventive actions**

Approved preventive actions are an input to the direct and manage project execution process.  Such actions reduce the probability of negative consequences associated with project risks.  Approved corrective actions, on the other hand, focus on ensuring that future performance will conform to the project management plan.

PMI®, *PMBOK® Guide,* 2004, 92

**3. b.  Can never conflict with the law**

Codes of ethics guide professional behavior on the basis of obligations to others and typically complement, but do not conflict with, applicable law. While the code of ethics may overlap the law of the country or community, it can never conflict with the law.

Cleland and Ireland 2002, 577

**4. a.  Value engineering**

Value engineering focuses on cost trade-offs and is an important aspect of system integration.  A product analysis technique, it is used in scope definition to translate specific project objectives into deliverables and requirements.

PMI®, *PMBOK® Guide,* 2004, 110; Meredith and Mantel 2006, 246

**5. b.  The configuration management system (CMS) is a subsystem of the overall PMIS**

The CMS provides a formal process for submitting, tracking, reviewing, and approving proposed changes, and is a subsystem of the overall PMIS.

PMI®, *PMBOK® Guide,* 2004, 90

### 6. c.  Developing contract clauses

First, developing contract clauses is done during contract formation, not contract administration, which begins at contract signing.  Second, contract specialists and attorneys—given their legal expertise—are typically the individuals who write contract clauses, not project managers.

Verma 1995, 63

### 7. c.  Vertical or horizontal

Requested changes are an output of the direct and manage project execution process and may change project scope, modify policies or procedures, modify the project cost or budget, or revise the project schedule.

PMI®, *PMBOK® Guide,* 2004, 93

### 8. d.  Change control system

The change control system defines how project deliverables and documentation are controlled, changed, and approved and is usually done through a set of formal documented procedures.  This is an example of what could be part of a change control system for an information technology project.

PMI®, *PMBOK® Guide,* 2004, 90

### 9. b.  Only the work required should be completed

Project scope management includes all the work—and only the work—required to complete the project successfully.  Gold plating, a practice in which more features are delivered than required by the customers or users, is to be avoided because it is out of the scope of the project.

PMI®, *PMBOK® Guide,* 2004, 103; Frame 1994, 102

### 10. b.  Continuous process improvement

Continuous process improvement provides an iterative means for improving the quality of all processes and is part of the definition of quality assurance.  Its objective is to reduce waste and eliminate nonvalue-added activities.

PMI®, *PMBOK® Guide,* 2004, 187–188

## 11. c. Serve as a statement as to what can be expected

A code of ethics can serve as a statement to clients, employees, and others that "this is what you can expect from us." Violations or perceived violations of the code often erode confidence in the person whose actions are questionable.

Cleland and Ireland 2002, 578–579

## 12. a. Identify the items to be used in evaluating the project outcome

It is often difficult to satisfy all stakeholders, given their different and sometimes contradictory requirements. When analyzing stakeholder needs, it is important to identify the items that will be used to evaluate project outcome first, followed by the identification of the stakeholders who will influence that criteria.

Verma 1995, 71

## 13. b. Kurt Lewin

Kurt Levin, who developed force field analysis, thought that change is not just an event but is a dynamic balance of opposing forces. He reasoned that any situation can reach a state of equilibrium resulting from a balance of forces pushing against each other. Mr. Levin advanced the idea that behavior change follows a three-step process: unfreezing, changing, and refreezing.

Verma 1997, 28–30

## 14. c. Scope management plan

The degree of rigor and detail regarding project scope must be commensurate with the project's size, complexity, and importance. A small or routine project, for example, will require less documentation and detail than a complex project. Scope management decisions should be documented in the project scope management plan.

PMI®, *PMBOK® Guide*, 2004, 107

## 15. d. Continuously monitor the project

The monitor and control project work process is performed throughout the project and includes collecting, measuring, and disseminating performance information and assessing measurements and trends to effect process improvement. Continuous monitoring is important because it provides insight into the project's health, highlighting areas requiring special attention.

PMI®, *PMBOK® Guide*, 2004, 94

**16. a. Payback period**

The payback period is the period of time needed for a company to recover its initial cost outlays for a project. Because the calculations are not adjusted for the time value of money, it is not as precise as other capital budgeting methods.

Kerzner 2005, 582

**17. d. A quality audit**

A quality audit is a tool and technique for the perform quality assurance process. It is primarily used to determine whether the project team is complying with organizational and project policies, processes, and procedures.

PMI®, *PMBOK® Guide*, 2004, 189

**18. a. Configuration status accounting**

Configuration status accounting captures, stores, and accesses the needed configuration information to manage products and product information effectively.

PMI®, *PMBOK® Guide*, 2004, 97

**19. c. Document the specific responsibilities of each stakeholder in the integrated change control process.**

Configuration management is an integral part of the integrated change control process. It is necessary because projects by their nature involve changes. The integrity of baselines must be maintained by releasing only approved changes for incorporation into the project's products or services and by maintaining their related configuration and planning documentation.

PMI®, *PMBOK® Guide*, 2004, 97

**20. b. Customer**

Roles and responsibilities of change control boards should be clearly defined within configuration control and change control procedures. They also should be agreed to by the sponsor, customer, and other stakeholders. If the project is being provided under a contract, some proposed changes will require customer approval.

PMI®, *PMBOK® Guide*, 2004, 98

**21. c. Scope management plan**

The scope management plan describes how project scope will be addressed by the project management team. Its components are the scope definition, WBS creation, scope verification, and scope control processes.

PMI®, *PMBOK® Guide*, 2004, 108

**22. a. Direct and manage project execution**

In the administrative closure procedure, the project team documents all the activities and interactions, and identifies the roles and responsibilities needed to execute all aspects of the closure procedure.

PMI®, *PMBOK® Guide*, 2004, 93

**23. a. Define the starting point or "baseline" configuration.**

Configuration management is a technique that is employed to control changes to a project. Because the impact of any change must be assessed relative to a baseline, accordingly, the baseline configuration must be established and agreed upon at the outset of the project.

Kerzner 2005, 455–456; PMI®, *PMBOK® Guide*, 2004, 97

**24. a. Root cause analysis**

Determining the root cause of the problem means to determine the origin of the problem. What may appear to be the problem on the surface is often revealed, after further analysis, not to be the real cause of the problem. One technique used in root cause analysis is to ask "why" five times.

PMI®, *PMBOK® Guide*, 2004, 189

**25. c. Scope management plan**

The scope management plan includes the processes, documentation, tracking systems, and approval levels necessary for authorizing changes.

PMI®, *PMBOK® Guide*, 2004, 121

**26. c. Conduct an immediate review of the work packages**

A thorough review of the work packages will provide a complete accounting of the physical progress achieved on the project. This is the first step in attempting to improve performance.

Cleland and Ireland 2002, 443

### 27. b. Quality assurance

Quality assurance is the management section of quality management. It is the collective term for the formal activities and managerial processes that attempt to ensure that products and services meet the required quality level. The project manager should establish administrative processes and procedures necessary to ensure and often prove that the scope statement conforms to the customer's actual requirements, to determine which processes will be used to ensure that stakeholders have confidence that the quality activities will be properly performed, and to ensure that all legal and regulatory requirements will be met.

Kerzner 2005, 846

### 28. a. Create an environment in which each stakeholder contributes appropriately

To garner support for the project among its stakeholders, the project team should involve all appropriate parties in project planning based on their influence on the project and its associated outcomes. They should be involved in project planning because they usually have the skills and knowledge that can be leveraged to develop the most realistic project management plan.

PMI®, *PMBOK® Guide,* 2004, 25, 46

### 29. c. Scope definition

In the planning process group, scope definition follows scope planning, which is the first process after develop project management plan. Stakeholder analysis needs to be conducted early in the project life cycle. Scope definition results in, among other things, a list of prioritized requirements, which are gathered from the various stakeholders.

PMI®, *PMBOK® Guide,* 2004, 110

### 30. d. Project team members are adequately trained for their jobs.

The purpose of the quality audit is to evaluate whether the project is conforming to the project's quality requirements and is following established quality procedures and policies. It looks at the outputs of the work processes and not on the individuals performing the job.

Kerzner 2005, 847

**31. c.  There are misunderstandings regarding what was agreed to**

Using a formal, documented approach to change management reduces the level of misunderstanding or uncertainty regarding the nature of the change and its impact on cost and schedule.  For large projects, change control boards are recommended.

Meredith and Mantel 2006, 574

**32. b.  Project A because its present value is $75,614**

Using a discount factor of 15%, the PV of Project A is $75,614, while the PV of Project B is $72,327.  Accordingly, a return of $100,000 in two years is worth more to the firm than a $110,000 return in three years.

Kerzner 2005, 584

**33. b.  Douglas McGregor**

Douglas McGregor's (Theory X & Y) views illustrate that leadership is not the property of a single individual factor, but is a complex relationship among these variables.

Cleland and Ireland 2002, 457

**34. d.  Determine the total float variance**

Variance analysis is a common tool and technique in schedule control and involves comparing target schedule dates with actual/forecast start and finish dates.  Once the variance is known, the project team can take corrective action to bring performance in line with the plan.

PMI®, *PMBOK® Guide*, 2004, 154

**35. a.  Cultural differences**

Certain words, terms, or gestures have different meanings and interpretations in different cultures.  When working in a multicultural environment, sensitivity to differing interpretations of words, terms, or gestures is important to promote good communication.

Verma 1996, 24–25

### 36. a. Recommend corrective action

A corrective action is anything that is done to bring expected future schedule performance in line with the schedule baseline. Regarding the project schedule, it usually means taking action to speed up the project. One way to determine why the schedule performance is not in line with the plan is root cause analysis, which may address schedule activities other than the activity that is actually causing the variance.

PMI®, *PMBOK® Guide,* 2004, 155

### 37. a. Be concerned because it entails a high risk

Customer satisfaction is often difficult to quantify. One can meet all the specifications yet have a dissatisfied client. As a result, it entails high risk. Remember that stakeholder analysis is a tool and technique in scope definition.

PMI®, *PMBOK® Guide,* 2004, 110

### 38. b. There are new stakeholders.

As long as the new stakeholders agree with the project's business case, the work should continue. However, if any of the other events occur, termination should be considered.

Cleland and Ireland 2002, 442

### 39. d. Detailed project scope statement

The scope statement describes the project's major objectives. Based on those objectives, the project team can then identify the major deliverables that need to be completed to satisfy the objectives and the resources required to complete the project. There are many tools that can be used to identify the deliverables, including expert judgment.

PMI®, *PMBOK® Guide,* 2004, 115

### 40. c. Provide the ability to show performance for a specified time period for trend analysis

Because schedule performance index (SPI) and cost performance index (CPI) are expressed as ratios, they can be used to show performance for a specific time period or trends over a long-time horizon. Additionally, there is no need to disclose confidential financial data to convey the project's status to one's customers; they should not have a need to know such information.

Kerzner 2005, 618–619

**41. a. 7%**

Albert Meharabian, a researcher, discovered that words alone account for just 7% of any message's impact. Vocal tones account for 38% of the impact and facial expressions account for 55% of the message. Thus, project managers should use nonverbal ingredients to complement verbal message ingredients whenever possible and should recognize that nonverbal factors generally have more influence on the total impact of a message than verbal factors. The lack of nonverbal cues makes project communications in a virtual environment more challenging.

Verma 1996, 19

**42. b. At -$200, the physical progress is being accomplished at a slower rate than is planned, indicating an unfavorable situation.**

Schedule variance is calculated: EV – PV or $1,000 – $1,200 = –$200. Because the SV is negative, physical progress is being accomplished at a slower rate than planned.

Kerzner 2005, 616

**43. d. Place emphasis on improving the productivity by which work was being performed**

CPI = EV/AC and measures the efficiency of the physical progress accomplished compared to the baseline. A CPI of .84 means that for every dollar spent, you're only receiving 84 cents of progress. Therefore, you should focus on improving the productivity by which work is being performed.

Kerzner 2005, 618

**44. d. Where the present value of the cash inflows exactly equals the initial investment**

IIR is a sophisticated capital budgeting technique and is the discount rate that equates the present value of the cash returns with invested cash.

Ward 2000, 106

**45. b. Material culture**

Material culture refers to tangible elements such as the physical objects or technologies created by people and often involves tools, skills, work habits, and work attitudes. Knowledge of material culture is especially helpful to project managers as they plan for negotiations with international partners.

Verma 1996, 150

**46. a.  Culture shock**

Project managers should focus on execution and not on convincing others of their own values or work styles.  Project managers need to be aware of possible culture shock so they can recognize its effects during negotiations.

Verma 1996, 152

**47. c.  (Percent complete)(budget at completion)**

Multiplying the percent complete by the budget at completion, or the total budget for the project, is the simplest formula to use.  The 50/50 rule, or the more conservative 0/100 rule, can eliminate the necessity for the continuous determination of percent complete.  Once percent complete is determined, it can be plotted against time expended.

Kerzner 2005, 623–624

**48. b.  An organizational breakdown structure**

The organizational breakdown structure (OBS) provides a hierarchically organized depiction of the project organization.  Its primary purpose is to relate work packages to the performing organizational units.

PMI®, *PMBOK® Guide,* 2004, 115, 117

**49. d.  Establish the basic purpose of the message**

The first step is to establish a general or specific purpose before starting to write.  There are many reasons to communicate.  Some examples include to direct, inform, inquire, or persuade.  Project managers should work closely with their team to develop a consensus on the purpose of the message.

Verma 1996, 20

**50. b.  Milestone method**

The milestone method is especially helpful for work packages of long duration that have interim milestones or a functional group of activities with a milestone established at specific control points.  In the EV system, value is earned when the milestone is completed.  In such cases, a budget is assigned to the milestone rather than to the work packages.

Kerzner 2005, 623–624

### 51. b.  Herzberg's Motivator-Hygiene Theory

Frederick Herzberg's Motivator-Hygiene Theory asserts that some job factors lead to satisfaction, whereas others can only prevent dissatisfaction. There are two types of factors associated to the motivation process: hygiene factors, which relate to the work environment, and motivators, which relate to the work itself.  Hygiene factors, if provided appropriately, can prevent dissatisfaction, while motivating factors can increase job satisfaction and are more permanent.

Verma 1996, 56, 64–65

### 52. c.  Phases

The WBS can be shown in different forms.  The first level of decomposition can be by deliverables, subprojects, or phases.  This is an example of a WBS that uses the phases of the project life cycle as the first level of decomposition, with the deliverables at the next level.

PMI®, *PMBOK® Guide,* 2004, 115–116

### 53. c.  Contract or memorandum of understanding

Upon completion of negotiations, a final contract or memorandum of understanding is prepared and signed by all parties.

Verma 1996, 153

### 54. b.  The number of levels for each component need not be the same

Not all elements of the WBS need to have the same levels of decomposition.  To determine the appropriate work package level, the work for some deliverables needs to be decomposed only to the next level, while others need greater levels of decomposition.

PMI®, *PMBOK® Guide,* 2004, 114

### 55. b.  David McClelland

According to David McClelland, there are three relevant motives or needs in work situations:  the need for achievement, power, and affiliation or association.  This theory supports the view that there is a high correlation between achievement, affiliation, and power motives and the overall motivation and performance achieved in a project.

Verma 1996, 68

### 56. c. Estimate at completion

EAC is the total amount of money estimated to be spent on the project. It can be calculated several different ways. However, the basic approach is to add the actual costs to date plus the estimate to complete.

Kerzner 2005, 626

### 57. c. EAC = [Actual to date] + [all remaining work to be done at the planned cost including remaining work in progress]

This formula assumes that all of the remaining work is independent of the burn rate incurred thus far. AC is $2,900 + [$500 + $1,000]. The $500 is from Activity B, and the $1,000 is from Activity C.

Kerzner 2005, 629

### 58. a. Average rate of return

The average rate of return is the ratio of the average annual profit (either before or after taxes) to the initial or average investment in the project. Because profits are not equivalent to cash inflows, the average rate of return does not usually equal the reciprocal of the payback period.

Meredith and Mantel 2006, 50

### 59. c. Concrete/sequential style

When closing a project, the project team is concerned with transferring the product and information to the users. The concrete/random style is recommended because the focus is on logical organization, evaluating alternatives, and fixing problems without losing sight of details and administrative issues.

Verma 1996, 49–51

### 60. d. Cost accounts

Work packages describe the work to be accomplished by a performing organizational unit or responsible individual. It is a natural subdivision of effort planned according to the way the work will be done and rolls up to a cost account.

Kerzner 2005, 417

**61. b. Expectancy Theory**

Developed by Victor Vroom, Expectancy Theory asserts that people think seriously about how much effort they should put into a task before doing it. Motivation is linked to an expectation of a favorable outcome. It is based on the concept that people choose behaviors that they believe will lead to desired rewards and outcomes.

Verma 1996, 73

**62. b. Prior to verification that the degree of decomposition of the work is necessary and sufficient**

There are five sequential activities in the decomposition process. First, the deliverables and required work are identified. Then, the WBS is structured and organized. Next, the upper WBS levels are decomposed into lower-level detailed components. Identification codes are then developed and assigned to components. The last step is to verify that the degree of decomposition of the work is necessary and sufficient.

PMI®, *PMBOK® Guide,* 2004, 115

**63. a. Make sure it is an independent, noncalculated estimate for the remaining work that considers resource performance or productivity**

The estimate to complete (ETC) is the estimate for completing the remaining work for the project, an activity, work package, or control account. To be reliable, it should be an independent, noncalculated ETC for the work remaining that considers performance or production of the resource(s) to date.

PMI®, *PMBOK® Guide,* 2004, 175

**64. d. Scope management plan**

The scope baseline is an output of the create WBS process. It consists of the detailed project scope statement and its associated WBS and WBS dictionary.

PMI®, *PMBOK® Guide,* 2004, 117

**65. d. Schedule**

In a study of sources of conflict by project life-cycle phase, seven different causes of conflict were identified. In the execution phase, the highest-ranking sources of conflict were schedules, technical issues, and manpower, in this order, followed by priorities, administrative procedures, cost, and personalities.

Verma 1996, 103–104

**66. c.   A WBS component below the control account but above the work package**

Planning packages are a category of planning components and are used for planning known work content that does not have detailed schedule activities.  Identifying these is part of the activity definition process.

PMI®, *PMBOK® Guide,* 2004, 129

**67. c.   Project management software**

Project performance reviews (a tool and technique for the cost control process) are conducted to compare cost performance over time, schedule activities or work packages that are overrunning and underrunning the budget or planned value, milestones due, and milestones met.  They are held to assess schedule activity, work package, and cost account status or progress, and typically are used in conjunction with variance analysis, earned value, and trend analysis.

PMI®, *PMBOK® Guide,* 2004, 176

**68. d.   The calculated CV, SV, CPI, and SPI values for WBS components are documented and communicated to stakeholders**

Performance measurements involve calculating CV, SV, CPI, and SPI values for WBS components.  This is critical project performance information that needs to be documented and communicated, most typically through performance reports.

PMI®, *PMBOK® Guide,* 2004, 177

**69. b.   Start to start, 6 days**

Start-to-start relationships are useful if a few key tasks are involved.  In this situation, the latest that the documentation can be completed is Day 6.  It is calculated by—

$LF_i = LS_j (\text{Day } 4) - SS_{ij} (2 \text{ days}) + Dur_i (4 \text{ days}) = \text{Day } 6$

PMI®, *PMBOK® Guide,* 2004, 132

**70. d.   GERT**

GERT, the graphical evaluation and review technique, is a method of constructing a project schedule network diagram that has been developed to a level of detail that cannot be handled by PERT/CPM.  It is a network analysis technique that allows for the conditional and probabilistic treatment of logical relationships (for example, some activities may not be performed).

Meredith and Mantel 2006, 414–415

**71. b.  1.2.1, 1.3.1, 1.3.2**

Total float is the total amount of time that a schedule activity may be delayed from its early start date without delaying the project finish date or without violating a scheduling constraint.  It is calculated by determining the difference between the early finish dates and the late finish dates or early start dates and late start dates.

PMI®, *PMBOK® Guide,* 2004, 378

**72. a.  1.3.2**

Free float is the amount of time that a schedule activity can be delayed without delaying the early start of any immediately following schedule activity.  Task 1.3.2 has three days of free float because the early start of the finish milestone is Day 16.

PMI®, *PMBOK® Guide,* 2004, 362

**73. b.  Performance measurement baseline (PMB)**

The PMB is a time-phased budget plan used to measure performance.  It is formed by the budgets assigned to schedule cost accounts and the applicable indirect accounts.  It typically integrates scope, schedule, and cost parameters of the project, but it may also include technical and quality parameters.

PMI®, *PMBOK® Guide,* 2004, 232; Ward 2000, 146

**74. a.  Smoothing**

Smoothing emphasizes areas of agreement while avoiding points of disagreement.  It tends to keep peace only in the short term.

Verma 1996, 118

**75. d.  Forcing**

Forcing and majority rule are represented by a strong desire to satisfy oneself rather than to satisfy others.  It involves imposing one viewpoint at the expense of another and is characterized by a win-lose outcome in which one party overwhelms the other.

Verma 1996, 118, 120

**76. a   Schedule**

In many projects, there is a rush to finish due to schedule slippages that develop in the execution/implementation phase.  Delays in schedules become cumulative and impact the project most severely in the final stages of the project.  While there are other sources of conflict, such as personalities and cost, attempting to finish on time is always on everyone's mind.

Verma 1996, 103, 105

**77. a.  Role ambiguity**

The main sources of stress are grouped into four categories of stress-creating factors:  those related to roles and relationships, those related to the job environment, personal factors, and factors related to the project environment or climate.  Role ambiguity is an example of factors related to roles and responsibilities.  It occurs when an individual is not clear about his or her job responsibilities.

Verma 1996, 180, 183–184

**78. c.  Discounted cash flow**

The discounted cash flow method, or net present value method, determines the present value of all cash flows by discounting them by the required rate of return.  The required rate of return is also known in many organizations as the hurdle rate or cutoff rate.

Meredith and Mantel 2006, 50

**79  c.  Use a control chart**

A control chart is one of the seven basic tools of quality that determines whether or not a process is stable or has predictable performance.  It also illustrates how a process behaves over time.  When a process is within acceptable limits, it need not be adjusted; when it is outside acceptable limits, an analysis should be conducted to determine the reasons why.

PMI®, *PMBOK® Guide*, 2004, 192

**80. d.  Collaborating**

Collaborating involves bringing people with opposing views together to reach a solution.  When there are too many people involved, it is more difficult to reach a solution, given the multiplicity of perspectives.  If the parties involved have mutually exclusive views, then forcing or compromise must be used.

Verma 1996, 119

### 81. a. Histogram

In a histogram, or bar chart, each column represents an attribute or characteristic of a problem or situation. The height of each column represents the relative frequency of the characteristic.

PMI®, *PMBOK® Guide*, 2004, 194

### 82. b. Linear responsibility charts

A linear responsibility chart relates the work to be done with one or more people who have anything to do with completing the work. A review of all tasks and persons associated with completion will help to pinpoint areas of potential conflict.

Kerzner 2005, 294

### 83. b. Pareto chart

The Pareto chart is a type of histogram, ordered by frequency of occurrence, to show how many defects were generated by the type or category of identified cause. It rank orders the problem areas and is used primarily to identify and evaluate nonconformities.

PMI®, *PMBOK® Guide*, 2004, 195

### 84. d. Run chart

A run chart shows the history and pattern of process variation. It shows trends, variation, declines, or improvements in a process over time. One benefit of using a run chart is it provides data that can be used for trend analysis.

PMI®, *PMBOK® Guide*, 2004, 196

### 85. b. Acknowledge that conflict exists

In order to address conflict, people must recognize and acknowledge that conflict exists. Next, it is important to establish common ground or shared goals and then to separate people from the problem.

Verma 1996, 126

### 86. d. Scope verification typically precedes quality control.

Scope verification focuses on accepting project deliverables. In order to be accepted, they must meet the requirements. Quality control is one way to ensure that the requirements have been met. That is why quality control is typically done before scope verification.

PMI®, *PMBOK® Guide*, 2004, 118

### 87. b. Aligning the personal inputs of different project participants

Intercultural team building is a major challenge on an international project. To align the personal inputs of the different project participants, a project manager must be aware of and appreciate cross-cultural differences and create an intercultural environment to capitalize on these differences.

Verma 1997, 105

### 88. a. Project B has a 7.1 ROS, which is higher than that of Project A.

ROS = [(revenues/costs) − 1] x 100 and is a nontime-dependant measure of profit or return as a percentage of a project's total cost. A negative return on sales indicates a loss. It is a ratio that expresses how much net income a company earns from each dollar of revenue. In this situation, Project B has a 7.1 ROS, while Project A has a 6.1 ROS.

Cohen and Graham 2001, 223; ESI *Risk Management* Class 1999

### 89. c. Clarify your expectations

To minimize conflict, you need to know your project team members by developing rapport and building trust. Other tactics to use are to discover their professional and personal goals, define control parameters, develop a tolerance for failure to encourage creativity, give positive feedback, and give timely praise and recognition.

Verma 1996, 136–137

### 90. c. Weighted Pareto analysis

The weighted Pareto analysis gives a measure of significance to factors that may not appear significant at first, using such additional factors as cost, time, and criticality. A basic Pareto analysis identifies the vital few contributors that account for most quality problems, and the comparative Pareto analysis focuses on any number of program options or actions.

Kerzner 2005, 855–856

### 91. d. Identify the problem

There are typically six steps in this process but the first and most important is to identify the problem. This step often involves the use of other statistical process control tools, such as Pareto analysis, the histogram, and control charts as well as brainstorming. The result of this step is a clear, concise problem statement.

Kerzner 2005, 853

**92. c.   It is used primarily for Level 1 of the WBS.**

Estimates are categorized according to accuracy and the time to prepare them.  Grassroots or engineering-type estimates are definite estimates and are prepared when detailed information about the project is available.  These estimates would use the work package level of the WBS.

Kerzner 2005, 542

**93. a.   Office power consumption**

Indirect costs are not project specific but support project activities in some way.  For example, the cost of capital equipment not charged per piece of output, advertising, salaries of owners, sales, office power consumption, and so on.

Meredith and Mantel 2006, 354

**94. d.   Withdrawal**

Confronting is considered to be the most effective resolution style, followed in order by compromising, smoothing, forcing or competing, and withdrawal.  Forcing is detrimental because it leads to win-lose outcomes and creates hard feelings.  Withdrawing tends to minimize conflict; however, it fails to resolve the conflict, which only causes further problems in the future.

Verma 1996, 139

**95. c.   Celebrating**

During the adjourning stage of team development, the emphasis is on tasks and relationships that promote closure and celebration.  There is recognition and satisfaction as the theme is moving on and separation.  Management skills involve evaluating, reviewing, and improving, while leadership qualities are celebrating and bringing closure.

Verma 1997, 40

**96. b.   Attribute chart**

There are two types of control charts:  variable charts, which are used with continuous data and attribute charts, for use with discrete data.  Attribute data have only two values (conforming/nonconforming, pass/fail, go/no-go, or present/absent).  In this situation, you are looking for the presence of the required food label.

Kerzner 2005, 862–863

### 97. c.  An output of activity resource estimating

The key output of activity resource estimating is the identification and description of the types and quantities of resources needed for each schedule activity in a resource, which are often depicted on an RBS.  It shows the resources by resource category and resource type in a hierarchical structure.

PMI®, *PMBOK® Guide,* 2004, 138

### 98. d.  Rough bargaining

Rough bargaining is the third stage in negotiations that occurs during the negotiation meeting phase.  It follows protocol and probing and is important for successful negotiations.

Verma 1996, 153

### 99. d.  Project performance appraisals

Lessons learned in managing a project team can include:  project organization charts, position descriptions, staffing management plans, ground rules, conflict management techniques, and recognition events that were particularly useful.  Performance appraisals document and record an individual project team member's contribution to the project measured against what was expected of him or her, and are a tool and technique used in this process.

PMI®, *PMBOK® Guide,* 2004, 219

### 100. b.  It is a professional obligation of every project manager to do so

Lessons learned should be conducted on all projects.  However, to ensure that failure or less-than-expected results are minimized on subsequent projects, PMI® asserts that every project manager is professionally obligated to do so.

PMI®, *PMBOK® Guide,* 2004, 230

### 101. b.  5.333 days

The formula to calculate three-point estimates using PERT, program evaluation and review technique, is [a + 4m +b]/6; a = the most optimistic time, b = the most pessimistic time, and m = the most likely time.  Three-point estimates are a tool and technique used in activity duration estimating.  The average often provides a more accurate estimate than the single point, most likely estimate because it requires more thorough deliberation and consideration of the task itself.

PMI®, *PMBOK® Guide,* 2004, 142; Kerzner 2005, 491

**102. c.  Between 3.3 and 7.3 days with a normal distribution**

The standard deviation is helpful to provide a range of estimates on task duration and to show any concerns that the project manager may have regarding specific tasks or the project as a whole, when the technique is so applied.  In this example, the normal distribution is used because the beta distribution would have a much higher incidence on the pessimistic end of the curve.

PMI®, *PMBOK® Guide,* 2004, 142; Kerzner 2005, 491–492

**103. c.  Face-to-face meetings**

Face-to-face meetings are considered to be the most effective way to resolve issues with stakeholders because there is a greater exchange of ideas in a shorter period of time, plus there is the dynamic of being together with the stakeholders in the same room.  If they are not warranted or practical, such as on an international project, then telephone calls, e-mail, and other communications methods can be used.

PMI®, *PMBOK® Guide,* 2004, 235

**104. b.  Accommodating**

Open subordination is much like an accommodating style of conflict management in which negotiators are more concerned about positive relationships than about substantive outcomes.  It can dampen hostility, increase support and cooperation, and foster more interdependent relationships.  This is an effective style for project managers to use with support staff.

Verma 1996, 157

**105. d.  Evaluate the return on capital percent versus the cost of capital percent**

Economic value added quantifies the value a company provides to its investors and seeks to determine if a company is creating or destroying value to its shareholders.  It is calculated by subtracting the expected return, represented by the capital charge, from the actual return that a company generates, represented by net operating profit after taxes.

Cohen and Graham 2001, 217; ESI *Risk Management* Class 1999

### 106. b.  Risk register

The risk monitoring and control process includes keeping track of those risks on the watch list.  Low-priority risks are inputs to the risk monitoring and control process and are documented in the risk register.  Other inputs that are part of the risk register include identified risks and risk owners, agreed-upon risk responses, specific implementation actions, symptoms and warning signs of risk, residual and secondary risks, and the time and cost contingency reserves.

PMI®, *PMBOK® Guide*, 2004, 264–265

### 107. b.  There is a high sensitivity to changing requirements

Life-cycle costing estimates the total cost of a process or product from research and development or inception through to disposition.  If requirements change frequently during execution, the life-cycle cost estimate developed at the project's outset will fluctuate wildly and therefore be of little use as a cost baseline.

Kerzner 2005, 576–577; *PMBOK® Guide*, 2004, 157

### 108. b.  Work performance information

Work performance information is an input to this process.

PMI®, *PMBOK® Guide*, 2004, 101

### 109. d.  C, A, F, and G

First, it is necessary to determine the critical path, which is A, C, F, and G. To determine the lowest weekly crashing cost, start with C at $1,500 per week.  The next activity is A, followed by F and G.

PMI®, *PMBOK® Guide*, 2004, 145; Kerzner 2005, 494–495

### 110. c.  Zero-sum game analysis

Achieving mutual gain during negotiations means that each party benefits by the decisions made.  A zero-sum game is where one side wins at the expense of the other.

Ward 2000, 243

### 111. d.  The information distribution process

This process is concerned with providing stakeholders with project information in a timely manner.  Lessons learned documentation is an example of project information.

PMI®, *PMBOK® Guide*, 2004, 230

**112. a. The company requires a continuous stream of projects to survive**

Organizations that rely on products for their revenue must constantly be introducing new products into the marketplace as old products are removed. Ideally, this should be an overlapping process to maintain balanced or increasing revenue over time. The closure phase evaluates the efforts of the total system and serves as input to the conceptual phase for new projects and systems. It also has an impact on other ongoing projects with regard to identifying priorities.

Kerzner 2005, 67–69

**113. c. Implementation**

Regardless of the many terms used across many industries, implementation would be considered a term used in the executing phase.

Kerzner 2005, 69–71

**114. d. Organizational standard processes**

Enterprise environmental factors and systems are from any or all of the enterprises involved in the project. Organizational standard processes, on the other hand, are process assets; in other words, the way things are done.

PMI®, *PMBOK® Guide*, 2004, 83, 360

**115. b. Structure**

Supportive behavior is relationship oriented and is the extent to which the leader engages in two-way communication, listens, provides support and encouragement, facilitates interaction, and involves the followers in decision making. Structure connotes a certain level of rigidity and inflexibility and is not a term associated with supportive behavior.

Verma 1996, 216–217

**116. a. Change master**

During the execution stage, the major attributes and emphasis is on realignment. The leadership style/blend that is most appropriate is one who is a decision maker, balances work and fun, is trustworthy, and promotes the team concept and synergy.

Verma 1996, 225

**117. c.  Norming; high supportive and low directive approach**

There are four stages of team development:  forming, storming, norming, and performing.  Different leadership styles in terms of the amount of required supportive and directive behavior are appropriate when a team is in a certain development stage.  At the norming stage, the third stage in team development, leaders provide high support and low direction.

Verma 1996, 227

**118. b.  A conflict of interest**

A conflict of interest is a situation where an individual is placed in a compromising position where the individual can gain personally based upon the decisions that are made.  As project managers, one is expected to abide by the PMI® Code of Professional Conduct, which makes it clear that project managers should conduct themselves in an ethical manner.

Kerzner 2005, 334–335

**119. b.  Business need**

Projects are usually chartered and authorized because of problems, opportunities, or business requirements.  They result from market demands, business needs, customer requests, technology advances, legal requirements, or social needs.  This example is representative of a business need, as it is based on a class to increase the company's revenues.

PMI®, *PMBOK® Guide*, 2004, 7, 81

**120. a.  Conduct a risk audit**

The risk audit is a tool and technique in the risk monitoring and control process and is used for two purposes:  to assess the effectiveness of risk responses and to evaluate the effectiveness of the risk management process.

PMI®, *PMBOK® Guide*, 2004, 266

**121. a.  The project's selection processes**

Before starting a project, the organization should document its business needs or requirements.  Unambiguous descriptions of the project objectives are developed, which includes the reason the project is the best solution to satisfy requirements.  The selection process that is used, therefore, serves to clarify the framework for the project.

PMI®, *PMBOK® Guide*, 2004, 43

**122. c. Technical performance measurement**

Technical performance measurement compares technical accomplishments to date compared to the project plan's schedule of technical achievement. Deviation, such as less functionality than planned at a key milestone, can help to forecast the degree of success in achieving the project scope.

PMI®, *PMBOK® Guide*, 2004, 266

**123. d. Direct and manage project execution and risk monitoring and control**

A work-around is a form of corrective action, which is an output of direct and manage project execution and risk monitoring and control processes.

PMI®, *PMBOK® Guide*, 2004, 93 and 267

**124. b. Demands**

Claims administration is a tool and technique in the contract administration process. When the buyer and seller can't agree, this is also called claims, disputes, or appeals and should be documented, processed, monitored, and managed throughout the contract life cycle.

PMI®, *PMBOK® Guide*, 2004, 293

**125. a. Buyer-conducted performance review**

Such a review is a tool and technique in the contract administration process, which can include a review of seller-prepared documentation and buyer inspections. It seeks to identify performance successes or failures, progress with respect to the contract statement of work, and contract noncompliance.

PMI®, *PMBOK® Guide*, 2004, 293

**126. d. Resource-limited schedule**

Resource leveling is a technique applied to a schedule that already has been analyzed by the critical path method. If you are working on a project with a finite and critical project resource, you can schedule this resource in reverse from the end date of the project. It is called a resource-limited or resource-constrained schedule because the dates are calculated based on available, known resources.

PMI®, *PMBOK® Guide*, 2004, 147

**127. c. Approval and funding for the project are handled external to the project boundaries.**

The develop project charter process is concerned with authorizing the project or a subsequent phase. Approval and funding are done before the decision is made to proceed with the project.

PMI®, *PMBOK® Guide*, 2004, 43

**128. a. Legitimate**

Legitimate power is formal authority based on a person's position within the organization. It comes with the right to give orders or make requests.

Verma 1996, 233

**129. d. Expert**

Expert power is earned/personal power when project personnel admire an individual's skills and want to follow him or her as a role model. In such situations, people willingly comply with the demands of such a person.

Verma 1996, 233–235

**130. b. Progressively elaborated**

The project's requirements, as documented in the product scope description, will have less detail during the initiation process and more detail during later processes. This process is known as progressive elaboration.

PMI®, *PMBOK® Guide*, 2004, 83

**131. b. Recognize that this is an example of an inappropriate connection and disclose it immediately to your company's executive management**

Connections with family or friends may be able to provide you with information or influence by which you could gain personally in a business situation. Examples include receiving insider information, receiving privileged information, or opening doors that you could not open by yourself, at least without difficulty. As a project manager, one should abide by the PMI® Code of Professional Conduct and conduct oneself in an ethical manner.

Kerzner 2005, 335

**132. d. Understanding of policies, operating procedures, and regulations of external stakeholder organizations**

Successful project managers are ones that have expertise and skills in leadership/interpersonal areas, project management/administration areas, and technical areas. The understanding of policies, operating procedures, and regulations of external stakeholder organizations is representative of project management/administrative skills.

Verma 1995, 27

**133. c. Identify the system's constraints**

Dr. Eliyahu M. Goldratt identified the following five steps in his Theory of Constraints: (1) Identify the system constraint, (2) decide how to exploit the constraint, (3) subordinate everything else to the above decision, (4) elevate the system's constraint, and (5) if in a previous step the system's constraint has been broken, return to Step 1.

PMI®, *PMBOK® Guide*, 2004, 147; Kerzner 2005, 912

**134. a. Who will do the task**

In a matrix environment, project resources (that is, people) come from the functional departments. Therefore, it is the functional manager's job to identify who will work on specific project tasks.

Verma 1995, 56–57

**135. d. Project files**

The organizational corporate knowledge base is part of the organizational process assets. In addition to project files, it contains the process measurement database, historical information and lessons learned knowledge base, issue and defect management database, configuration management knowledge base, and financial database.

PMI®, *PMBOK® Guide*, 2004, 85

**136. d. Behavioral-oriented reasons**

Behavioral reasons, rather than quantitative reasons, account for more project terminations because it is much more difficult to manage people than things. Issues such as poor morale, poor human relations, poor labor productivity, and no commitment from those involved in the project combine to thwart project success in many industries.

Kerzner 2005, 432

**137. a. A cost estimating tool and technique used to examine the price of individual deliverables when a project is won under competitive processes**

Vendor bid analysis is used to help determine the cost of the total contract.

PMI®, *PMBOK® Guide*, 2004, 165

**138. d. Preparing personnel performance evaluations**

The project manager, or whomever supervised the work of each individual team member, should prepare the personnel evaluations because they have an intimate understanding of the work performed by the team members. The termination manager focuses instead on the administrative requirements of termination and the environment within which the project will be operating if it is continued in any way.

Meredith and Mantel 2006, 638–640

**139. d. Performing**

The performing stage of team development is noted by a theme of productivity. Management skills involve consensus building, problem solving, decision making, and rewarding, with leadership shown through management by walking around, stewardship delegation, mentoring, being a futurist, and being a cheerleader/champion.

Verma 1997, 40

**140. b. $90,000**

In this situation the fixed-fee of $10,000 does not change but now represents a seller profit of 12.5% on incurred costs. This means that the total cost to the project is $90,000.

Fleming 2003, 97

**141. c. $118,000**

In this situation, there is a $10,000 overrun from the target costs. Applying the 80/20 share ratio, the seller's share of the overrun is 20% of $10,000 or a minus $2,000 in earned fee. The final value of this procurement is $110,000 in costs plus a seller fee of $10,000 less $2,000 or $8,000 for a final price of $118,000.

Fleming 2003, 92

**142. b. Initiator**

To initiate something means to get it started. In the project environment, that typically means a task.

Verma 1997, 78–79

**143. a. A kickoff meeting is recommended**

Even if team members already know one another, a kickoff meeting should still be held because the meeting always includes more than meeting team members. Specific expectations for the project can be discussed as well as other important administrative details. It also gives people an opportunity to express their commitment to the project's objectives.

Verma 1997, 135

**144. c. Develop project charter**

The PMIS is used by the project team to help prepare the project charter; facilitate feedback as the charter is refined; control changes to it; and release the final, approved document.

PMI®, *PMBOK® Guide*, 2004, 86

**145. b. Lateral**

Lateral or horizontal communication is between the project manager and his or her peers and will be where most of the communications will occur. Accordingly, it is essential for success in a highly competitive environment and requires diplomacy, experience, and mutual respect.

Verma 1997, 136

**146. a. Consider every meeting a team meeting, not the project manager's meeting**

Team building should be made as important a part of every project activity as possible. Given that there are many meetings on projects, each team member should be made to feel that it is his or her meeting and not just the project manager's meeting. This will foster greater contribution by each team member.

Verma 1997, 137

### 147. d. Project management methodology (PMM)

The PMM is an organization-approved approach for project management that is used on every project. It is not part of the develop preliminary project scope statement process, which addresses and documents the project and deliverable requirements, product requirements, project boundaries, methods of acceptance, and high-level scope control.

*PMI®, PMBOK® Guide,* 2004, 45, 86

### 148. c. Tight matrix

A "tight" matrix refers to team members working in close proximity to one another. Studies have demonstrated that such a team approach facilitates concurrent engineering by having designers working next to manufacturing engineers to help ensure that the project is designed in such a manner that it is also cost-effective to manufacture.

Verma 1997, 169

### 149. b. Cost aggregation

Other cost estimating tools and techniques are: analogous estimating, determining resource cost rates, bottom-up estimating, parametric estimating, and vendor bid analysis.

*PMI®, PMBOK® Guide,* 2004, 166

### 150. c. You and your supplier should decline the gifts since gifts are not permitted by your organization's code of ethics, and your company is the prime contractor

Many companies have written policies addressing gift acceptance. Regardless of company policy and the country in which one is working, it is usually advisable to avoid all gifts.

Kerzner 2005, 335

### 151. a. A recommendation for changing current practice should be made and defended

It is important to capture lessons learned, which then can be used on subsequent projects. The more detailed the lessons the better. However, when it comes to personnel lessons learned, the information should be handled in a confidential manner.

Meredith and Mantel 2006, 642–643

**152. a. Inconsistencies in the solicitation of the contract shall be resolved in a given order of procedure**

The order of precedence specifies that any inconsistency in the contract shall be resolved in a given order. This avoids confusion and debate, which could lead to litigation.

Kerzner 2005, 819

**153. a. Earn and maintain the confidence of team members, colleagues, employees, employers, customers/clients, the public, and the global community**

The Project Management Institute is dedicated to the development and promotion of the field of project management. Accordingly, it has a Member Code of Ethics, which defines and clarifies ethical responsibilities for all PMI® members, present and future. PMI® members pledge to: maintain high standards of integrity and professional conduct, accept responsibility for one's actions, enhance professional capabilities, practice with fairness and honesty, and encourage others in the profession to act in an ethical and professional manner.

PMI®, PMP® Code of Professional Conduct, 1

**154. a. Authorizes each project phase**

The develop project charter process is not only concerned with authorizing the project, it focuses on individual phases in a multiphase project as well. When used in a multiphase project, this process validates the decisions made during the project's original chartering.

PMI®, *PMBOK® Guide*, 2004, 45, 82

**155. a. Project sponsor**

The initiator or sponsor provides the information needed to develop the preliminary project scope statement. It then is refined by the project management team in the scope definition process.

PMI®, *PMBOK® Guide*, 2004, 87

**156. c. Consensus**

Project managers tend to use four basic decision styles: command, consultation, consensus, and coin flip or random. If acceptance and quality are both important, the consultation style is preferred. It allows for some involvement of team members but allows project managers to maintain control over the final decision. In this style, team members are free to express their opinions, but the project manager makes the final decision.

Verma 1997, 178

**157. c. Not part of the project cost baseline but included in the project budget**

A management contingency reserve is a budget reserved for unplanned, but potentially required, changes to the project, otherwise called "unknown unknowns." Usually the project manager must obtain approval before obligating or spending this reserve. While it is not part of the project cost baseline, it is included in the project budget. Because it is not distributed as budget, it cannot be used in earned value calculations.

PMI®, PMBOK® Guide, 2004, 169

**158. c. That while you want to manage this project, your resume cannot be submitted at this time**

According to the PMP® Code of Professional Conduct, you are responsible for providing accurate, truthful advertising and representations concerning qualifications, experience, and performance of services. This also applies in terms of responsibilities to customer and the public. Your resume, therefore, should not be submitted.

PMI®, PMP® Code of Professional Conduct, 1

**159. b. Contract or agreement between the project and line organizations**

Many organizations consider the project charter as a "legal" agreement between the project manager and the company. As such, they often supplement the charter with a "contract" that functions as an agreement between the project and line organizations. This is done to raise the level of commitment for both parties to the project's completion.

Kerzner 2005, 448–449

### 160. b.  Internal failure costs

Rework, scrap, reengineering, repair, downtime, corrective actions, and so on always provide the greatest area of savings to an organization.  Such costs are considered internal failure because they are discovered and connected by the organization and not by its clients.

Kerzner 2005, 849, *PMBOK® Guide*, 2004, 186

### 161. c.  Juran

This concept is attributed to Joseph Juran.  The implication here is that zero defects may not be a practical solution since the total cost of quality would not be minimized.

Kerzner 2005, 850

### 162. d.  Design of experiments

Design of experiments is a quality planning tool and technique, which helps identify the factors that may influence specific variables of a product or process under development or in production.  Design of experiments highlights the factors that influence results and illustrates the presence of interactions and synergisms among the factors.  Consequently, it can help the organization optimize its processes.

PMI®, *PMBOK® Guide*, 2004, 185

### 163. d.  There is integrity in the relationship and prior history with the vendor

When people know and trust one another, and in particular have worked with each other before, the negotiation process can be significantly shortened.  Three major factors of negotiation should be followed: compromise ability, adaptability, and good faith.

Kerzner 2005, 808

### 164. a.  A company uses sealed bids

When using the sealed bid method, competitive market forces determine the price, and the award goes to the lowest bidder, provided all other terms and conditions of the contract are met.

Kerzner 2005, 808

**165. d. Contract terms and conditions are reviewed before the proposal is submitted to the client**

The contracts (legal) representative is responsible for the preparation of the contract portion of the proposal. Generally, contracts with the legal department are handed through or in coordination with the proposal group. Before the proposal is submitted to the client, contract terms and conditions should be reviewed and approved.

Kerzner 2005, 823

**166. b. Confront Kim and ask her whether she provided her management with the local chapter's membership list.**

While it seems possible that Kim may be using the membership list to assist her company, you cannot be certain until you talk with Kim and obtain additional information. This should be your first step. In your discussion, you should point out the need to take responsibility for one's actions and the importance of maintaining high standards of integrity and professional conduct. Once Kim explains whether or not she has used the membership list inappropriately, you can then determine whether other actions are warranted.

PMI®, PMP® Code of Professional Conduct, 1; PMI®, Member Ethical Standards, 1

**167. b. Linear responsibility chart**

The linear responsibility chart is used to clarify the responsibilities of those involved in the project. While it is very similar in concept to a responsibility matrix, it shows the interfaces between work packages and organizational positions. It helps people understand how they relate to the work packages and becomes a model for the intended formal relationship in the project.

Verma 1995, 114–115

**168. c. Project expeditor**

A variation of the weak matrix organizational structure, the project expeditor has no formal authority to make or enforce decisions. Nonetheless, the project expeditor must be able to persuade those in authority to maintain the project's visibility so that resources will be allocated as needed to meet the project's schedule, budget, and quality constraints. This approach is considered to be effective in high-technology and research and development environments.

Verma 1995, 153–154

**169. a.** **Have the project manager and the functional manager work together to complete performance evaluations**

In a matrix environment, project team members have two bosses: the project manager and their functional line manager. People often are unclear as to which manager is their "real" boss, as there may be a continual shifting balance of power. To avoid confusion regarding performance issues, it is a good idea to have the project manager and functional line manager complete the individual's performance evaluations. Also, greater weight should be given to the project manager's assessment for the time the individual actually worked on the project.

Verma 1995, 178

**170. a.** **A tool and technique in the acquire project team process**

Using the virtual team process opens many possibilities regarding team members. The virtual team is defined as a group of people with a shared goal, who fulfills its role primarily using communications techniques and media that do not include face-to-face meetings.

PMI®, *PMBOK® Guide,* 2004, 211

**171. b.** **You may need to compensate the seller for seller preparations and for any completed or accepted work**

Early termination of a contract is a special case of contract closure. The rights and responsibilities of the parties are contained in a termination clause of the contract. Typically such a clause allows the buyer to terminate the whole contract or a portion of it for cause or convenience at any time. In doing so, the buyer may need to compensate the seller for seller's preparations and for any completed and accepted work related to the terminated part of the contract.

PMI®, *PMBOK® Guide,* 2004, 295

**172. a.** **Commence as scheduled as stated in the staffing management plan**

Training is a tool and technique for the develop project team process, the requirements and schedule for which should be stated in the staffing management plan. Project team members' skills can be developed as part of the project activities.

PMI®, *PMBOK® Guide,* 2004, 213

### 173. c. Updates to organizational process assets

The three outputs of the acquire project team process are project staff assignments (assigning the appropriate people to work on the project); resource availability (documenting the time period each team member can work on the project); and staffing management plan updates (incorporating changes that are needed as specific people fill the project roles and responsibilities).

PMI®, PMBOK® Guide, 2004, 212

### 174. b. 105

This is determined through the formula: $n(n-1)/2$, where n = the number of stakeholders: $15(15-1)/2 = (15)(14)/2 = 105$. It is important to note that project managers need to plan the project's communications requirements carefully, limiting who will communicate with whom given the potential for confusion when there are multiple communications channels.

PMI®, PMBOK® Guide, 2004, 226

### 175. d. Confusion of establishing a project in the matrix management environment

During project formation, there is always an element of confusion or lack of clarity regarding the balance of power between the project manager and functional managers. If not resolved, such confusion manifests itself in conflicts regarding technical decisions, resource allocation, and scheduling later in the project.

Meredith and Mantel 2006, 303

### 176. c. You need to tell your colleague that he has violated the PMP® Code of Professional Conduct and you now must report him to PMI®

Your colleague has just violated the PMP® Code of Professional Conduct as stated in Section I (A) 1. "Responsibility to provide accurate and truthful representations concerning all information directly or indirectly related to all aspects of the PMI® Certification Program, including but not limited to the following examination applications, test item banks, examinations, answer sheets, candidate information, and PMI® Continuing Certification Requirements Program reporting forms."

PMI®, PMP® Code of Professional Conduct, 1

### 177. d. Establish ground rules

Ground rules are a tool and technique for the develop project team process and help to establish clear expectations among team members regarding acceptable behavior. Ground rules that are established and agreed to at the outset will save many hours of discussion later, as team members will act to enforce the rules during the project's duration.

PMI®, *PMBOK® Guide*, 2004, 214

### 178. a. Expert

Expert power is a function of knowledge, skills, and reputation possessed by the project manager. In such situations, project personnel will do what the project manager wants because they believe he or she knows best and they trust and respect the project manager.

Verma 1996, 233; Verzul 2005, 54

### 179. c. List of risks requiring near-term responses

The primary outputs from risk identification are initial entries into the risk register. It ultimately contains outcomes of other risk management processes as they are conducted. As an output of risk identification, it should contain: a list of identified risks, a list of potential responses, root causes that gave rise to the identified risks, and updated risk categories.

PMI®, *PMBOK® Guide*, 2004, 249

### 180. b. Increased staff availability

Team effectiveness is measured by factors such as turnover, competencies, and improvements. Increased staff availability provides no insight into how well a team is performing. It is the project manager's responsibility to conduct assessments in this area and to take corrective action when needed. Team performance assessment is an output of the develop project team process.

PMI®, *PMBOK® Guide*, 2004, 215

### 181. d. It includes a specific contract management plan.

A contract management plan is not part of a contract. It is used to identify how the contract will be administered.

PMI®, *PMBOK® Guide*, 2004, 289–290

### 182. c.  The information distribution process

The lessons learned process is a tool and technique in the information distribution process.  It describes the importance of lessons learned sessions throughout the project life cycle with the project team and key stakeholders identifying lessons learned and compiling, formalizing, and storing them throughout the project's duration.

PMI®, *PMBOK® Guide,* 2004, 230

### 183. c.  $6.42 million

Test:  $5M + $960K + $460K = $6.42M; Don't Test:  $7M

PMI®, *PMBOK® Guide,* 2004, 257; ESI *Risk Management* Class 1999

### 184. a.  Conduct a procurement audit

A procurement audit is a tool and technique for the contract closure process.  It is conducted to identify the strengths and weaknesses of all aspects of the contract.  As such, knowledge gained from the process can be used in other contracts.

PMI®, *PMBOK® Guide,* 2004, 296

### 185. b.  Authorized contracts administrator

The buyer, through its authorized contract administrator, is responsible for providing the seller with formal written notice of contract completion. The contract administrator does so when the seller has met all contractual requirements as articulated in the contract.

PMI®, *PMBOK® Guide,* 2004, 297

### 186. d.  Airline B at $1,105.00

Based on use of decision tree analysis, Airline B is the more financially advantageous solution as it costs the project $1,105 per average trip, versus $1,170 on Airline A.  Airline A:  $750 + EV of $420 = $1170. Airline B:  $1,000 + EV of $105 = $1,105.

PMI®, *PMBOK® Guide,* 2004, 257; ESI *Risk Management* Class 1999

### 187. c.  Establish a contingency reserve

A contingency reserve is time, money, or resources set aside to implement a contingency plan should a known risk or opportunity occur.

PMI®, *PMBOK® Guide,* 2004, 263

**188. d. Configuration management system**

As an output of the close project process, organizational process assets are updated. The configuration management system is used to develop the index and location of project documents.

PMI®, *PMBOK® Guide*, 2004, 102

**189. d. Project review meetings**

Bidders conferences are meetings with prospective sellers prior to the preparation of a bid or proposal to answer questions and clarify issues. They are a tool and technique in the request sellers process. Project review meetings are conducted to assess project performance and status.

PMI®, *PMBOK® Guide*, 2004, 285

**190. c. Decline the invitation since it is a conflict of interest**

By participating in a CAPM™ exam writing session, you would know which questions would be on the exam. Given your organization helps people prepare for the exam, your knowledge, if used in your training materials, would give your company an unfair advantage.

PMI®, Conflict of Interest Policy, 2; PMI®, PMP® Code of Professional Conduct, 1

**191. b. $10,928**

The total point of assumption is that point after which all additional costs are borne by the contractor. In this example, it is when the cost reaches $10,928.00. At this point, the final price of $11,500 is reached. If the cost continues to increase, then all profits may disappear, and the contractor may be forced to pay the majority of the overrun.

Kerzner 2005, 816–817

**192. c. Definition of required product verification and administrative closure of contract records**

Required product verification and administrative closure of contract records is part of the contract closure procedure. All other answers are part of the administrative closure procedure.

PMI®, *PMBOK® Guide*, 2004, 101–102

### 193. b. All potential sellers are given equal standing

Bidders conferences are conducted to ensure all prospective sellers have a clear and common understanding of the requirements. They are not used to prequalify vendors. Thus, all vendors are treated equally.

PMI®, *PMBOK® Guide*, 2004, 285

### 194. d. To establish minimum requirements of performance for one or more of the evaluation criteria

Weighting systems are developed and used to help select the best vendor. By assigning a numerical weight to each evaluation criteria, the buyer can emphasize one area as being more important than another. It is a tool and technique in the select seller process.

PMI®, *PMBOK® Guide*, 2004, 288

### 195. b. Cost-plus-fixed fee

On a firm-fixed-price contract, the seller absorbs 100% of the risks, while on a cost-type contract, the buyer carries the most risk. Cost-plus-fixed-fee contracts have less risk to sellers than cost-plus-award-fee or cost-plus-incentive-fee contracts because the fee is fixed based on costs, so the seller is guaranteed a certain level of profit.

PMI®, *PMBOK® Guide*, 2004, 277–278, Kerzner 2005, 818

### 196. b. Technical and management details to be included

Expert judgment is a tool and technique in the develop preliminary project scope statement process. It is applied to any technical or management details to be included in the preliminary scope statement.

PMI®, *PMBOK® Guide*, 2004, 86

### 197. b. Contract administration process

During contract administration, seller performance is assessed and documented. Such information can be used by the buyer to determine whether the seller should be used on another contract.

PMI®, *PMBOK® Guide*, 2004, 289

**198. a. Open items list**

Issues or an open item list are examples of inputs if contract negotiation is an independent process. Outputs are documented decisions. While contract negotiations may need to be a separate process for complex procurements, for simple procurement items, the terms and conditions of the contract can be fixed and nonnegotiable.

PMI®, *PMBOK® Guide*, 2004, 288

**199. c. Expert judgment and some form of evaluation criteria**

Expert judgment is a tool and technique used in the select sellers process. It, along with some form of evaluation criteria as developed during the plan contracting process, is used to rate and score proposals. This does not preclude the use of other tools and techniques, but these tools and techniques are used in all evaluations.

PMI®, *PMBOK® Guide*, 2004, 289

**200. c. Tell your CEO that this action by your company constitutes a violation of the PMP® Code of Professional Conduct in the section titled: "Qualifications, Experience, and Performance of Professional Services"**

The PMP® Code of Professional Conduct specifically states that a PMP® is responsible for providing accurate and truthful representation to the public. This obligation applies to the preparation of estimates concerning costs, services, and expected results. Therefore, such an action in terms of not using the audited overhead rates would violate this responsibility.

PMI®, PMP® Code of Professional Conduct, 1

# APPENDIX
# STUDY MATRIX

## Overview

In 2000, the Project Management Institute (PMI®) published *the Project Management Professional (PMP®) Role Delineation Study (RDS)*. This study serves as the foundation for the PMP® certification examination. The study also serves as the foundation for our 200-question practice test.

The role delineation study identified six broad performance domains and determined how the 200 questions on the PMP® exam would be distributed according to these domains. The distribution is as follows:

| | | |
|---|---|---|
| I | Initiating the Project | 22 questions |
| II | Planning the Project | 46 questions |
| III | Executing the Project | 54 questions |
| IV | Monitoring and Controlling the Project | 42 questions |
| V | Closing the Project | 18 questions |
| VI | Professional and Social Responsibility | 18 questions |
| | | 200 questions |

The matrix beginning on page 373 identifies each practice test question according to its performance domain and its knowledge area in the *PMBOK® Guide*.

The matrix is designed to help you—

- Assess your strengths and weaknesses in each of the performance domains

- Identify those areas in which you need additional study before you take the PMP® exam

Here is an easy way to use the matrix:

**Step 1**  Circle all the questions you missed on the practice test in Column 1.

**Step 2**  For each circled question, note the corresponding process or professional and social responsibility in Column 2.

**Step 3**  To determine whether any patterns emerge indicating weak areas, tally the information you obtained from the matrix.

**Step 4**  To ensure that you have a good understanding of the major management processes that define a particular knowledge area, including the input, tools and techniques, and output, refer to the appropriate knowledge area in the *PMBOK® Guide*.

The last column in the matrix is provided for your notes.

## Study Matrix

| Practice Test Question Number | Performance Domain (Process or Professional and Social Responsibility) | Knowledge Area | Study Notes |
|---|---|---|---|
| 1 | Planning | Integration | |
| 2 | Executing | Integration | |
| 3 | Professional and Social Responsibility | | |
| 4 | Planning | Scope | |
| 5 | Planning | Integration | |
| 6 | Monitoring and Controlling | Procurement | |
| 7 | Executing | Integration | |
| 8 | Planning | Integration | |
| 9 | Planning | Scope | |
| 10 | Executing | Quality | |
| 11 | Professional and Social Responsibility | | |
| 12 | Monitoring and Controlling | Procurement | |
| 13 | Monitoring and Controlling | Integration | |
| 14 | Planning | Scope | |
| 15 | Monitoring and Controlling | Integration | |
| 16 | Initiating | Integration | |
| 17 | Executing | Quality | |
| 18 | Monitoring and Controlling | Integration | |
| 19 | Monitoring and Controlling | Integration | |

| Practice Test Question Number | Performance Domain (Process or Professional and Social Responsibility) | Knowledge Area | Study Notes |
|---|---|---|---|
| 20 | Monitoring and Controlling | Integration | |
| 21 | Planning | Scope | |
| 22 | Closing | Integration | |
| 23 | Monitoring and Controlling | Integration | |
| 24 | Executing | Quality | |
| 25 | Monitoring and Controlling | Scope | |
| 26 | Closing | Integration | |
| 27 | Executing | Quality | |
| 28 | Planning | Integration | |
| 29 | Planning | Scope | |
| 30 | Executing | Quality | |
| 31 | Monitoring and Controlling | Integration | |
| 32 | Initiating | Integration | |
| 33 | Executing | Human Resources | |
| 34 | Monitoring and Controlling | Time | |
| 35 | Professional and Social Responsibility | | |
| 36 | Monitoring and Controlling | Time | |
| 37 | Planning | Scope | |
| 38 | Closing | Integration | |
| 39 | Planning | Scope | |
| 40 | Monitoring and Controlling | Cost | |

| Practice Test Question Number | Performance Domain (Process or Professional and Social Responsibility) | Knowledge Area | Study Notes |
|---|---|---|---|
| 41 | Executing | Human Resources | |
| 42 | Monitoring and Controlling | Cost | |
| 43 | Monitoring and Controlling | Cost | |
| 44 | Initiating | Integration | |
| 45 | Professional and Social Responsibility | | |
| 46 | Professional and Social Responsibility | | |
| 47 | Monitoring and Controlling | Cost | |
| 48 | Planning | Scope | |
| 49 | Executing | Communications | |
| 50 | Monitoring and Controlling | Cost | |
| 51 | Executing | Human Resources | |
| 52 | Planning | Scope | |
| 53 | Professional and Social Responsibility | | |
| 54 | Planning | Scope | |
| 55 | Executing | Human Resources | |
| 56 | Monitoring and Controlling | Cost | |
| 57 | Monitoring and Controlling | Cost | |
| 58 | Initiating | Integration | |
| 59 | Closing | Integration | |
| 60 | Planning | Scope | |
| 61 | Executing | Human Resources | |

| Practice Test Question Number | Performance Domain (Process or Professional and Social Responsibility) | Knowledge Area | Study Notes |
|---|---|---|---|
| 62 | Planning | Scope | |
| 63 | Monitoring and Controlling | Cost | |
| 64 | Planning | Scope | |
| 65 | Executing | Human Resources | |
| 66 | Planning | Time | |
| 67 | Monitoring and Controlling | Cost | |
| 68 | Monitoring and Controlling | Cost | |
| 69 | Planning | Time | |
| 70 | Planning | Time | |
| 71 | Planning | Time | |
| 72 | Planning | Time | |
| 73 | Monitoring and Controlling | Cost | |
| 74 | Executing | Human Resources | |
| 75 | Executing | Human Resources | |
| 76 | Closing | Human Resources | |
| 77 | Professional and Social Responsibility | | |
| 78 | Initiating | Integration | |
| 79 | Monitoring and Controlling | Quality | |
| 80 | Executing | Human Resources | |
| 81 | Monitoring and Controlling | Quality | |
| 82 | Executing | Human Resources | |

| Practice Test Question Number | Performance Domain (Process or Professional and Social Responsibility) | Knowledge Area | Study Notes |
|---|---|---|---|
| 83 | Monitoring and Controlling | Quality | |
| 84 | Monitoring and Controlling | Quality | |
| 85 | Executing | Human Resources | |
| 86 | Monitoring and Controlling | Scope | |
| 87 | Professional and Social Responsibility | | |
| 88 | Initiating | Integration | |
| 89 | Executing | | |
| 90 | Monitoring and Controlling | Quality | |
| 91 | Monitoring and Controlling | Quality | |
| 92 | Planning | Cost | |
| 93 | Planning | Cost | |
| 94 | Executing | Human Resources | |
| 95 | Closing | Human Resources | |
| 96 | Monitoring and Controlling | Quality | |
| 97 | Planning | Time | |
| 98 | Executing | Human Resources | |
| 99 | Monitoring and Controlling | Human Resources | |
| 100 | Professional and Social Responsibility | | |
| 101 | Planning | Time | |
| 102 | Planning | Time | |

| Practice Test Question Number | Performance Domain (Process or Professional and Social Responsibility) | Knowledge Area | Study Notes |
|---|---|---|---|
| 103 | Monitoring and Controlling | Communications | |
| 104 | Executing | Human Resources | |
| 105 | Initiating | Integration | |
| 106 | Monitoring and Controlling | Risk | |
| 107 | Initiating | Integration | |
| 108 | Closing | Integration | |
| 109 | Planning | Time | |
| 110 | Executing | Human Resources | |
| 111 | Closing | Communications | |
| 112 | Closing | Integration | |
| 113 | Closing | Integration | |
| 114 | Initiating | Integration | |
| 115 | Executing | Human Resources | |
| 116 | Executing | Human Resources | |
| 117 | Executing | Human Resources | |
| 118 | Professional and Social Responsibility | | |
| 119 | Initiating | Integration | |
| 120 | Monitoring and Controlling | Risk | |
| 121 | Initiating | Integration | |
| 122 | Monitoring and Controlling | Risk | |
| 123 | Monitoring and Controlling | Risk | |

| Practice Test Question Number | Performance Domain (Process or Professional and Social Responsibility) | Knowledge Area | Study Notes |
|---|---|---|---|
| 124 | Monitoring and Controlling | Procurement | |
| 125 | Monitoring and Controlling | Procurement | |
| 126 | Planning | Time | |
| 127 | Initiating | Integration | |
| 128 | Executing | Human Resources | |
| 129 | Executing | Human Resources | |
| 130 | Initiating | Integration | |
| 131 | Professional and Social Responsibility | | |
| 132 | Executing | Human Resources | |
| 133 | Planning | Time | |
| 134 | Executing | Human Resources | |
| 135 | Initiating | Integration | |
| 136 | Closing | Integration | |
| 137 | Planning | Cost | |
| 138 | Closing | Integration | |
| 139 | Executing | Human Resources | |
| 140 | Monitoring and Controlling | Procurement | |
| 141 | Monitoring and Controlling | Procurement | |
| 142 | Executing | Human Resources | |
| 143 | Executing | Human Resources | |
| 144 | Initiating | Integration | |
| 145 | Executing | Communications | |

| Practice Test Question Number | Performance Domain (Process or Professional and Social Responsibility) | Knowledge Area | Study Notes |
|---|---|---|---|
| 146 | Executing | Human Resources | |
| 147 | Initiating | Integration | |
| 148 | Executing | Human Resources | |
| 149 | Planning | Cost | |
| 150 | Professional and Social Responsibility | | |
| 151 | Closing | Integration | |
| 152 | Monitoring and Controlling | Procurement | |
| 153 | Professional and Social Responsibility | | |
| 154 | Initiating | Integration | |
| 155 | Initiating | Integration | |
| 156 | Executing | Human Resources | |
| 157 | Planning | Cost | |
| 158 | Professional and Social Responsibility | | |
| 159 | Initiating | Integration | |
| 160 | Planning | Quality | |
| 161 | Planning | Quality | |
| 162 | Planning | Quality | |
| 163 | Executing | Procurement | |
| 164 | Executing | Procurement | |
| 165 | Executing | Procurement | |
| 166 | Professional and Social Responsibility | | |
| 167 | Planning | Human Resources | |

| Practice Test Question Number | Performance Domain (Process or Professional and Social Responsibility) | Knowledge Area | Study Notes |
| :---: | :---: | :---: | :---: |
| 168 | Planning | Human Resources | |
| 169 | Planning | Human Resources | |
| 170 | Executing | Human Resources | |
| 171 | Closing | Procurement | |
| 172 | Executing | Human Resources | |
| 173 | Executing | Human Resources | |
| 174 | Planning | Communications | |
| 175 | Initiating | Integration | |
| 176 | Professional and Social Responsibility | | |
| 177 | Executing | Human Resources | |
| 178 | Initiating | Integration | |
| 179 | Planning | Risk | |
| 180 | Executing | Human Resources | |
| 181 | Executing | Procurement | |
| 182 | Executing | Communications | |
| 183 | Planning | Risk | |
| 184 | Closing | Procurement | |
| 185 | Closing | Procurement | |
| 186 | Planning | Risk | |
| 187 | Planning | Risk | |
| 188 | Closing | Integration | |
| 189 | Executing | Procurement | |
| 190 | Professional and Social Responsibility | | |
| 191 | Planning | Procurement | |

| Practice Test Question Number | Performance Domain (Process or Professional and Social Responsibility) | Knowledge Area | Study Notes |
|---|---|---|---|
| 192 | Closing | Integration | |
| 193 | Executing | Procurement | |
| 194 | Executing | Procurement | |
| 195 | Planning | Procurement | |
| 196 | Initiating | Integration | |
| 197 | Executing | Procurement | |
| 198 | Executing | Procurement | |
| 199 | Executing | Procurement | |
| 200 | Professional and Social Responsibility | | |

# References

Acker, David D. *Skill in Communication: A Vital Element in Effective Management.* 2d ed. Ft. Belvoir, Va.: Defense Systems Management College, 1992.

Adams, John R., and Bryan W. Campbell. *Roles and Responsibilities of the Project Manager.* Upper Darby, Penn.: Project Management Institute, 1982.

AGCA (*see* The Associated General Contractors of America).

The Associated General Contractors of America. *Construction Planning and Scheduling.* Washington, D.C.: The Associated General Contractors of America, 1994.

Bell, Chip R. *Managing as Mentors: Building Partnerships for Learning.* San Francisco: Berrett-Koehler, 1996.

Bicheno, John. *The Quality 50.* Melbourne, Australia: Nestadt Consulting Party, 1994.

Bockrath, Joseph T. *Contracts, Specifications, and Law for Engineers.* 4th ed. New York: McGraw-Hill, 1986.

Brake, Terence, Danielle Medina Walker, and Thomas (Tim) Walker. *Doing Business Internationally: The Guide to Cross-Cultural Success.* 2d ed. Boston: McGraw-Hill, 2002.

Cable, Dwayne, and John R. Adams. *Organizing for Project Management.* Upper Darby, Penn.: Project Management Institute, 1982.

Carter, Bruce, Tony Hancock, Jean-Marc Morin, and Ned Robins. *Introducing RISKMAN Methodology: The European Project Risk Management Methodology.* Oxford, England: NCC Blackwell, 1994.

Cavendish, Penny, and Martin D. Martin. *Negotiating and Contracting for Project Management.* Upper Darby, Penn.: Project Management Institute, 1987.

Cibinic, John, Jr., and Ralph C. Nash, Jr. *Cost-Reimbursement Contracting.* 2d ed. Washington, D.C.: The George Washington University, National Law Center, Government Contracts Program, 1993.

Cleland, David I., and Lewis R. Ireland. *Project Management: Strategic Design and Implementation.* 4th ed. New York: McGraw-Hill, 2002.

Cohen, Dennis J., and Robert J. Graham. *The Project Manager's MBA: How to Translate Project Decisions into Business Success.* San Francisco: Jossey-Bass, 2001.

Corbin, Arthur L. *Corbin on Contracts.* St. Paul, Minn.: West Publishing, 1952.

Covey, Stephen R. *The Seven Habits of Highly Effective People: Powerful Lessons in Personal Change.* New York: Simon and Schuster, 1989.

Crosby, Philip B. *Quality Without Tears: The Art of Hassle-Free Management.* New York: McGraw-Hill, 1984; reprint, New York: Penguin Books, 1985.

Crosby, Philip B. *Quality Is Free: The Art of Making Quality Certain.* New York: McGraw-Hill, 1979.

Defense Systems Management College. *Risk Management: Concepts and Guidance.* Ft. Belvoir, Va.: Defense Systems Management College, 1989.

DeMarco, Tom, and Timothy Lister. *Peopleware: Productive Projects and Teams.* New York: Dorset House Publishing, 1987.

Dinsmore, Paul C., M. Dean Martin, and Gary T. Huettel. *The Project Manager's Work Environment: Coping with Time and Stress.* Upper Darby, Penn.: Project Management Institute, 1985.

Dinsmore, Paul C., and Manuel M. Benitez. "Challenges in Managing International Projects." *AMA Handbook of Project Management,* edited by Paul C. Dinsmore. New York: AMACOM Books, 1993, 463–464.

Dobler, Donald W., and David N. Burt. *Purchasing and Supply Management: Text and Cases.* 6th ed. New York: McGraw-Hill, 1996.

Dreger, J. Brian. *Project Management: Effective Scheduling.* New York: Van Nostrand Reinhold, 1992.

ESI International. *Contracting for Project Managers.* Arlington, Va.: ESI International, May 2001.

———. *Risk Management.* Arlington, Va.: ESI International, 1999.

———. *PMI® Exam Preparation.* Arlington, Va.: ESI International, October 2001.

Evans, James R., and William M. Lindsay. *The Management and Control of Quality.* 5th ed. Cincinnati: South-Western, 2001.

Ferraro, Gary P. *The Cultural Dimension of International Business.* 3rd ed. Upper Saddle River, N.J.: Prentice Hall, 1998.

Filley, Alan C. *Interpersonal Conflict Resolution.* Glenview, Ill.: Scott, Foresman, and Co., 1975.

Fisher, Roger, William Ury, and Bruce Patton. *Getting to Yes: Negotiating Agreement Without Giving In.* 2d ed. New York: Penguin Books, 1991.

Fleming, Quentin W. *Cost/Schedule Control Systems Criteria: The Management Guide to C/SCSC.* Chicago: Probus Publishing, 1988.

Fleming, Quentin W. *Project Procurement Management Contracting, Subcontracting, Teaming.* Tustin, Ca.: FMC Press, 2003.

Fleming, Quentin W., and Joel M. Koppelman. *Earned Value Project Management.* 2nd ed. Newtown Square, Penn.: Project Management Institute, 2000.

Forsberg, Kevin, Hal Mooz, and Howard Cotterman. *Visualizing Project Management.* New York: John Wiley and Sons, 1996.

Frame, J. Davidson. *Managing Projects in Organizations: How to Make the Best Use of Time, Techniques, and People.* Rev. ed. San Francisco: Jossey-Bass, 1995.

———. *The New Project Management: Tools for an Age of Rapid Change, Corporate Reengineering, and Other Business Realities.* San Francisco: Jossey-Bass, 1994.

Friedman, Jack P. *Dictionary of Business Terms.* 2d ed. Hauppauge, N.Y.: Barron's Educational Series, Inc., 1994.

Garrett, Gregory A. *World-Class Contracting.* Arlington, Va.: CCH Incorporated, 2001.

Hirsch, William J. *The Contracts Management Deskbook.* Rev. ed. New York: American Management Association, 1986.

Imai, Masaaki. *Kaizen: The Key to Japan's Competitive Success.* New York: McGraw-Hill, 1986.

Ireland, Lewis R. *Quality Management for Projects and Programs.* Drexel Hill, Penn.: Project Management Institute, 1991.

Jentz, Gaylord A., Kenneth W. Clarkson, and Roger LeRoy Miller. *West's Business Law.* 2d ed. St. Paul, Minn.: West Publishing, 1984.

Katzenbach, Jon R., and Douglas K. Smith. *The Wisdom of Teams.* New York: HarperBusiness, 1994.

Kerzner, Harold. *Project Management: A Systems Approach to Planning, Scheduling, and Controlling.* 9th ed. New York: John Wiley & Sons, Inc., 2005.

Kirchof, Nicki S., and John R. Adams. *Conflict Management for Project Managers.* Upper Darby, Penn.: Project Management Institute, 1989.

Kostner, Jaclyn. *Knights of the Tele-Round Table: Third Millennium Leadership.* New York: Warner Books, 1994.

Lewis, James P. *Project Planning, Scheduling, and Control.* Chicago: Probus Publishing, 1991.

Mansir, Brian E., and Nicholas R. Schacht. *An Introduction to the Continuous Improvement Process: Principles and Practices.* Bethesda, Md.: Logistics Management Institute, 1988.

Martin, Martin D., C. Claude Teagarden, and Charles F. Lambreth. *Contract Administration for the Project Manager.* Upper Darby, Penn.: Project Management Institute, 1990.

Maslow, Abraham H. *Motivation and Personality.* New York: Harper and Row, 1954.

McGregor, Douglas. *The Human Side of Enterprise.* New York: McGraw-Hill, 1960.

Meredith, Jack R., and Samuel J. Mantel, Jr. *Project Management: A Managerial Approach.* 6th ed. New York: John Wiley and Sons, 2006.

Pennypacker, James S., ed. *Principles of Project Management: Collected Handbooks from the Project Management Institute.* Sylva, N.C.: Project Management Institute, 1997.

PMI® (*see* Project Management Institute Standards Committee).

Pritchard, Carl L., ed. *Risk Management: Concepts and Guidance.* 2d ed. Arlington, Va.: ESI International, 2001.

Project Management Institute Standards Committee. *A Guide to the Project Management Body of Knowledge,* third edition (PMBOK® Guide). Newtown Square, Penn.: Project Management Institute, 2004.

Project Management Institute. *Project Management Experience and Knowledge Self-Assessment Manual.* Newtown Square, Penn.: Project Management Institute, 2000.

Project Management Institute. *Project Management Professional (PMP®) Certification Handbook.* http://www.pmi.org/

Project Management Institute. Project Management Professional (PMP®) Code of Professional Conduct. http://www.pmi.org/

Project Management Institute. PMI® Conflict of Interest Policy. http://www.pmi.org/

Project Management Institute. PMI® Member Ethical Standards: Member Code of Ethics and Member Standards of Conduct. http://www.pmi.org/

Project Management Institute. PMP® Member Ethics Case Procedures. http://www.pmi.org/

Project Management Institute. *Project Management Professional (PMP®) Role Delineation Study.* Newtown Square, Penn.: Project Management Institute, 2000.

Rose, Kenneth H. *Project Quality Management: Why, What and How.* Boca Raton, Fla.: J. Ross Publishing, 2005.

Rosen, Robert, Patricia Digh, Marshall Singer, and Carl Phillips. *Global Literacies: Lesson on Business Leadership and National Cultures.* New York: Simon & Schuster, 2000.

Schmauch, Charles H. *ISO 9000 for Software Developers*. Milwaukee: ASQC Quality Press, 1994.

Soin, Sarv Singh. *Total Quality Control Essentials: Key Elements, Methodologies, and Managing for Success*. New York: McGraw-Hill, 1992.

Stuckenbruck, Linn C., ed. *The Implementation of Project Management: The Professional's Handbook*. Reading, Mass.: Addison-Wesley, 1981.

Stuckenbruck, Linn C., and David Marshall. *Team Building for Project Managers*. Upper Darby, Penn.: Project Management Institute, 1985.

———. "Team Building for Project Managers." In *Principles of Project Management: Collected Handbooks from the Project Management Institute*. Sylva, N.C.: Project Management Institute, 1997.

Thamhain, Hans J., and David L. Wilemon. "Conflict Management in Project Life Cycles." *Sloan Management Review* 16, no. 3 (Spring 1975): 31–50.

Verma, Vijay K. *Human Resource Skills for the Project Manager*. Vol. 2 of *The Human Aspects of Project Management*. Upper Darby, Penn.: Project Management Institute, 1996.

———. *Managing the Project Team*. Vol. 3 of *The Human Aspects of Project Management*. Upper Darby, Penn.: Project Management Institute, 1997.

———. *Organizing Projects for Success*. Vol. 1 of *The Human Aspects of Project Management*. Upper Darby, Penn.: Project Management Institute, 1995.

Verzuh, Eric. *The Fast Forward MBA in Project Management*. Hoboken, N.J.: John Wiley & Sons, 2005.

Vroom, Victor H. *Work and Motivation*. San Francisco: Jossey-Bass, 1995.

Ward, J. LeRoy. *Project Management Terms: A Working Glossary*. 2d ed. Arlington, Va.: ESI International, 2000.

Wideman, R. Max, ed. *Project and Program Risk Management: A Guide to Managing Project Risks and Opportunities*. Preliminary ed. Drexel Hill, Penn.: Project Management Institute, 1992.

Willborn, Walter, and T. C. Edwin Cheng. *Global Management of Quality Assurance Systems*. New York: McGraw-Hill, 1994.

Youker, Robert. "Communication Styles Instrument: A Team Building Tool." In *The Project Management Institute 1996 Proceedings: Revolutions, Evolutions, Project Solutions*, 27th Annual Seminars and Symposium, Papers Presented October 7–9, 1996, Boston, Massachusetts, 796–799. Upper Darby, Penn.: Project Management Institute, 1996.

# A NOTE TO OUR READERS

Preparing for the PMP® exam is strenuous and time consuming. We hope this tool significantly maximizes your study time. We tried to be as accurate and complete as possible, carefully checking the text and the references. But, given the nature of this collaborative work, some of the material may have fallen short of the mark.

The true test of this book's usefulness, however, is how well it helps you get ready for the PMP® exam. So let us know how it works for you. We welcome your comments and your suggestions for making the next edition even more useful. E-mail your comments to ESIbooks@esi-intl.com.